DATE DUE			
Mar 26 '86			

FREUD AND EDUCATION

Publication Number 930

AMERICAN LECTURE SERIES®

A Monograph in

AMERICAN LECTURES IN PHILOSOPHY

Edited by

MARVIN FARBER
State University of New York at Buffalo

□□□□□□□□□□□□□□□□□□□□□□□□□□□□□

FREUD
AND
EDUCATION

□□□□□□□□□□□□□□□□□□□□□□□□□□□□□

By

SEYMOUR FOX, Ph.D.

Associate Professor of Education
Director
School of Education
The Hebrew University of Jerusalem

CHARLES C THOMAS · PUBLISHER
Springfield · Illinois · U.S.A.

Published and Distributed Throughout the World by

CHARLES C THOMAS • PUBLISHER
BANNERSTONE HOUSE
301-327 East Lawrence Avenue, Springfield, Illinois, U.S.A.

© 1975 by CHARLES C THOMAS • PUBLISHER
ISBN 0-398-03009-X
Library of Congress Catalog Card Number: 73-14892

With THOMAS BOOKS *careful attention is given to all details of manufacturing and design. It is the publisher's desire to present books that are satisfactory as to their physical qualities and artistic possibilities and appropriate for their particular use.* THOMAS BOOKS *will be true to those laws of quality that assure a good name and good will.*

Printed in the United States of America
N-1

Library of Congress Cataloging in Publication Data

Fox, Seymour.
   Freud and education.

   (American lecture series, publication no. 930. A monograph in American lectures in philosophy)
   Bibliography: p.
   1. Freud, Sigmund, 1856-1939. 2. Educational psychology. 3. Personality. I. Title.
LB775.F772F69   370.15   73-14892
ISBN 0-398-03009-X

for
Sarah, David, Eitan, and Daniel

ACKNOWLEDGMENTS

THIS BOOK WAS WRITTEN over several years and in different places—Chicago, New York and Jerusalem.

I wish to thank Professor Joseph Schwab, whom I first met at the University of Chicago, where he was my teacher, and whose influence upon me as mentor and colleague continues to be profound. Of course he bears no responsibility for my errors; otherwise, my debt to him is apparent on every page of this book. Above all, thanks are due him for having taught me what it means to read a text.

In New York, I should like to thank my colleagues at the Jewish Theological Seminary, and especially Mrs. Sylvia Ettenberg. It was she, who by undertaking many of my responsibilities, provided me the opportunity to do the research for this book. I am also extremely grateful to my colleague of many years, Mrs. Rose Wishner, for her gracious and efficient help in so many matters throughout this period. In New York, I was privileged to know the late Dr. Lillian Kaplan, a profound student of Freud. When others were discouraging, she encouraged me to persist in my line of inquiry, even when it led in a direction distasteful to most of her colleagues.

In Jerusalem, I wish to thank my colleagues at The Hebrew University who listened to and discussed my ideas with me. I owe a special debt in this regard to Mrs. Nechama Moshaieff, a member of the Curriculum Department, who devoted many hours to reading, editing and commenting on the text. Thanks also to Muriel Hurovitz, who saw the manuscript through several revisions and provided the index.

For his encouragement, patience and cordiality, I thank my editor, Professor Marvin Farber.

The author gratefully acknowledges permission of authors and publishers to reprint passages from the following:

Sigmund Freud were used with the permission of Liveright, Publishers, New York. Copyright James Strachey 1961.

Excerpts from GROUP PSYCHOLOGY AND THE ANALYSIS OF THE EGO by Sigmund Freud were used with the permission of Liveright, Publishers, New York. (C) Sigmund Freud Copyrights, Ltd. 1959; translation and notes (C) James Strachey 1959.

Excerpts from A GENERAL INTRODUCTION TO PSYCHOANALYSIS by Sigmund Freud were used with the permission of Liveright, Publishers, New York. Copyright (C) renewed 1963 by Joan Riviere.

S.F.

CONTENTS

FREUD AND EDUCATION

Chapter One

□

INTRODUCTION

EDUCATIONAL THEORY AND PRACTICE must draw heavily upon the ideas that are developed in the humanities, the social and natural sciences. These ideas must be adapted for education from their original habitats in disciplines such as philosophy, psychology, sociology, political science, economics and biology.

Translation from theory in the disciplines to educational theory and practice is not easily accomplished. At least two serious problems must be met. The first involves the complications introduced by the multi-disciplinary nature of education, and the second, the complexities involved in the application of the fruits of scholarship developed in theoretical disciplines to education, which must be viewed in large measure as a practical field.

The Multi-disciplinary Nature of Education

An educational problem requires concurrent consideration of issues concerning students, their teachers, the "societies" of which they are members and the subject matter to be taught. At present, each of these—students, teachers, society and subject matter—is treated in one or more of the academic disciplines. No one discipline treats all of them together. Education cannot omit consideration of any one of them. The frames of reference of the scholars and researchers in the humanities, the natural and the social sciences are often not coherent with each other, nor are they easily joined for the purpose of a common attack on a problem. Yet educational theory and practice must find a way to join these issues. If they do not,

3

the most serious kinds of distortion will result.[1]

The deliberations, decisions and products for the curriculum reforms of the 1950's and 1960's would have been very different had the efforts of scholars in the natural sciences been supplemented by those of philosophers and representatives of diverse schools of psychology and sociology. The deliberations should also have included a sophisticated concern for the varieties of teachers and students to be found in the schools. Many of these reforms were based on Bruner's concept of *structure of knowledge* as the sole guiding principle for selection of subject matter. Structure itself was to be taught in a particular manner, the method of *discovery* or *inquiry*. One interpretation of Piaget was adopted to justify the early and universal introduction of this approach in the subjects taught in the elementary school. There were even suggestions of a particular way—called *spiraling*—to organize and sequence the structures that were to be taught by inquiry.[2] Yet it is well-known that the *structure of knowledge* has long been debated by philosophers. There is no possibility of pretending that there is one conception of structure that is universally acceptable. The various conceptions of structure should have been examined prior to the adoption of one of them. The decision to have all children learn by the methods of *inquiry,* and the suggestion that these methods could be used for long periods of the school day required deliberation before curricula were prepared and implemented. Even more serious was the failure to examine the assumption that teachers could be expected to teach the structures of various disciplines by the methods of inquiry. In many cases teachers had never heard

[1]There are those, such as Marc Belth and John Walton (see Belth, Marc: *Education as a Discipline.* Boston, Allyn and Bacon, 1965; Walton, John and Kuethe, James L. (Eds.): *The Discipline of Education.* Madison, U. Wisconsin Pr., 1963), who have responded to this problem by arguing for a discrete discipline of education, which would develop its own psychology, sociology, etc. But even they would admit that this is a distant prospect.

[2]For a critical analysis of the use of the concept *structure* for the curriculum see Lukinsky, Joseph S.: "Structure" in educational theory. *Educational Philosophy and Theory,* 2:15-31, 1970; *3:29-36, 1971; Martin, Jane R.: The disciplines and the curriculum. In Martin, Jane R. (Ed.): *Readings in Philosophy of Education: A Study of Curriculum.* Boston, Allyn and Bacon, 1970; see also Cremin, Lawrence A.: Curriculum making in the United States. *Teachers College Record, 73:* 2, 207-220, 1971.

of these concepts or had distorted notions of them.

Compensatory education was the name given to many different programs that were initiated to meet the crisis in the education of the disadvantaged child. In the beginning, each of the programs was based upon a particular conception of learning theory or child development or socialization. When these programs failed to yield their intended results, elements were added to attain greater breadth or depth. These components were added without concern for coherence or compatibility with the earlier components. Programs in compensatory education did not have to concentrate on the student (or more precisely one aspect of the student, his cognitive development) and then consider his milieu and then later further supplement these programs by retraining the teacher. Each of these factors (as well as others, such as the affective development of the child) is an indispensable part of an educational deliberation and all could have been treated concurrently from the very outset.

The educational researcher himself has often indiscriminately adopted methods imported from psychology and sociology for the purpose of educational evaluation. This research has sometimes been dominated by input-output models, by an experimental design appropriate to the laboratory conditions of psychology or by the highly theoretical constraints of sociology and economics. The input-output model, however, does not contribute a great deal to the explanation of educational results. It does not tell us very much about what actually happens to the input when teachers undertake new programs in the classroom. The model does not explain why success or failure occurs, and therefore does not help the policy maker decide among alternative plans or even help him diagnose the difficulty he is encountering. Proposed educational research of this type must face the problems of design and methodology before research is undertaken. Facing up to the realities and practicalities of the classroom and teaching may cause great difficulty for those who must develop and invent an experimental design—but it cannot be avoided.[3]

---

[3]See James Coleman: *The Evaluation of Equality of Educational Opportunity.* (Santa Monica, Rand, 1968.)

The problem of translation from theory in the disciplines to theory in education is further complicated by the nature of research and scholarship within the disciplines. Freud's treatment of personality or of child development is quite different from Sullivan's or Maslow's. Parsons, Eisenstadt and Coleman conceive of the various student and teacher milieus in different terms. These theoretical controversies have their practical counterpart; that is, the diversity of ideas in psychology and sociology offer competing and sometimes contradictory advice to the educator. Before the educator adopts the conclusions of one theory of personality or of cognitive development, he must have dependable information about what he is adopting (or adapting). The use of Jean Piaget's work for education is a case in point. Piaget's theory is the basis of a great many programs in early childhood education.[4] Yet several of Piaget's basic ideas play little or no role in the programs claiming to be Piagetian. The problems involved in the use of Piaget for education seem to have been minimized or even ignored. As David Elkind has pointed out:

> Of particular note is the fact that Piaget nowhere points to the practical implications of his work. Indeed he seems to feel that a solid foundation of genetic research and theory is necessary before useful practical implications can be drawn. If one looks carefully through Piaget's writings, one seldom, if ever, finds an attempt to deal with concrete problems or pedagogy or child. This is an important point. Some educators have engaged in certain teaching practices in the name of Piaget. What should always be made clear in such cases is that it is the educator's interpretation of Piaget which is being utilized and not Piaget's own ideas about educational practice. If Piaget has such, he seldom voices them.[5]

We suspect that educational programs resulting from a careful

---

[4]". . . the significance of his contribution has literally had the effect of a bomb . . . in educational and psychological circles during very recent times. Hardly a major curriculum development project has failed to draw upon his ideas. . . . It is his work, more than any other, that promises to form the basis for an eventually workable theory of instruction." (Frost, Joe L.: The rediscovery of Piaget. In Frost, J. L. (Ed.): *Early Childhood Education Rediscovered*. Readings. New York, Holt, Rinehart and Winston, 1968, p. 129.)

[5]Jean Piaget, *Six Psychological Studies* (New York, Random, 1967). Intro., xv-xvi.

examination of Piaget's genetic and epistemological ideas would have differed significantly from the present programs.

Education as a Practical Field

The uniqueness of each educational situation is such that it escapes the net of any theory. Even if a comprehensive theory of human nature existed it could not be directly applied to the problems of the teacher in the classroom.[6,7]

The practical nature of education makes it necessary to agree upon the problem before trying to apply the insights of theory to its solution. Often apparent consensus is reached, and theoretical insights applied, and only then is it discovered that the wrong problem has been treated. As Schwab has put it,

> Practical problems do not present themselves wearing their labels around their necks. Problem situations, to use Dewey's old term for it, present themselves to consciousness, but the character of the problem, its formulation, does not. The character of the problem depends on the discerning eye of the beholder.[8]

After identification of the problem, a decision must be made as to which theories can contribute to the solution. A first indispensable step in the preparation of theories—both for educational theory and for practice—is the careful analysis of a theory so as to disclose its underlying assumptions and methods. Through such an analysis, we can reveal the extent to which a theory partially or

---

[6]Ernest Hilgard has indicated that learning theory must be radically adjusted if it is to make a contribution to the practice of education. Hilgard, Ernest: A perspective on the relationship between learning theory and educational practice. In *Theories of Learning and Instruction.* The Sixty-Third Yearbook of the National Society for the Study of Education. Chicago, National Society for the Study of Education, 1964. See also, Scheffler, Israel: Philosophy and the curriculum. In *Reason and Teaching.* London, Routledge and Kegan, 1973, 31-41.

[7]James Coleman, Lee Cronbach and Patrich Suppes have been grappling with the difficult problems involved in developing techniques of educational research that could make a significant contribution to educational policy decisions. Coleman, James S.: *Policy Research in the Social Sciences.* New York, General Learning Press, 1972; Cronbach, Lee and Suppes, Patrick (Eds.): *Research for Tomorrow's Schools.* New York, Macmillan, 1969.

[8]Joseph J. Schwab. The practical: a language for curriculum. In NEA Center for the Study of Instruction (Pub.): *Schools for the 70's,* Auxiliary Series. Washington, D.C., NEA, 1970.

fully treats its subject. Disclosing the architectonic of a theory will not only make clear its strengths and weaknesses, but will also enable educators to judge the theory's coherence with the values, practices and prejudices that guide current educational policy. We will then be in a position to decide what combinations can be made among theories so that the richest possible defensible eclectic can be created. Application of the eclectic combination of theories to the peculiarities of an educational problem will require constant dialogue between theoretician and practitioner. The practitioner will have to insist that the theory include as much as possible of the richness of the practical situation and the theoretician must guarantee that theory is not distorted and does not promise what it cannot deliver.[9]

In this volume we undertake the first step in the translation from theory in a discipline to theory in education—the disclosure of the architectonic of a theory. We have selected Sigmund Freud's theory of personality for analysis. Freud has made one of the significant contributions to personality theory in this century. His theory has been the basis for supporting or rejecting various practices in education. It is therefore important to disclose the terms and principles Freud imposed upon his subject matter in developing his theory. After we have uncovered his theoretical framework we will be in a position to consider the uses of his personality theory for education. This we do in our final section. The actual application of Freud to *practical* educational situations will require

---

[9]Schwab has distinguished and expounded three steps in the process of preparing theories for their use in education, after disclosure of their architectonic: 1) Eclectic A where theories within a discipline are adjusted to each other; 2) Eclectic B, where theories between disciplines are used to complement each other; and 3) Practical deliberation, where theories from several disciplines are brought to bear on particular educational situations. See Schwab, Joseph J.: The practical: A language for curriculum. NEA Center for the Study of Instruction (Pub.): *Schools for the 70's.* Auxiliary Series. Washington, D.C., NEA, 1970; *Idem.:* The Practical: Arts of the eclectic. *School Review 79,* 493-542; *Idem.:* The Practical 3: Translation into curriculum. *School Review,* August 1973, 501-522. For a fuller treatment of the problems of preparing theories in the disciplines for educational theory and practice, see Seymour Fox: "From theory into practice in education." In *A Memorial Volume for Zalman Arrane* (late Minister of Education, Israel), being prepared for publication by the School of Education, The Hebrew University of Jerusalem, Israel, 1975.

complex deliberation in a group competent to consider the realistic alternatives and resources available to a given school, student body, teaching staff and community.[10]

Lest we mislead the reader, it is important to specify the material under analysis, for there are several different bodies of material commonly referred to as Freudian theory, but only one of these is the subject of our inquiry.

The community of psychoanalysts is so closely knit, both to one another and in their loyalty to Freud, that their *cumulative* contributions are often referred to as Freudian theory. This Freudian theory is not the subject of our investigation. Some of it exists as part of the orally communicated wisdom of the profession. A very large part of it has been diversely formulated by many different analysts. The diversity of formulation and the oral traditional form of some of it pose such formidable barriers to anlysis that we have not dared to undertake one. This is most regrettable, for it is probably this Freudian theory that contains the best tested and most beneficial material associated with Freud. Its importance, unfortunately, is not matched by it accessibility to analysis.

Neither are we interested in analyzing the stages in the development of Freud's theory. Such an analysis would be concerned with the evolution of a theory or with the adventure of inquiry of which it is the expression. Although we have scrutinized all of Freud's written work, his early theoretical works, containing ideas later disavowed or reformulated, were examined not for their historical interest but rather for the light they throw on the mature theory.[11]

There is a third Freudian theory with which we are not con-

---

[10]Seymour Fox, A practical image of the practical. *Curriculum Theory Network*, *10*, Fall 1972; Schwab, Joseph J. The practical 3: translation into curriculum. *School Review*, August 1973, 501-522.

[11]For example, *Sexuality in the Aetiology of the Neuroses* (1898), S.E., Vol. III, in which he merely suggests the existence of a sexual aetiology for neurosis; Instincts and their vicissitudes, in *Papers on Metapsychology*, S.E., XIV, where he proposes ego instincts and sexual instincts as the source of conflict in mental life, concepts later reformulated, in *Beyond the Pleasure Principle* (1921), S.E., XVIII, to life and death instincts; and in *The Ego and the Id* (1923), S.E., XIX, where he discards his earlier division of the psyche into Conscious and Unconscious in favor of a tri-partite psyche: id, ego and super-ego.

cerned. This consists of the therapeutic techniques and insight developed by Freud and other psychoanalysts, some of it a part of the oral tradition of psychoanalysis and communicated principally through didactic and control analyses. We name this *therapeutic Freud*. It is our tentative conclusion that much of this therapeutic insight stands or falls in its own right; its soundness or unsoundness is independent of the theory. As in the case of Freud's early theoretical works, we have examined the *therapeutic Freud*, but again with a view to better understanding the theory from which some of these techniques and insights are derived.

There is a fourth Freud as well. Here we do not have a group of papers and books, but rather many indications throughout his works of how Freud might have developed or reformulated his theory had he lived longer. For Freud, unlike many scientists, did not think he had discovered *the* theory or *the whole* theory of human personality. Though this Freud is not the focus of our attention, we will indicate at certain points how we believe Freud might have reformulated some of his ideas. What this Freud would have been, we will never know.

The fifth Freud is the subject of our analysis. It is essentially the content of those works whose clear intent is to provide us with a description of the parts of the human personality, their organization and their operation as expressed in the behavior, the testimony and the *inner life* of the human individual.

We are, then, concerned with a very small part of what is often called, *Freud*. Within this part we shall be principally concerned to disclose the terms, the distinctions and the first principles[12] by means of which Freud determines what facts to look for in his inquiries, and what meanings to assign to them. (See Chapter Two.) This is to say that we are not concerned with the adequacy of his data, nor with the soundness of his conclusions, except as the latter follow from the soundness and coherence of his terms, distinctions and first principles.

On occasion we shall contrast Freudian terms, distinctions or principles with those of others. These contrasts are intended to

---

[12]By first principles, we mean those notions capable of statement and propositions which are treated by Freud as *basic concepts*.

show that there are viable alternatives to those of Freud. It does not follow from the fact that there are viable alternatives that Freud's choices were either the best or the worst of these alternatives. Consequently, our contrasts should not be taken as either invidious or complimentary. There is one exception to the last statement: we treat the conception of education extrapolated from Freud's personality theory as, in some sense, a test of the theory and see through this test a theory which is inadequate in many respects as a view of *normal* man.

Each of our theses will be defended by passages drawn from several of Freud's works.[13] We have analyzed all of his theoretical works and have included as Appendices four examples of these analyses, in the form of Protocols: *Beyond the Pleasure Principle, Group Psychology and the Analysis of the Ego, The Ego and the Id* and *Civilization and Its Discontents.*[14]

The volume has been organized in three parts: Part I, "The Frame of Analysis," describes how we shall attack the problem; Part II, "The Structure and the Content of Freud's Theory," discloses the architectonic of Freud's theory; and Part III, "Freud's Personality Theory and Education," presents a translation of Freud's theory of personality for education.

---

[13]All citations are from *The Standard Edition of the Complete Psychological Works of Sigmund Freud* (hereafter referred to as S.E.), James Strachey (Tran. and Ed.) in collab. with Anna Freud. 24 vols. London, Hogarth Press and the Institute of Psycho-Analysis, 1953-1974.

[14]The protocols are designed to demonstrate how Freud's architectonic may be disclosed through textual analysis. Of necessity, these analyses are presented in note form and are intended for reading in parallel with these four works of Freud.

PART I

THE FRAME OF ANALYSIS

Chapter Two

□

THE FRAME OF ANALYSIS

THERE IS A VERY WIDE RANGE of views held as to the nature of human personality. Some investigators have viewed man's personality as a non-material organism with parts, analogous to the physiological and anatomical parts of the body. Others conceive of personality as the dynamic interplay of relationships established with other humans, beginning at birth and continuing throughout life. Still others consider human personality to be that which society writes on what, initially, is a near *tabula rasa*. These diverse conceptions refer to the same subject—man's personality. How can the same subject matter give rise to such diverse understandings?

We claim that this diversity is the consequence of different starting points of inquiry, or of different conceptions of inquiry. Some of these differing conceptions concern issues of scientific method, but most of them, and all of those important to this work, involve presuppositions concerning the nature of the subject matter itself, in this case, the human personality. In short, the diversity which shall concern us in this work is a diversity in *forms of principle* for inquiry.[1]

By principles of inquiry, we mean the ideas which instigate, direct and control any investigation. These principles determine the character of the subject matter to be investigated, by defining what is relevant and important for the investigation.

Principles not only determine what we shall investigate, but also how we shall proceed with the inquiry. They do this by pro-

---

[1]This discussion of the role and character of principles closely follows that in the monograph by Joseph J. Schwab: What do scientists do? *Behavioral Science*, 5(1): 1-27, 1960.

15

viding the terms in which to couch the problem. These terms discriminate between acceptable and unacceptable data and between procedures for gathering and organizing data. Finally, principles determine how data are to be interpreted.

The investigator may or may not be aware of the principles that guide his investigation. He may believe that there is but one way to recognize or limit a subject matter and investigate it. Or he may be aware of the doctrines involved in the principles he chooses to use in his research. He may even disclose his principles and indicate how he reformulates and refines them in the process of investigation.

Since principles have such a determining character for inquiry, it will be important for us to discover and analyze the principles guiding Freud's investigation into personality. For this purpose, I have decided to use Schwab's classification of the kinds of forms of principles.

Schwab classifies five forms of principles:[2] reductive, holistic, rational, anti-principle and primitive.

Reductive principles

Reductive principles lie back of investigations which seek an explanation for the behavior of their subject matter in terms of the properties or behavior of constituents. For example, some sociology would explain a *social* phenomenon in terms of the character of individuals. The reductive biologist would try to account for the behavior of the organism in terms of the properties or reactions of the chemicals which constitute the organism.

Schwab distinguishes two kinds of reductive principles: atomic and molecular. Atomic reduction is the most frequently used and the most effective. It is a reduction to constituents which belong to an *order of phenomena* different from that of the subject matter of interest, e.g. socials reduced to individuals or biologicals reduced to chemicals. (The examples cited in the previous paragraph are instances of atomic reduction.) In molecular reduction, the reduction is to the minimal or simplest unit of the order of phenomena which is of interest, e.g. the attempt to see all social

---

[2]*Ibid.*, pp. 3-12.

phenomena through the study of the interrelations of two persons or of the family or the attempt to understand all biologicals by a study of what is alleged to be the limiting life unit, the cell.

Holistic principles

We shall contend that Freud's place in this scheme of forms of principles lies at the formal-material holistic locus, one subtype of the holistic form of principle. We shall therefore be interested in a fuller description of this general form and its subtypes. For this, we quote from Schwab:

> Holistic principles are most conspicuous in the frankly taxonomic sciences—zoology, botany, minerology and in physiology from William Harvey to recent times. Holistic principles require an account of the subject-matter of interest in terms of the combination of qualities or constituents which, as organized, sets that subject-matter apart from all others. Parts or constituents are used, as in atomic reductive principles, but the properties of the constituent factors do not provide an adequate or complete account of the whole. *That* is sought in the whole itself, as well as in the parts. Indeed, some properties of the constituents are sometimes treated as conferred by their place in the organization of which they are parts. For this reason, such principles are sometimes called "organic." The original Aristotelian prescription of such principles is still viable:
>
> '. . . the organizing principle is the starting point in natural things as it is in those things which are made by man. Consider how the physician or the builder sets about his work. He starts by setting for himself a definite picture, the physician, of health, the builder, of a house. This picture he uses as the guide and explanation of each subsequent step that he takes. . . . In the works of nature, the organizing principle is even more dominant than in works of art such as these. . . .
>
> '. . . there is also a factor manifested which may be called contingent necessity. For if a house or other such object is to be realized, it is necessary that such and such material shall exist; and it is necessary that first this and then that shall be produced—and so on. . . . So also is it with the production of nature. The starting point for living things is that which is to be. But this, being of such-and-such characters necessitates the previous existence or production of this and that antecedent . . .
>
> 'The fittest mode, then, of treatment is to say, a man has such and such parts because the organization of man includes their presence and because they are necessary conditions of his existence.' (Paraphrased from *Parts of Animals*, Bk. I, Chapter I).

And from Maslow (1954):

'One essential characteristic of holistic analysis of the personality . . . is that there be a preliminary study or understanding of the total organism, and that we then proceed to study the role that our part of the whole plays in the organization and dynamics of the total organism.'

Formal-material holistic principles. Formal-material holistic principles follow the Aristotelian prescription in assigning roles to both the material constituents and to the organized whole. For example,

'The atom, we now find, is . . . a mechanism or organism in which the properties of the whole depend not *solely* on the nature of its parts but *also* on the peculiar relatedness of its parts; while an organic molecule . . . is, again a mechanism or organism in which the properties of the whole depend upon the relatedness of its parts as well as upon their nature. Now for *descriptive* purposes, and for visualization, the parts of the atom or molecule must be in our minds; and we cannot therefore dispense with the results of analysis. Yet in spite of such knowledge of the parts certain fundamental properties of the *whole* will elude us in each case unless we study it while intact. We can only properly define the whole in terms of its activities. . . . In all cases structure, internal events and functions must be thought of as inseparable if we are to grasp the essential nature of such systems . . . (Needham & Baldwin, 1949, pp. 179-190).

In a less dramatic form, such a principle is seen in a physiology which first assigns certain necessary activities to the organism (e.g. ingestion, digestion, excretion, reproduction, etc.) and then describes each organ, tissue and enzyme-system by reference to what it contributes to one or another of these defining activities and how it does so.

Formal holistic principles. When the distinguishing character of the subject of interest is treated as capable of embodiment in any one of a variety of materials or sets of parts, the holistic principle becomes formal. Enquiry guided by such a view may use material parts as evidence of the character of the whole since they are taken as effects or requisites of it but the stable object of enquiry is the pattern, organization or form exhibited *via* the material. For example:

'Democracy—like forms of group living—cannot be defined adequately by isolated elements of conduct, rules or institutions; it is the larger *pattern* of group life and the group atmosphere which determines how society is to be classified.' (Lewin, 1954).

And from Maslow (1954) again,

'Since these specificities have the same source or function or aim, they are interchangeable and may actually be thought to be psychological synonyms of one another . . .'

Such enquiries entail a search for a variety of embodiments. One set of material parts, being only one means of expression, may, as stubborn matter, either fail to express the full pattern or mix its own properties with it. Hence, the nature of culture is sought in cross-cultural study. The nature of the organism is sought through numerous experiments in which parts are altered and the coordinate changes in all other parts are scrutinized in order to determine the stable pattern which is reconstituted by all such sets of changes (J. S. Haldane, 1932).

Needless to say, the exponents of such principles, dubbed mystics, do as they are done by, especially to atomic reductionists; e.g.,

'. . . The orthodox credulity with which so many writers continue to refer to the *mechanisms* of various living activities is to my mind pathetic in its blind clinging to what has come to be regarded as a sacred scientific authority.' (Haldane, 1932).

It is worth noting that holistic principles share with molecular reductions an emphasis on the apartness of the subject of interest. It must be studied 'in its own terms.' I suspect, however, that a factor analytic study would show that scientists' adhesion to holistic principles is heavily loaded with a passion for wholeness or something of which wholeness is symbolic rather than with a need to create an independent domain of investigation.[3]

Rational principles

If, with reductive principles, we lose sight of the whole, or see it in terms of its parts, and with holistic principles we see the parts as servants of the whole, then with rational principles we treat *wholes* as the consequence of relationships with other wholes, instead of explaining a thing in terms of parts. In short, the whole ceases to be whole, but becomes a part. "Principles of this kind require that the subject of interest be seen as given its character by its place in some larger determinative whole or by some *ratio* imposed from without."[4]

An important distinction between rational and formal holistic principles is that the *ratio* in formal holistic principles is im-

---

[3]*Ibid.*, pp. 6-8, citing (a) Aristotle: Parts of Animals. Book I, Chapter I; (b) Maslow, A. H.: *Motivation and Personality.* New York, Harper, 1954; (c) Needham, J. and Baldwin, E. (Eds.): *Hopkins and Biochemistry, 1861-1947.* Cambridge, W. Heffer, 1949; (d) Lewin, Kurt: Group living: autocratic, democratic, and laissez-faire. In Ebenstein, W. (Ed): *Modern Political Thought.* New York, Rinehart, 1954, pp. 89-97; (e) Maslow, *op. cit.;* (f) Haldane, J. S.: The universe in its biological aspect. In *Materialism.* London, Hodder & Stoughton, 1932; (g) *ibid.*

[4]Schwab: *ibid.*, p. 8.

bedded in or unique to the whole, that is, the subject matter, while the ratio in rational principles lies in larger and varying subject matters. In theories using rational principles, causal efficacy is assigned upward, ". . . whether to the configuration of a material 'whole' of which the subject of interest is a 'part' or to a Platonic-Cartesian ratio."[5] By a *Platonic-Cartesian ratio,* Schwab means the abstract set of relations responsible for the configuration of the material whole, as against the material as configured. An example would be the "information" contained in the gene set of a fertilized egg, or in the competitiveness relating N individuals, regardless of the character of the individuals *per se.*

Anti-principles

Here, the investigation disavows or refuses to attempt to organize scientific knowledge in terms other than the data. In this view, science must avoid principles and deal with "facts."

Primitive principles

Immature sciences and sciences in moments of frustration and re-regression often refresh their enquiries by renewed contact with the earth of common sense. Conceptual frames which never were or which seem to be exhausted are replaced by numerous *ad hoc* investigations framed in the terms of the queries which would normally speak to practical problems.

For example, one current investigation of cancer discards all conceptions of the micro-chemistry and biology of the cell in favor of *ad hoc* tests of the effects of an array of chemicals chosen almost at random.[6]

We shall argue in Chapter Three that Freud adopted the formal-material holistic principle to guide his inquiry into personality. Having concluded our general examination of forms of principles for inquiry, we shall now return to elaborate upon positions of emphases within the formal-material subtype that have important consequences for personality theory.

---

[5]*Ibid.,* p. 8.
[6]*Ibid.,* pp. 11-12.

PARTS AND WHOLES IN THEIR RELATION TO EACH OTHER[7]

This subtitle indicates that what we have been calling *formal-material holistic* may be equally termed *part-whole*. The change of name reflects the fact that the subspecies of such theories can be conveniently differentiated in terms of the differing relations between the whole and its parts, especially with respect to the degree of potency assigned to the whole or to the parts.

The Whole as the Sum of Independent Parts

This view represents one extreme of the entire scheme of part-whole theories, in that the whole virtually disappears as an object of investigation. It is treated as if it were no more than the co-existence of separate, independently acting parts. The commonest use of such an extreme emphasis on parts embodies the use of causal lines or antecedent-consequent connections as the part. Again, to use a biological analogy after Schwab, such a view would be represented by a study of embryology which treated the flow of events instigated by each separate gene as if the organism were simply the area in space and time where each of these sequences reached its terminus; therefore, data are collected and interpreted without concern for the interaction of parts with each other. In biological experimentation, this view makes it possible to remove an organ and compare the performance of the animal with a missing organ with that of a whole animal. The difference between the two animals is interpreted as due entirely to the missing part. This concept of causal lines leads to the mode of inquiry most commonly known as the controlled experiment.

The Parts as Servants of the Whole or the Concept of Functional Part

This kind of part-whole theory represents a nearly opposite emphasis in that the whole is given special weight, and the parts

[7]The material on part-whole theories is drawn from the following works by Prof. Schwab: (a) Problems, topics, and issues. In Elam, Stanley (Ed.): *Education and the Structure of Knowledge.* Chicago, Rand, 1964; (b) Supvr.: *Biology Teacher's Handbook,* New York, J. Wiley, 1963.

are seen in terms of the needs of the whole, each serving the whole. This principle asserts that the whole has a central character or nature. This character or nature is expressed through recognizable activities. Investigation of an animal, for example, would begin with the identification of a typical whole organism through its characterizing activity systems: ingestion, digestion, reproduction, etc.

> The character or nature of a specific animal would be expressed through specific versions of these generic traits, plus certain others which set that species apart from other species.[8]

Only when these characteristic sustaining activities have been identified, would the investigation proceed to a study of parts. The parts would then be investigated by attempting to determine what role or function each plays in the whole. In such investigations, it must be assumed that the structure, location and action of each part are all appropriate to the role that they play for the whole. With this assumption, knowledge of structure, location and activity become data from which the role can be inferred. Further data are supplied by the physical relationships of parts to one another. It should be added that two points of such an investigation bear (or should bear) a complementary relationship to one another. The list of the basic activities of the whole given us by the first investigation becomes the subprinciples which enable us to interpret the data about structure and location as evidence of function. Conversely, the investigation of organ-parts will amend or add to the perceived activities by disclosing part actions which have no place in our original list of the characteristic whole activities.

The Whole as Determiner of its Parts

The conception of the functional part assumes a fixed structure, a fixed function for each part and a fixed relationship among parts and between parts and the whole. The subtype we shall now describe introduces a flexibility in each part and in the whole by presupposing that changes are possible in the parts as well as in

---

[8]Idem. (Supvr.): *Biology Teacher's Handbook.* New York, John Wiley and Sons, 1963, p. 188.

the whole. The principle assumes that the whole and each organ possess a range or repertory rather than a fixed structure or function. This repertory, in the case of the organism, may include changes even in architecture and in cellular arrangement. Such changes would be induced by changing needs arising from changed external circumstances imposed upon the organism. Enquiries proceeding on the basis of this view would look for (1) the conditions that evoke changes in the part; (2) the process by which changes are evoked; (3) the range of conditions which can be met within the repertory, i.e. what can be adjusted to and what cannot; (4) the items in the repertory, i.e. the sets of alternatives available for meeting and mastering vicissitudes. We look for the flexibility of the parts, and for the flexibility of the whole as well. For changes in parts, with their altered integration, would result in a different whole, insofar as the whole is seen as the integration of its parts. Obviously, there would be some anchoring stability in the midst of this flux, but it might be no more than "survival" or, in the case of the personality, continued "satisfactory living." Notice that this view of functional part would allow for radical changes in the *personality*. This kind of flexibility could leave room, for example, for radical personality changes appropriate to radical change in culture or subculture membership.

PART-WHOLE THEORIES AND THEIR RELATIONSHIP TO BEGINNINGS

Part-whole theories not only differ as to their concept of the part, the whole and their relationship to each other, but also in terms of their notion of originating factors or "beginnings."

With respect to a part-whole theory, the most obvious difference in *beginnings* is based on whether one or more parts or the whole is taken as the beginning. In the case of the whole as the sum of individual parts, the parts are obviously taken as the beginning; indeed, there are nothing but parts. In the case of the functional part conception, the whole is taken as the beginning, its character becomes the guiding principle in describing and accounting for the parts. In the case of the view of the whole as determining its parts, the whole is again the beginning, but with even greater hegemony over the parts than in the functional part case. In the latter, the whole "selects and organizes" its parts. In the former, the whole not only selects and organizes once, but continually "reselects and reorganizes." As we shall see in discussing personality theories, this matter of the potency of the beginning as well as the matter of what is taken as the beginning, becomes a very important issue.

In the case of biological organisms and in the case of many personality theories, some kind of embryogeny or development is crucially involved. In such cases, the question of beginnings becomes especially poignant. Here, one issue of principle among theories of personality will concern the extent to which the mature presonality and late stages in its development, either do or do not continue to bear the stigma of the beginning. In classical biological embryology, the beginning is paradoxically the end. That is, the condition of the embryo at any given time is studied and understood as a step or stage toward the mature organism. This assignment of beginnings is, of course, typical of the functional part view. It is possible, however, to treat the condition of the embryo at any given time not as a stage or step toward the mature organism, but as a consequence ensuing from the originating matter. Such a view obviously treats "beginnings" as extremely potent. Several personality theories adopt the latter procedure. We emphasize this matter of potency of beginnings especially with respect to an embryology because of its cogency to Freud. In his view, the beginning is located among the parts, specifically in one part; furthermore, this part is in itself a "given" or "beginning" and all further development bears its stigma.

PART-WHOLE THEORIES WITH RELATIONSHIP TO RANK-ORDER OF PARTS

Emphases within the formal-material holistic form of principle may be considerably qualified and shaded as the investgator comes to decisions about how to rank parts, if they are to be ranked, as they function in the mature organism or in any significant plateaus of development. Two gross choices are available to the investigator. On the one hand, he may treat parts as co-

ordinate, affecting equally the behavior of the matured or pla-
teaued whole. On the other hand, he may set them in some rank-
order.

Should he choose a hierarchy, finer graded choices are available to him. The hierarchy may be simply linear or two or more
parts may occupy the same rank while a third or fourth part ranks
lower or higher. Among theories which have identified the same
part, there are obviously alternatives as to which of these shall be
ranked first, second, third, and so on.

PASSIVITY VS. ACTIVITY

One further issue of principle distinguishes the theories we
shall deal with, an issue by no means wholly independent of the
issues treated so far, but which can be described independently
and in its own terms. This issue we shall call the issue of passivity-
activity. The issue is an ancient and familiar one. It concerns the
extent to which the investigator assigns to his "organism" any
"self-possessed" capacities for initiating, choosing, or controlling
its present or future.[9]

At one extreme lies the conception of the organism as a nineteenth century machine. ". . . each one of these bodies is inert,
that is, it is incapable of putting itself into action; to do this, it
must always enter into relations with another body for which it
receives a stimulus . . . They never break into vital activity unless
some foreign influence invites them."[10]

The other extreme involves not merely assigning some
"stimuli or initiators to the organism," as in the case of the
Freudian instincts, but consists in assigning to the organism another and quite different nineteenth century ideal, "mastery of
its fate." In the case of personality theory, it would be illustrated
by assigning such powers to the ego that it could choose its own
ideals and then proceed to condition, modulate and reorder itself
toward a reasonable approximation of this ideal. In a humbler
form, the activity extreme would be illustrated by a personality

---

[9]Joseph J. Schwab: excerpt from a discussion.

[10]Claude Bernard: *An Introduction to the Study of Experimental Medicine.*
New York, Dover, 1957, p. 78.

theory which assigned powers of self-diagnosis and some capacity for self-therapy. It is highly probable that Carl Rogers takes something of this view.[11]

The issue of activity-passivity will be crucial in distinguishing personality theories and will be equally critical in distinguishing theories of education.

THE CONCEPT OF COMMONPLACES

What we have described thus far is almost adequate for a frame of analysis. Two elements are lacking. In the first place, our frame considers only the formal structure of part-whole theories. That is, it discusses the relations of parts to one another, the relations of parts to whole, and the relations of part or whole to starting points. But it does not discuss the kind of thing which can serve as a part or whole. It cannot, because this matter is obviously contingent on the particular area of inquiry, the subject-matter, which is to be treated. Thus, the parts and whole of personality must be radically different from parts and whole of a material, living organism, and both of these will differ radically from the parts or organs of a polity or society.

The second inadequacy lies in the fact that, by default, we seem to convey the notion that there is little "real" or "certain" about scientific knowledge. That is, we have talked exclusively to the question of the differences of knowledge which arise as we take one or another position on different issues of principle. Knowledge, however, is not merely restatement of principles. It is the product which arises as principles are brought to bear on a subject matter. Though it must be granted that principles will determine one's choice and interpretation of data, data are chosen, they are disclosed by close scrutiny of the subject matter, and they constitute the ground on which the finished theory rests. A discussion of the force of the subject matter, and how it is expressed,

[11]Carl Rogers: *Client-Centered Therapy; Its Current Practice, Implications and Theory.* Boston, Houghton Mifflin, 1951. A conception between the two extremes can be found in a monograph by Magda B. Arnold; An excitatory theory of emotion. In Reymart, Martin L. (Ed.): *Feeling and Emotion.* New York, McGraw, 1950.

despite (and by the way of) the terms in which it is investigated, will enable us to complete our discussion of principles.

The key to these matters—the material character of parts and wholes and the role of subject matter in an enquiry—lies in the conception of a *topic* or *commonplace*.[12]

A commonplace is to be understood as one of a system of points (common-places) that evidence their durability and neutrality with respect to different purposes by occurring and recurring among theories about an almost-common subject-matter, however disparate the theories may be in principle and however remote in time and place.

What we have in mind becomes obvious in the case of physics. Newtonian physics has its own concept of *time, space, mass,* and *motion.* Relativity has its specific view of these same four concepts. Each system of mechanics assigns widely different properties and definitions to these four, but the four do occur in both systems.

We take the position that so long as a theory of mechanics continues to treat these four, that in itself shall be taken as sufficient evidence that their common subject matter (bodies of motion) requires them to do so. In general, then, the terms which occur and recur among diversities of theory about an approximately similar subject matter are their commonplaces and are taken to represent their common focus of attention, the subject matter. Among personality theories we discover seven commonplaces. They are: (1) a social factor, e.g. Sullivan's interpersonal relations, Freud's super-ego; (2) a biological factor, e.g. Aristotle's appetitive parts, Freud's id, Sullivan's primacy needs; (3) a rational part, e.g. Freud's ego, Plato's rational, Aristotle's deliberative scientific and philosophical faculties; (4) an energy factor, e.g. Freud's libido; (5) a factor of pleasure or satisfaction; (6) an additional emotive or affective factor, e.g. Plato's shame, Freud's

---

[12]See Joseph J. Schwab: Problems, topics and issues. In Elam, Stanley (Ed.): *Education and the Structure of Knowledge.* Chicago, Rand McNally, 1964, pp. 4-42; and Idem.: *The practical: arts of the eclectic. School Review, (79):*493-541, 1971.

guilt, Sullivan's anxiety; and (7) the therapist.[13]

In the following chapters I will describe Freud's investigation into human personality and indicate how the principles he adopted guided his investigation. I will then give an account of Freud's treatment of commonplaces of personality with a view to discovering the opportunities, limits and difficulties his theory poses for the theory and practice of education.

---

[13]We no not treat "the therapist" in this volume. Schwab points out that any commonplace may play any role in a theory. For example, emotion (see Chapter 7 on affect) could be used by an ingenious theorizer as one of the constitutive elements or organs of the soul. In the same way "the therapist" could be made a constitutive element in a theory bent on emphasizing self-therapy. However, most Western theories after Plato use the biological, the social and the rational as constitutive elements and attach energy and pleasure to one or more of these in different ways. This is most certainly the case for Freud. Further, as we shall indicate in Chapter Nine, Freud does not treat teaching and the teacher *qua* teacher as entire or partial equivalents of therapy and the therapist. Consequently, we shall confine the bulk of our treatment to these five commonplaces, give appropriate attention to emotion in Chapter Seven, and suggest the uses and limits of the analogue therapist-teacher in our final section.

Chapter Three

☐

FREUD'S PRINCIPLES

I T IS CLEAR THAT FREUD did not work with primitive or anti-principle principles. His metapsychological papers are an attempt to present a coherent and consistent frame of reference to guide the investigation into human personality.

We have often heard it maintained that sciences should be built up on clear and sharply defined basic concepts. In actual fact no science, not even the most exact, begins with such definitions. The true beginning of scientific activity consists rather in describing phenomena and then in proceeding to group, classify and correlate them. Even at the stage of description it is not possible to avoid applying certain abstract ideas to the material in hand, ideas derived from somewhere or other but certainly not from the new observations alone. Such ideas—which will later become the basic concepts of the science —are still more indispensable as the material is further worked over. They must at first necessarily possess some degree of indefiniteness; there can be no question of any clear delimitation of their content. So long as they remain in this condition, we come to an understanding about their meaning by making repeated references to the material of observation from which they appear to have been derived, but upon which, in fact, they have been imposed. Thus, strictly speaking, they are in the nature of conventions—although everything depends on their not being arbitrarily chosen but determined by their having significant relations to the empirical material, relations that we seem to sense before we can clearly recognize and demonstrate them. It is only after more thorough investigation of the field of observation that we are able to formulate its basic scientific concepts with increased precision, and progressively so to modify them that they become serviceable and consistent over a wide area. Then, indeed, the time may have come to confine them in definitions. The advance of knowledge, however, does not tolerate any rigidity even in definitions. Physics furnishes an excellent illustration of the way in which even 'basic concepts' that have been established in the form of definitions are constantly being altered in their content.

> A conventional basic concept of this kind, which at the moment is still somewhat obscure but which is indispensable to us in psychology, is that of an 'instinct'.[1]

Freud also did not employ rational principles, for he views the personality as an entity. That is, personality for Freud is a "something" (though obviously not a material "something"), an organization of describable parts with functions relative to one another.

> For we picture the unknown apparatus which serves the activities of the mind as being really like an instrument constructed of several parts (which we speak of as 'agencies'), each of which performs a particular function and which have a fixed spatial relation to one another: . . .[2]

Freud's principles are not reductive, for the constituents, or elements of the personality, have no existence apart from their existence in parts. Further, the notion of the id as a collection of mere wishes taken entirely apart from perceptions of the external world and the capacity of acting with respect to what is perceived makes no sense. In the same way, structures of the super-ego are enseless without wishes or impulses to repress. Finally, Freud does not discuss a reduction of mind or personality to smaller particles or constituents.[3]

Freud's tri-partite personality is clearly an instance of a part-whole theory, specifically one which is formal-material. The formality consists of the role or function of each part relative to the whole personality. The "material" consists of the wishes, the introjected or internalized values or attitudes, the sensory input and accumulation of meanings, etc. which are their content.

Part-whole theories, as we have indicated, are of several sub-types, differing as to their relationship of parts to each other and to the whole. It is clear that Freud does not view his parts as independent of one another. Two of them develop from the third part and continue to bear the mark of their origin.

The ego develops from the id. "Under the influence of the real external world around us, one portion of the id has undergone a

---

[1]Instincts and their Vicissitudes. In *Papers on Metapsychology*, S.E., XIV, 117-118.

[2]*The Question of Lay Analysis* (hereafter abbreviated to *Lay Analysis*), S.E., XX, 194.

[3]There is the possibility of a reduction to the chemical constituents of the part. See *Beyond the Pleasure Principle*, S.E., XVIII, 60 and our discussion on p. 52.

special development. . . . To this region of our mind we have given the name of *ego*."[4]

The super-ego is a division of the ego. "The long period of childhood, during which the growing human being lives in dependence on his parents, leaves behind it as a precipitate the formation in his ego of a special agency in which this parental influence is prolonged. It has received the name of *super-ego*. In so far as this super-ego is differentiated from the ego or is opposed to it, it constitutes a third power which the ego must take into account."[5] Not only are parts not separate, but in their mutuality continue to act with reference to the past. To put it briefly for the pesent, ego and super-ego act and exist primarily in relation to the id. This is to say that the id is not only primitive in terms of the ontogeny of the parts, but also a primary and potent force in their mature functioning.

Since, as we have indicated above, two of the parts arise from the third, we may suspect that Freud in no way conceived these parts as capable of any important qualitative change in response to needs of the whole. (Freud does not use the flexible subtype where the whole is the determiner of the parts.) On the contrary, Freud is beginning-oriented. He begins with the parts or, rather, one part, and leaves little room for the kind of radical change in the personality that would be characteristic of the functional-part view.

For similar reasons, we can say that Freud is not working with a concept of *the parts as servants of the whole*. In order to develop a part-as-servant conception, the inquiry must begin with a study of the whole and develop a view of its central character and nature. Only then can it turn to an examination of parts, even if these parts can be recognized by characteristics of their own, for parts are understood only as "organs" that contribute to the whole. In the case of a personality theory the parts cannot be recognized even as items in their own right, as in the case of the anatomical parts of the body. Consequently, a part-as-servant personality theory must, a fortiori, be characterized by an investigation which first provides a description of the central character and nature of the whole. As we shall show, Freud, by contrast, is beginning-oriented for he takes

[4]*An Outline of Psycho-Analysis*, S.E., XXIII, 145.
[5]*Ibid.*, p. 146.

the parts or one part as his beginning.[6] "We have arrived at our knowledge of this psychical apparatus by studying the individual development of human beings. To the oldest of these psychical provinces or agencies we give the name of *id*. It contains everything that is inherited, that is present at birth, that is laid down in the constitution—above all, therefore, the instincts, which originate from the somatic organization and which find a first psychical expression here [in the id] in forms unknown to us."[7]

However, Freud's beginning-orientation is more inclusive. His reliance on biology—makes him emphasize the *generic* over the *specific*. Man is *alive* first and *man* second. To be alive is to have needs and wants and to have a machine or apparatus capable of satisfy these needs and wants.[8] "The power of the id expresses the true purpose of the individual organism's life. This consists in the satisfaction of its innate needs."[9]

His beginnings have roots deeper even than the animate. Not only does he take the generic in man to be prior to and more potent than the specific in man, but he recognizes the importance of a pre-generic factor, prior to living—the inorganic. In some passages we find the inanimate dominating the living and an appeal to a vague notion of entropy. That is, the organism is seen as striving toward an equilibrium to be found through death as the doorway to the inorganic. The conceptual culmination of this notion is Freud's invention of a death instinct as one of the prime movers of life.

These generic and earlier stages—the inorganic, the id, the early life of the individual—are basic, potent and determining. Indeed, all later stages of development are shaky and in constant danger of regression.

In *Beyond the Pleasure Principle,* in which Freud describes the conservative nature of the life and death instincts, he characterizes the power balance between them thus:

> Let us suppose, then, that all the organic instincts are conservative, are acquired historically and tend towards the restoration of an earlier state of things. It follows that the phenomena of organic devel-

---

[6]See pp. 23-24.

[7]*An Outline of Psycho-Analysis*, S.E., XXIII, 145.

[8]The other parts, the ego and the super-ego, as we shall see, serve this purpose for the id.

[9]*An Outline of Psycho-Analysis*, S.E., XXIII, 148.

opment must be attributed to external disturbing and diverting influences. The elementary living entity would from its very begining have had no wish to change; if conditions remained the same, it would do no more than constantly repeat the same course of life. In the last resort, what has left its mark on the development of organisms must be the history of the earth we live in and of its relation to the sun. Every modification which is thus imposed upon the course of the organism's life is accepted by the conservative organic instincts and stored up for further repetition. Those instincts are therefore bound to give a deceptive appearance of being forces tending towards change and progress, whilst in fact they are merely seeking to reach an ancient goal by paths alike old and new. Moreover it is possible to specify this final goal of all organic striving. It would be in contradiction to the conservative nature of the instincts if the goal of life were a state of things which had never yet been attained. On the contrary, it must be an *old* state of things, an initial state from which the living entity has at one time or other departed and to which it is striving to return by the circuitous paths along which its development leads. If we are to take it as a truth that knows no exception that everything living dies for *internal* reasons—becomes inorganic once again—then we shall be compelled to say that *'the aim of all life is death'* and, looking backwards, that *'inanimate things existed before living ones'*.

The attributes of life were at some time evoked in inanimate matter by the action of a force of whose nature we can form no conception. It may perhaps have been a process similar in type to that which later caused the development of consciousness in a particular stratum of living matter. The tension which then arose in what had hitherto been an inanimate substance endeavoured to cancel itself out. In this way the first instinct came into being: the instinct to return to the inanimate state. It was still an easy matter at that time for a living substance to die; the course of its life was probably only a brief one, whose direction was determined by the chemical structure of the young life. For a long time, perhaps, living substance was thus being constantly created afresh and easily dying, till decisive external influences altered in such a way as to oblige the still surviving substance to diverge ever more widely from its original course of life and to make ever more complicated *détours* before reaching its aim of death. These circuitous paths to death, faithfully kept to by the conservative instincts, would thus present us to-day with the picture of the phenomena of life. If we firmly maintain the exclusively conservative nature of instincts, we cannot arrive at any other notions as to the origin and aim of life.[10]

---

[10]*Beyond the Pleasure Principle*, S.E., XVIII, 37-39. The Lamarckist influence, so obvious in this passage, is discussed on pp. 71-75. The emphasis in this quotation is mine.

In analogous fashion, Freud will contend that later developments of the personality, or those parts which develop last, the
parts that express the individuality of man, are the most shaky and
least dependable.

> Each of the mental differentiations that we have become acquainted
> with represents a fresh aggravation of the difficulties of mental func-
> tioning, increase its instability, and may become the starting-point for
> its breakdown, that is, for the onset of a disease. Thus, by being born
> we have made the step from an absolutely self-sufficient narcissism to
> the perception of a changing external world and the beginnings of
> the discovery of objects. And with this is associated the fact that we
> cannot endure the new state of things for long, that we periodically
> revert from it, in our sleep, to our former condition of absence of
> stimulation and avoidance of objects. It is true, however, that in this
> we are following a hint from the external world, which, by means of
> the periodical change of day and night, temporarily withdraws the
> greater part of the stimuli that affect us. The second example of such
> a step, pathologically more important, is subject to no such qualifica-
> tion. In the course of our development we have effected a separation
> of our mental existence into a coherent ego and into an unconscious
> and repressed portion which is left outside it; and we know that the
> stability of this new acquisition is exposed to constant shocks. In
> dreams and in neuroses what is thus excluded knocks for admission
> at the gates, guarded though they are by resistances; and in our wak-
> ing health we make use of special artifices for allowing what is repres-
> sed to circumvent the resistances and for receiving it temporarily into
> our ego to the increase of our pleasure. Jokes and humour, and to
> some extent the comic in general, may be regarded in this light. Every-
> one acquainted with the psychology of the neuroses will think of simi-
> lar examples of less importance; but I hasten on to the application I
> have in view.
>   It is quite conceivable that the separation of the ego ideal from
> the ego cannot be borne for long either, and has to be temporarily un-
> done. In all renunciations and limitations imposed upon the ego a
> periodical infringement of the prohibition is the rule; this indeed is
> shown by the institution of festivals, which in origin are nothing less
> nor more than excesses provided by law and which owe their cheerful
> character to the release which they bring.[11]

Only the beginning or origin is durable. The developments
due to later differentiations do not really reflect man's "basic na-

---

[11]*Group Psychology and the Analysis of the Ego* (hereafter referred to as *Group
Psychology*), S.E., XVIII, 130-131.

ture." They cannot be tolerated for very long periods of time. This view of the specific or recent as unstable, coupled with the fact that man himself is a recent development in the biological world, commits Freud to the importance of what is generic in man, namely his wants and needs. His problem then must be, what role do any of the parts of the whole play relative to wants and needs.

If we are correct in our interpretation of Freud as beginning-oriented, then the first part should contain the generic characteristics of the organism, the needs and wants, and should be most potent. This first part, the id, does indeed have this content and potency for Freud. The passage we have cited from *An Outline of Psycho-Analysis* (see page 32) unequivocally describes such a content. The footnote attached to it is equally clear as to the degree of the id's potency: "This oldest portion of the psychical apparatus remains the most *important*[12] throughout life; moreover, the investigations of psychoanalysis started with it."[13]

The other parts, as we have indicated, are seen as developing embryogenically from the id and as consequences of or as means toward fulfilling the needs of the id.

> Under the influence of the real external world around us, one portion of the id has undergone a special development. From what was originally a cortical layer, equipped with the organs for receiving stimuli and with arrangements for acting as a protective shield against stimuli, a special organization has arisen which henceforward acts as an intermediary between the id and the external world. To this region of our mind we have given the name of *ego*.
>
> *Here are the principal characteristics of the ego.* In consequence of the pre-established connection between sense perception and muscular action, the ego has voluntary movement at its command. It has the task of self-preservation. As regards *external* events, it performs that task by becoming aware of stimuli, by storing up experiences about them (in the memory), by avoiding excessively strong stimuli (through flight), by dealing with moderate stimuli (through adaptation) and finally by learning to bring about expedient changes in the external world to its own advantage (through activity). As regards *internal* events, in relation to the id, it performs that task by gaining control over the demands of the instincts, by deciding whether they are to be allowed satisfaction, by postponing that satisfaction to times and

---

[12]Emphasis mine.
[13]*An Outline of Psycho-Analysis*, S.E. XXIII, 145, n. 2.

circumstances favourable in the external world or by suppressing their excitations entirely. It is guided in its activity by consideration of the tensions produced by stimuli, whether these tensions are present in it or introduced into it. The raising of these tensions is in general felt as *unpleasure* and their lowering as *pleasure*. It is probable, however, that what is felt as pleasure or unpleasure is not the *absolute* height of this tension but something in the rhythm of the changes in them. The ego strives after pleasure and seeks to avoid unpleasure. An increase in unpleasure that is expected and foreseen is met by a *signal of anxiety;* the occasion of such an increase, whether it threatens from without or within, is known as a *danger*. From time to time the ego gives up its connection with the external world and withdraws into the state of sleep, in which it makes far-reaching changes in its organization. It is to be inferred from the state of sleep that this organization consists in a particular distribution of mental energy.[14]

The role of the second part, the ego, is to serve the first part, the id, and its wants and desires. It is the sense organ of the id, the mediator of what goes out of and into the organism. It represents the id to the external world and serves as navigator for the id through its stormy environment. It tries to fulfill the id's wants or pleasures and still protect the id from the environment.

The organism develops in an environment. The crucial shaping unit of that environment is the family in which the child grows and develops. Later, other adults can serve as surrogates of the family. Freud designates the super-ego as the part of the psyche that represents this influence.

The long period of childhood, during which the growing human being lives in dependence on his parents, leaves behind it as a precipitate the formation in his ego of a special agency in which this parental influence is prolonged. It has received the name of *super-ego*. In so far as this super-ego is differentiated from the ego or is opposed to it, it constitutes a third power which the ego must take into account.

An action by the ego is as it should be if it satisfies simultaneously the demands of the id, of the super-ego and of reality—that is to say, if it is able to reconcile their demands with one another. The details of the relation between the ego and the super-ego become completely intelligible when they are traced back to the child's attitude to its parents. This parental influence of course includes in its operation not only the personalities of the actual parents but also the family, racial

[14]*Ibid.*, pp. 145-146.

and national traditions handed on through them, as well as the demands of the immediate social *milieu* which they represent. In the same way, the super-ego, in the course of an individual's development, receives contributions from later successors and substitutes of his parents, such as teachers and models in public life of admired social ideals. It will be observed that, for all their fundamental differences, the id and the super-ego have one thing in common: they both represent the influences of the past—the id the influence of heredity, the super-ego the influence, essentially, of what is taken over from other people—whereas the ego is principally determined by the individual's own experience, that is by accidental and contemporary events.[15]

Restraint, values, conscience, these are the content of the super-ego. They are, however, nothing in their own right but only the price the id or organism must pay for living in a society. It should be borne in mind that the conduct of the super-ego is not only a consequence of the organism's dependence on environment, but also expresses some of the id's most basic needs.[16]

The id is not only the first part, and in the light of Freud's beginning-orientation, the most potent, but *inflexible* as well. The id can be guided and channeled by the ego but it cannot be controlled or changed. "Often a rider, if he is not to be parted from his horse, is obliged to guide it where it wants to go; so in the same way the ego is in the habit of transforming the id's will into action as if it were its own."[17]

The id's desires may not be fulfilled directly but they must be expressed. That is, the desire persists and will find expression in some substitute form or other. "It may be that by this introjection, which is a kind of regression to the mechanisms of the oral phase, the ego makes it easier for the object to be given up or renders that process possible. It may be that this identification is the *sole*[18] condition under which the id can give up its objects."[19]

The ego may control or repress an instinctual wish, but this

[15]*Ibid.*, 146-147.

[16]There are two identifications involved in super-ego formation: (1) a direct identification from the id to the father; (2) an introjection due to an unfulfilled object cathexis of the id to the mother. These identifications represent the most basic expressions of the id. See *The Ego and the Id*, S.E., XIX, 31.

[17]*The Ego and the Id*, S.E., XIX, 25.

[18]Emphasis mine.

[19]*The Ego and the Id*, S.E. XIX, 29.

does not eliminate the wish. "Although the act of repression demonstrates the strength of the ego, in one particular it reveals the ego's powerlessness and how impervious to influence are the separate instinctual impulses of the id."[20]

If a substitute or alternative expression of an instinctual need is not available, then a neurotic symptom is likely to result. "The main characteristics of the formation of symptoms have long since been studied and, I hope, established beyond dispute. A symptom is a sign of, and a substitute for, an instinctual satisfaction which has remained in abeyance; it is a consequence of the process of repression."[21]

The id is also strong, inflexible and persistently influential because of its connection with the archaic heritage of man.

> Through the forming of the ideal, what biology and the vicissitudes of the human species have created in the id and left behind in it is taken over by the ego and re-experienced in relation to itself as an individual. Owing to the way in which the ego ideal is formed, it has the most abundant links with the phylogenetic acquisition of each individual—his archaic heritage.[22]

The id is not only first and inflexible, but the other parts are dependent on it. This dependence is due to the conception of embryogenic development that Freud adopted. Freud's embryogenesis sees the embryo not as a step towards the mature organism but as the result of and dependent on the originating matter. For Freud, this dependency is so far-reaching as to deny entirely the very notion of an embryo as a step or stage toward the mature organism. On the contrary, embryogeny is seen as no more than the expression of the dynamism of the originating matter, the id. All developing parts will be dependent on the original part and bear its stigma.

The ego is formed out of the id and derives its energy only from the id. "The ego is after all only a portion of the id, . . . From a dynamic point of view it is weak, it has borrowed its energies from the id, and we are not entirely without insight into the methods—

---

[20]*Inhibitions, Symptoms and Anxiety* (hereafter referred to as *Anxiety*), S.E., XX 97.

[21]*Ibid.*, p. 91.

[22]*The Ego and the Id*, S.E., XIX, 36.

we might call them dodges—by which it extracts further amounts of energy from the id."[23]

The super-ego is dependent on the id in two senses:

(1) As a precipitate of the ego it is a secondary derivative of the id. "Thus in the id, which is capable of being inherited, are harboured residues of the existences of countless egos; and, when the ego forms its super-ego out of the id, it may perhaps only be reviving shapes of former egos and be bringing them to resurrection."[24]

(2) It is contact with the deepest and most fundamental parts of the id. "Through the forming of the ideal, what biology and the vicissitudes of the human species have created in the id and left behind in it is taken over by the ego and re-experienced in relation to itself as an individual."[25]

We have already indicated how far Freud is beginning-oriented, even phylogenetically. First, there is his emphasis on the pull of encompassing inorganic matter of the universe, expressed as a battle waged between the life and death instincts. In addition, there is his emphasis on the origin of the ego and super-ego out of the id. The origin of one part is left unaccounted for, the origin of the id. The lack of such an account is strictly analogous to the problem of the origin of life as it would appear to the biologist.

In one sense there is more than mere analogy or parallelism here. That is, the id comes into being as the prime necessity for the existence of life. Life exists and can continue to exist only to the extent that it can "recognize" and select from the environment what it needs for its persistence and reject what is inimical to its continued organization. This is precisely Freud's conception of the id. "Thus it may in general be suspected that the *individual* dies of his internal conflicts but that the *species* dies of its unsuccessful struggle against the external world if the latter changes in a fashion which cannot be adequately dealt with by the adaptation which the species has acquired."[26]

---

[23]*New Introductory Lectures on Psycho-Analysis* (hereafter referred to as *New Introductory Lectures*), S.E., XXII, 76-77.

[24]*The Ego and the Id*, S.E., XIX, 38.

[25]*Ibid.*, p. 36.

[26]*An Outline of Psycho-Analysis*, S.E., XXIII, 150.

Just as the id represents what would have to come about in order for there to be any evolution of life from non-life, so there must be the same kind of contact with the environment for an evolution of ego and super-ego out of the id. The ego is developed as a result of contact with the environment.

> We need scarcely look for a justification of the view that the ego is that portion of the id which was modified by the proximity and influence of the external world, which is adapted for the reception of stimuli and as a protective shield against stimuli, comparable to the cortical layer by which a small piece of living substance is surrounded. The relation to the external world has become the decisive factor for the ego; it has taken on the task of representing the external world to the id—fortunately for the id, which could not escape destruction if, in its blind efforts for the satisfaction of its instincts, it disregarded that supreme external power.[27]

The ego thus adds the factor of thought or intelligence to life and we have not only an animal, but an animal that thinks as well.

Similarly, the super-ego develops as a result of the organism's growth in a human environment, i.e. the family. It is as a result of the influence of his relationship to his parents and later parent-substitutes that the child is socialized. The development of the super-ego makes it possible for us to speak of social life as against a mere being alive in the way of a one-celled organism.

However, Freud's extreme emphasis on beginning, coupled with the importance to him of the environment, could contain elements of a kind of residual end-orientation. This would be possible if we assume that everything to be found in man's nature at present was there in some form at the beginning of human history. It would require the further assumption that the present environment is identical with his earlier environment.

In fact, Freud does seem to indicate that all of the elements that constitute man's nature were present at the beginning and have not undergone any radical change.

> Religion, morality, and a social sense—the chief elements in the higher side of man—were originally one and the same thing. According to the hypothesis which I put forward in *Totem and Taboo* they were acquired phylogenetically out of the father-complex: religion and moral restraint through the process of mastering the Oedipus

---

[27]*New Introductory Lectures*, S.E., XXII, 75.

complex itself, and social feeling through the necessity for overcoming the rivalry that then remained between the members of the younger generation. . . . Even to-day the social feelings arise in the individual as a superstructure built upon impulses of jealous rivalry against his brothers and sisters.[28]

Consequently, whatever evolved from that earlier environment would be adaptive with respect to the present environment and therefore, by a curious tour de force, carrying beginning-orientation as far as he does, would give him a kind of end-orientation. This is precisely the sort of end-orientation one can see in *Civilization and Its Discontents*[29] and in *The Future of an Illusion*,[30] in which Freud describes work or more specifically the origin of work.

There is a similar orientation in his description of the origin of the higher side of man:

Perhaps we may begin by explaining that the element of civilization enters on the scene with the first attempt to regulate these social relationships. If the atempt were not made, the relationships would be subject to the arbitrary will of the individual: that is to say, the physically stronger man would decide them in the sense of his own interests and instinctual impulses. Nothing would be changed in this if this stronger man should in his turn meet someone even stronger than he. Human life in common is only made possible when a majority comes together which is stronger than any separate individual and which remains united against all separate individuals. The power of this community is then set up as 'right' in opposition to the power of the individual, which is condemned as 'brute force'. This replacement of the power of the individual by the power of a community constitutes the decisive step of civilization. The essence of it lies in the fact that the members of the community restrict themselves in their possibilities of satisfaction, whereas the individual knew no such restrictions. The first requisite of civilization, therefore, is that of justice—that is, the assurance that a law once made will not be broken in favour of an individual. This implies nothing as to the ethical value of such a law. The further course of cultural development seems to tend towards making the law no longer an expression of the will of a small community—a caste or a stratum of the population or a racial group—which, in its turn, behaves like a violent individual towards other, and perhaps more numerous, collections of people. The

[28]*The Ego and the Id*, S.E., XIX, 37.
[29]*Civilization and its Discontents*, S.E., XXI, 99-101.
[30]*The Future of an Illusion*, S.E., XXI, 3-39.

final outcome should be a rule of law to which all—except those who are not capable of entering a community—have contributed by a sacrifice of their instincts, and which leaves no one—again with the same exception—at the mercy of brute force.[31]

It is, however, only a *residual* end-orientation since he has not decided to view work as basic to man in environment, but as the modification of man caused by environment. Nor does he view the higher side of man as basic but as a modification caused by living in an environment.

Furthermore, this conjecture collapses entirely if his premise of the identity or similarity of the early and current environment is tested and fails. And, of course, it does fail. Not only is there very good reason to suppose that the physical environment of the last hundreds of thousands of years differs radically from the environment in which life had its origin, but also the contemporary social environment is different from the social environment of primitive man and contemporary environments themselves differ radically. Therefore, if we try to take this argument as a magnificient tour de force, in which by pushing the beginning-orientation to its limit we get end-orientation, we fail; that is, we do not come up with a view of the nature of man as a whole. Rather, we come up with a view of the nature of man which is culture bound, and only if we assume that the culture Freud knew is the universal culture would it be a true nature of man.

We have indicated[32] that one issue which would distinguish theories of personality is the degree to which the organism is seen as passive or active.

Freud's view of personality cannot simply be classified as passive in the conventional biological sense of the term. By this we refer to the tendency in biology to treat living things as passive creatures to surrounding events. They move only in response to external stimuli. For Freud life is continuous in the id and requires no external stimulus. Freud describes the id in the following manner: "We approch the id with analogies: we call it a chaos, a cauldron full of seething excitations. We picture it as being open at its end to somatic influences, and as there taking up into itself instinctual

---

[31]*Civilization and its Discontents*, S.E., XXI, 95.
[32]Chapter Two, pp. 25-26.

needs which find their psychical expression in it, but we cannot say in what substratum."[33] There is self-generating activity in Freud's id, for its instinctual demands are constantly striving for expression. However, if we are to view the self or self-generating activity as self-aware and free to choose its deals, then Freud's theory must be viewed as passive.

The super-ego, the source of ideals and values, is developed as a result of the Oedipal conflict, and represents an environmentally induced structure. " 'Very true,' " we can say, " 'and here we have that higher nature, in this ego ideal or super-ego, the representative of our relation to our parents. When we were little children we knew these higher natures, we admired them and feared them; and later we took them into ourselves.' "[34] What appear to be stimuli arising from the super-ego are the moment's expression of pre-Oedipal stages.

As a derivative structure, the ego also does not possess the power to stimulate or instigate. It can merely process stimuli from without. "This system is turned towards the external world, it is the medium for the perceptions arising thence . . . It is the sense-organ of the entire apparatus; moreover, it is receptive not only to excitations from without but also to those arising from the interior of the mind."[35] "The ego is after all only a portion of the id, a portion that has been expediently modified by the proximity of the external world with its threat of danger. From a dynamic point of view it is weak, it has borrowed its energies from the id."[36c] Only through therapy can the individual aspire to any kind of important change or self direction. However, the idea of therapy itself, though it acknowledges a rational capacity for self discovery—"Accordingly, the first part of the help we have to offer is intellectual work on our side and encouragement to the patient to collaborate in it."[37]—has for its basic component an instinctually derived factor: the trans-between the patient and the analyst.

At this point what turns the scale in his struggle is not his intellectual insight—which is neither strong enough nor free enough for

---

[33]*New Introductory Lectures,* S.E., XXII, 73.

[34]*The Ego and the Id,* S.E., XIX, 36.

[35]*New Introductory Lectures,* S.E., XXII, 75.

[36]*Ibid.,* pp. 76-77.

[37]*An Outline of Psycho-Analysis,* S.E., XXIII, 177.

such an achievement—but simply and solely his relation to the doctor. In so far as his transference bears a 'plus' sign, in clothes the doctor with authority and is transformed into belief in his communications and explanations. In the absence of such a transference, or if it is a negative one, the patient would never even give a hearing to the doctor and his arguments. . . . a man is only accessible for the intellectual side too, in so far as he is capable of a libidinal cathexis of objects . . .[38]

It is already reasonably clear that as a result of Freud's beginning-orientation he will organize his parts in an order that is hierarchical. The dependence of the ego and super-ego on the id must place the id at the top of the hierarchy.[39] The close relationship of the super-ego to the id would place the super-ego second in the rank order, thus leaving the ego at the bottom of the hierarchy. "Thus the super-ego is always close to the id and can act as its representative *vis-à-vis* the ego. It reaches deep down into the id and for that reason is farther from consciousness than the ego is."[40] The super-ego is destined to rule over the ego as well. "Although it is accessible to all later influences, it nevertheless preserves throughout life the character given to it by its derivation from the father-complex—namely, the capacity to stand apart from the ego and to master it."[41] Freud treats most of the commonplaces.[42] The emotive or affective factor, however, does not emerge clearly. From the standpoint of the subject matter itself, this neglect is hard to understand, for when we view man non-theoretically an emotive or affective factor is— perhaps by its very nature—conspicuously and insistently present. It is undeniable that people express feelings— love, fear, hope, dread, anxiety, terror, hunger, joy, sadness, etc., and little less undeniable that they have them. There certainly was a period in psychology when an emotive or affective factor was the focus of attention, e.g. in the writings of William James and Walter B. Cannon. In Freud this commonplace is difficult to circum-

---

[38]*Introductory Lectures on Psycho-Analysis*, S.E., XVI, 445-446.

[39]Chapter Two, pp. 24-25.

[40]*The Ego and the Id*, S.E., XIX, 48-49.

[41]*Ibid.*, p. 48.

[42]Biological, social, rational, pleasure, energy, and emotive or affective factor and the therapist. See Chapter Two, pp. 26-28 and note 13, p. 28.

scribe.[43] Why is this factor neglected in Freud?

It may be that Freud neglects this commonplace because of his commitment to more "basic" phenomena. His heavy dependence on biology, as embodied in his conception of the id, will force him to view all phenomena that are not early and immediately related to the biological instinct as epi-phenomena. Moreover, his decision to favor an instinct theory will direct him to reduce all complex feelings to simple elements, such as love and hate to representatives of life and death.

The other commonplaces are seen very clearly. In fact, Freud's choice of a part-whole theory emphasizes the role of the commonplaces. We shall see that he assigns each part of the "psyche" to one commonplace: the id to the biological; the super-ego to the social; the ego to the rational; while pleasure and energy are in the first instance to be found only in one of the parts, the id.

---

[43]The 'emotive' will be shown to be a highly complicated notion. See Chapter Eight.

PART II

THE STRUCTURE AND CONTENT
OF FREUD'S THEORY

Chapter Four

□

THE BIOLOGICAL COMMONPLACE

WE HAVE DEMONSTRATED that Freud elevated the generic over the specific, which is to say that man is animal first, and human only second, and that he is characteristically pulled (as is all life) in the direction of the inorganic. We have also demonstrated Freud's beginning-orientation and the fact that the beginning is embodied in the id. If we can now establish the character of the id as essentially biological, we shall have established the thoroughgoing biological character of Freud's personality theory. The evidence for Freud's commitment to a biological emphasis is the burden of this chapter. This biological emphasis is seen—

A. In his explicit commitment to see mental life from the biological point of view.

B. In the extent to which his theory is saturated with biological terms, analogies and formulations. These are found principally in:

(1) His instinct theory and especially in his insistence on the conservative nature of the instincts.

(2) His conception of pleasure and even more emphatically in his insistence on the supremacy of the pleasure principle.

(3) His conception of energy as being of only one kind and originating in the id.

(4) His stress on conflict. A conception of conflict, based on nineteenth century evolutionary theory, as found within man as well as between men, and between man and his environment.

(5) His concern for man's phylogenetic endowment.

(6) His emphasis on infancy and childhood.

(7) His account of man's psychological development

in biological terms.

(8) His use of a *Lamarckian* evolutionary concept.

(9) His overbearing biological and psychological determinism.

(10) His contention that an organism is in constant danger of regression.

(11) His treatment of rationality, group psychology, religion and morality as derivative phenomena.

A. EXPLICIT COMMITMENT TO BIOLOGY

Freud freely admits his dependence on biology for explanatory principles. Throughout his writings, Freud credits biology with providing him useful psychological hypotheses and formulations. He also asserts the hegemony of life phenomena, biological subject matter, over the subject matter of psychology. In fact, he looks forward to seeing his psychological terminology replaced by physiological and chemical terminology. Freud's appeal to the hegemony of the biological over the psychological can be seen in the following passage:

> The present development of human beings requires, as it seems to me, no different explanation from that of animals. What appears in a minority of human individuals as an untiring impulsion towards further perfection can easily be understood as a result of the instinctual repression upon which is based all that is most precious in human civilization.[1]

He again appeals to biology in his justification for introducing an instinct theory into psychology:

> There are various points in favour of the hypothesis of there having been from the first a separation between sexual instincts and others, ego-instincts, . . . But, in the first place, the distinction made in this concept corresponds to the common, popular distinction between hunger and love. In the second place, *there are biological considerations in its favour*.[2]

The argument for his instinct theory continues in this vein:

> Thirdly, we must recollect that all our provisional ideas in psychology will presumably some day be based on an organic substructure. This

[1]*Beyond the Pleasure Principle*, S.E., XVIII, 42.

[2]*On Narcissism: an Introduction* (hereafter referred to as *Narcissism*), S.E., XIV, 78. Emphasis mine.

makes it probable that it is special substances and chemical processes which perform the operations of sexuality and provide for the extension of individual life into that of the species. We are taking this probability into account in replacing the special chemical substances by special psychical forces. [sic!]

I try in general to keep psychology clear from everything that is different in nature from it, even biological lines of thought. For that very reason I should like at this point expressly to admit that the hypothesis of separate ego-instincts and sexual instincts (that is to say, the libido theory) rests scarcely at all upon a psychological basis, but derives its principal support from biology.[3]

In discussing his theory of narcissism Freud tells us, ". . . I know that these different lines of development correspond to the differentiation of functions in a highly complicated biological whole; . . . ."[4] His appeal to the hegemony of biology is emphasized also in the following passage:

The contribution which biology has to make here certainly does not run counter to the distinction between sexual and ego-instincts. Biology teaches that sexuality is not to be put on a par with other functions of the individual; for its purposes go beyond the individual and have as their content the production of new individuals—that is, the preservation of the species. It shows, further, that two views, seemingly equally well-founded, may be taken of the relation between the ego and sexuality. On the one view, the individual is the principal thing, sexuality is one of its activities and sexual satisfaction one of its needs; while on the other view the individual is a temporary and transient appendage to the quasi-immortal germ-plasm, which is entrusted to him by the process of generation. The hypothesis that the sexual function differs from other bodily processes in virtue of a special chemistry is, I understand, also a postulate of the Ehrlich school of biological research.[5]

---

[3]*Ibid.*, pp. 78-79. However, it is important to recognize that Freud is not an unqualified Comtean reductionist of psychology to biology. He concludes this section by indicating that he would be willing to abandon a biological hypothesis should his psychoanalytic work prove otherwise. "But I shall be consistent enough [with my general rule] to drop this hypothesis if psychoanalytic work should itself produce some other, more serviceable hypothesis about the instincts." (*Ibid.*, p. 79).

[4]*Ibid.*, p. 89.

[5]Instincts and their vicissitudes, S.E., XIV, 124-125. Although he presents the two views as "seemingly" well-justified, Freud resolves the issue for himself in a definite preference for the view of the individual as transitory. See the numerous references, *passim*, to Freud's emphasis on Lamarckism, other phylo-evolutionary factors and the hegemony of the instincts.

Throughout *Beyond the Pleasure Principle,* Freud continues this appeal to the findings of biology to substantiate his psychological theories. "We must therefore turn to biology in order to test the validity of the belief."[6] Further, Freud believed that one day, he would be able to replace his biological description with a chemical one. "The deficiencies in our description would probably vanish if we were already in a position to replace the psychological terms by physiological or chemical ones."[7]

This appeal to biology continues even where the subject is no longer confined to the frankly biological factors, pleasure and the instincts. In the Preface to *The Ego and the Id,* Freud states:

> In the following pages these thoughts are linked to various facts of analytic observation and an attempt is made to arrive at new conclusions from this conjunction; in the present work, however, there are no fresh borrowings from biology, . . .[8]

Freud will even assert that the ego represents an expression of man's biological nature: "It is as if we were thus supplied with a proof of what we have just asserted of the conscious ego; that it is first and foremost a body-ego."[9] The trend continues into his final works. When arguing the necessity for the distinction conscious-unconscious, Freud claims, ". . . there would thus be no alternative left to assuming that there are physical or somatic processes which are concomitant with the psychical ones . . . If so, it of course becomes plausible to lay stress in psychology on these somatic processes, to see in *them* the true essence of what is psychical. . . ."[10]

B. EVIDENCE FROM BIOLOGICAL TERMS, ANALOGIES AND FORMULATIONS

B1. The Instinct Theory

Freud's personality theory is saturated with biological terms, analogies and formulations. We shall begin with a consideration

---

[6]*Beyond the Pleasure Principle,* S.E., XVIII, 45. The entire seventh chapter is replete with similar statements.

[7]*Ibid.,* p. 60.

[8]*The Ego and the Id,* S.E., XIX, 12.

[9]*Ibid.,* p. 27.

[10]*An Outline of Psycho-Analysis,* S.E., XXIII, 157.

of the instinct theory. For Freud, what is common to all men is their instinctual nature. Among men there are genetic differences as well as differences in the way they develop an inhibitional system which enable them to live in a society that is at odds with man's instinctual nature.[11] Further, instinct for Freud, as we shall show, is a first cause or principle, that which is irreducible, or in Freud's language, a "basic concept." Hence, if we show that the instincts, Eros and Death, are purely biological in nature and their relations to each other are seen in biological terms, we have in effect again demonstrated that Freud is fundamentally biological in his orientation.

Because of his beginning-orientation[12] Freud not only emphasizes the "animal" over the "human" but recognizes the greater importance of a pre-generic factor, the inorganic. The decision to view the inorganic as prior to the organic will force Freud to view the instincts as conservative and not easily amenable to change.

Let us examine some of the characteristics of the concept instinct as seen by Freud.

For Freud, instincts are fundamental to the whole man. They represent "the true purpose" of the individual organism's life. "The power of the id expresses the true purpose of the individual organism's life. This consists in the satisfaction of its innate needs. . . ." "The forces which we assume to exist behind the tensions caused by the needs of the id are called *instincts*."[13]

When Freud describes the removal of that which is unique to the individual (inhibition), what is disclosed is what is common to men, the instincts: ". . . and this result [group membership] can only be reached by the removal of those inhibitions upon his instincts which are peculiar to each individual, and by his resigning those expressions of his inclinations which are especially his own."[14] Because instincts are so basic most attempts at denials of them are not possible in the Freudian system. "Attempts at flight

---

[11]We have indicated in Chapter Three, pp. 32-34, that the common and generic takes precedence over the specific or particular.

[12]See Chapter Three, pp. 31-35.

[13]*An Outline of Psycho-Analysis*, S.E., XXIII, 148.

[14]*Group Psychology*, S.E., XVIII, 88.

from the demands of instinct are, however, in general useless, . . ."[15]

For Freud instinct is a first cause or principle. "A conventional basic concept of this kind, which at the moment is still somewhat obscure but which is indispensable to us in psychology, is that of an 'instinct'."[16]

Instinct is not only a "basic" concept or principle but it cannot be reduced.[17] "Nevertheless, we should not neglect to ask ourselves whether instinctual motives like these, which are so highly specialized on the one hand, do not admit of further dissection in accordance with the *sources* of the instinct, so that only primal instincts—those which cannot be further dissected—can lay claim to importance."[18] This irreducibility of the primal instincts is seen further in his criticism of a "herd instinct." "When once natural continuity has been severed in this way, if a breach is thus made between things which are by nature interconnected, it is easy to regard the phenomena that appear under these special conditions as being expressions of a special instinct that is *not further reducible*—the social instinct 'herd instinct,' 'group mind', which does not come to light in any other situations."[19]

Freud holds that this most basic concept, instinct, is of a biological nature. "We have already alluded to the most important of these [postulate of the instincts], and all we need now do is to state it expressly. This postulate is of a biological nature, and makes use of the concept of 'purpose' . . ."[20] Or consider the following more explicit statement by Freud. "If we now apply ourselves to considering mental life from a *biological* point of view,

---

[15]The Unconscious. In *Papers on Metapsychology*, S.E., XIV, 184.

[16]Instincts and their vicissitudes, S.E., XIV, 117-118.

[17]This is apparently a fundamental irreducibility. That is, in discussing the behavior of a human being nothing further can be said by way of explanation after one has attributed an action to an instinct. However, Freud is perfectly well prepared to see the mature instinct develop from a "component instinct," at least in the maturation of the individual. It may be that Freud would conceive this sort of development as taking place in phylogenesis as well. See pp. 62-65.

[18]Instincts and their vicissitudes, S.E., XIV, 124.

[19]*Group Psychology*, S.E., XVIII, 70. Emphasis mine. *See also* The Protocol, *Group Psychology and the Analysis of the Ego*, chapter iv, par. 3, p. 198.

[20]Instincts and their vicissitudes, S.E., XIV, 120.

an 'instinct' appears to us as a concept on the frontier between the mental and the somatic . . ."[21] Freud sees the sources of instinct to be somatic. "By the source [*Quelle*] of an instinct is meant the somatic process which occurs in an organ or part of the body and whose stimulus is represented in mental life by an instinct."[22]

Freud continued to develop his instinct theory and came to conclude that there are only two instincts, Eros and Death. In several places, however, he alluded to the possibility of there being more than these two instincts. For example, in one of his last works, *An Outline of Psycho-Analysis*, Freud states: "After long hesitancies and vacillations we have decided to assume the existence of only two basic instincts, . . ."[23] The possibility of additional instinct is suggested in other sources also.[24]

Can it be that the force of the subject matter (i.e. data) made Freud consider the possibility of there being more than the two instincts that he postulated? Freud concludes his volume, *Beyond the Pleasure Principle*, in a manner that suggests his readiness to consider this possibility:

> Here might be the starting point for fresh investigations. Our consciousness communicates to us feelings from within not only of pleasure and unpleasure but also of a peculiar tension which in its turn can be either pleasureable or unpleasurable. . . . We must be patient and await fresh methods and occasions of research. We must be ready, too, to abandon a path that we have followed for a time, if it seems to be leading to no good end.[25]

However, in later theoretical works, Freud continues to explain this "peculiar tension" in terms of the two basic instincts.

We do not know whether the above examples represent (a) a rethinking by Freud of the possibility of additional instincts or (b) a manner of stating that the many instincts that have been considered by others can be subsumed under *his* own two. In either case the examples cited disagree with the position adopted

---

[21]*Ibid.*, pp. 121-122.
[22]*Ibid.*, p. 123.
[23]*An Outline of Psycho-Analysis*, S.E., XXIII, 148.
[24]Instincts and their vicissitudes, S.E., XIV, 132.
[25]*Beyond the Pleasure Principle*, S.E., XVIII, 63-64.

by Freud in such works as *Group Psychology and the Analysis of the Ego* and *Civilization and Its Discontents* where the group instincts or horde instinct, religion or, for that matter, any primary feeling besides those of the pleasure-pain series are denied.[26] The introduction of additional instincts would have opened up interesting possibilities for the reformulation of Freud's theory.

When we examine the two instincts that Freud finally chose, Eros and Death, we discover that these instincts and their components are of a distinctly biological nature.

Eros, the life instinct, has, according to Freud, three aspects: self-preservation, ego-love and object love. (These are not separate components to which the instinct can be reduced.) All three aspects are clearly biological in nature. Self-preservation need not be discussed. Love, whether the object be one's self or the other, is first and foremost "sexual" or "libidinal" in nature. *"Being in love* is based on the simultaneous presence of directly sexual impulsions and of sexual implusions that are inhibited in their aims, while the object draws a part of the subject's narcissistic ego-libido to itself. It is a condition in which there is only room for the ego and the object."[27]

And:

> There can be no question but that the libido has somatic sources, that it streams to the ego from various organs and parts of the body. This is most clearly seen in the case of that portion of the libido which, from its instinctual aim, is described as a sexual excitation. The most prominent of the parts of the body from which this libido arises are known by the name of 'erotogenic zones,' though in fact the whole body is an erotogenic zone of this kind. The greater part of what we know about Eros—that is to say, about its exponent, the libido—has been gained from a study of the sexual function, which, indeed, on the prevailing view, even if not according to our theory, coincides with Eros. We have been able to form a picture of the way in which the sexual urge, which is destined to exercise a decisive influence on our life, gradually develops out of successive contributions from a number of component instincts, which represent particular erotogenic zones.[28]

---

[26]See *The Protocol: Civilization and Its Discontents,* Chap. i par. 4., p. 233.
[27]*Group Psychology,* S.E., XVIII, 142.
[28]*An Outline of Psycho-Analysis,* S.E., XXIII, 151.

The Death Instinct is seen in biological terms as well:

> Starting from speculations on the beginning of life and from biological parallels, I drew the conclusion that, besides the instinct to preserve living substance and to join it into even larger units, there must exist another, contrary instinct seeking to dissolve those units and to bring them back to their primaeval, inorganic state.[29]

In *The Ego and the Id,* Freud makes this point even more explicitly: "On the basis of theoretical considerations, supported by biology, we forward the hypothesis of a death instinct, . . ."[30]

Freud viewed the relationship of the instincts to each other in a distinctly biological manner. "On this view, a special physiological process (of anabolism or catabolism) would be associated with each of the two classes of instincts; both kinds of instinct would be active in every particle of living substance, though in unequal proportions, so that some one substance might be the principal representative of Eros."[31] One especially telling association between the instincts and physiological process is found in *The Ego and the Id.*

> It [the id] does so in the first place by complying as swiftly as possible with the demands of the non-desexualized libido—by striving for the satisfaction of the directly sexual trends. But it does so in a far more comprehensive fashion in relation to one particular form of satisfaction in which all component demands converge—by discharge of the sexual substances, which are saturated vehicles, so to speak, of the erotic tensions. The ejection of the sexual substances in the sexual act corresponds in a sense to the separation of soma and germ-plasm. This accounts for the likeness of the condition that follows complete sexual satisfaction to dying, and for the fact that death coincides with the act of copulation in some of the lower animals. These creatures die in the act of reproduction because, after Eros has been eliminated through the process of satisfaction, the death instinct has a free hand for accomplishing its purposes.[32]

The instincts not only work against each other but they fuse,

---

[29]*Civilization and Its Discontents,* S.E., XXI, 118. Freud's dependence upon biology is especially observable in his discussion of instincts in *Beyond the Pleasure Principle,* S.E., XVIII, Chap. VI, pp. 44-61. See *The Protocol: Beyond the Pleasure Principle,* Chap. vi, pp. 188-190.

[30]*The Ego and the Id,* S.E., XIX, 40.

[31]*Ibid.,* p. 41.

[32]*Ibid.,* p. 47.

blend and are alloyed with each other.[33] As we indicated previously, human manifestations such as religion, morality, the social sense, do not require that Freud postulate any more than the two basic instincts. "This concurrent and mutually opposing action of the two basic instincts gives rise to the whole variegation of the phenomena of life. The analogy of our two basic instincts extends from the sphere of living things to the pair of opposing forces—attraction and repulsion—which rule in the inorganic world."[34]

In Freud's theory the instincts remain as a conservative force and their conservative nature has biological roots. "Acting in this way, both the instincts would be conservative in the strictest sense of the word, since both would be endeavoring to re-establish a state of things that was disturbed by the emergence of life."[35] Similarly, Freud explains the "compulsion to repeat"[36] as a basic tendency of the instincts to restore an earlier state of things that has been disturbed by external forces, i.e. as an indication of the conservative nature of the instincts. To justify this assertion Freud draws a biological analogy:

> *It seems, then, that an instinct is an urge inherent in organic life to restore an earlier state of things* which the living entity has been obliged to abandon under the pressure of external disturbing forces; that is, it is a kind of organic elasticity or, to put it another way, the expression of the inertia inherent in organic life.
>
> This view of instincts strikes us as strange because we have become used to seeing in them a factor impelling towards change and development, whereas we are now asked to recognize in them the precise contrary—an expression of the *conservative* nature of living substance. On the other hand we soon call to mind examples from animal life

---

[33]Here Freud appears to be adopting the nineteenth century chemical view of elements. Thus Freud can preserve his coherence since the chemical elements which lose their identity when in combination can be recovered in the elemental state by their history of previous union.

[34]*An Outline of Psycho-Analysis*, S.E., XXIII, 149.

[35]*The Ego and the Id*, S.E., XIX, 40.

[36]See *Beyond the Pleasure Principle*, S.E., XVIII, 36; *The Protocol: Beyond the Pleasure Principle*, Chap. v, pp. 185-187; and *An Outline of Psycho-analysis*, S.E., XXIII, 149. The significance of this remark lies in the fact that it represents Freud's notion of the biological evolutionary process as one in which antecendent organs, etc. remain in the individual like fallen cities beneath the foundation of the modern structure. This conception will be discussed later. See our section on regression, pp. 76-77.

which seem to confirm the view that instincts are historically determined. Certain fishes, for instance, undertake laborious migrations at spawning-time in order to deposit their spawn in particular waters far removed from their customary haunts. In the opinion of many biologists what they are doing is merely to seek out the localities in which their species formerly resided but which in the course of time they have exchanged for others. The same explanation is believed to apply to the migratory flights of birds of passage. . .[37]

B2. Pleasure

Freud views pleasure as a diminution of excitation, and unpleasure as an increase of excitation. The excitation arises somatically and constitutes the impulse or motivation of the instincts. Therefore, for Freud, pleasure is necessarily only of one kind, biological. Life is governed by the pleasure principle and all manifestations of pleasure which appear to be beyond the pleasure principle are either prior to it or in its service.

Freud admits that he borrowed his concept of pleasure directly from biology. "This postulate is of a biological nature, . . . the nervous system is an apparatus which has the function of getting rid of the stimuli that reach it, or of reducing them to the lowest possible level; . . ."[38] As to his quantitative view (increase and diminution of excitation): "We have decided to relate pleasure and unpleasure to the quantity of excitation that is present in the mind but is not any way 'bound'; and to relate them in such a manner that unpleasure corresponds to an *increase* in the quantity of excitation and pleasure to a *diminution*."[39] This excitation is caused by the needs, which in turn are caused by the instincts. "The forces which we assume to exist behind the tensions caused by the needs of the id are called *instincts*."[40]

Freud assumed that life is governed by the pleasure principle: "In the theory of psycho-analysis we have no hesitation in assuming that the course taken by mental events is automatically regulated by the pleasure principle."[41] To the question, whether there

---

[37]*Beyond the Pleasure Principle*, S.E., XVIII, 36-37. The Lamarckian influence is clear here as it is in other passages that will be discussed later.

[38]Instincts and their vicissitudes, S.E., XIV, 120.

[39]*Beyond the Pleasure Principle*, S.E., XVIII, 7-8.

[40]*An Outline of Psycho-Analysis*, S.E., XXIII, 148.

[41]*Beyond the Pleasure Principle*, S.E., XVIII, 7.

is a "beyond the pleasure principle," Freud responds in the negative. He explains those cases that appear to be beyond the pleasure principle as essentially being in the service of the pleasure principle.[42]

B3. Energy

The tensions introduced by the instincts are viewed by Freud as a kind of energy. If the instincts are biological in nature then their energy would of necessity have to be biological. Such in fact is the case. Libido at first is pure "id energy" and even "ego energy" will be shown to be of libidinal or sexual origin. "In our discussion so far we have dealt with the repression of an instinctual representative, and by the latter we have understood an idea or group of ideas which is cathected with a definite quota of psychical energy (libido or interest) coming from an instinct."[43] Even ego energy for Freud is somatic, "libidinal" or sexual in origin.

> At the very beginning, all the libido is accumulated in the id, while the ego is still in process of formation or is still feeble. The id sends part of this libido out into erotic object-cathexes, whereupon the ego, now grown stronger, tries to get hold of this object-libido and to force itself on the id as a love-object. The narcissism of the ego is thus a secondary one, which has been withdrawn from objects.
>
> Over and over again we find, when we are able to trace instinctual impulses back, that they reveal themselves as derivatives of Eros.[44]

B4. Conflict

For Freud, man's intellectual and social capacities are developed so as to handle the conflict between man's instinctual nature and reality, physical and social, including the reality of

---

[42]*The Protocol: Beyond the Pleasure Principle,* Chap. i, pars, 6-9, p. 181 as well as Chap. vii, pars. 1 and 5, p. 191.

We are concerned here only with the biological character of pleasure. A more thorough treatment of pleasure as a commonplace will be presented in Chapter Seven.

[43]Repression, in *Papers on Metapsychology,* S.E., XIV, 152.

[44]*The Ego and the Id,* S.E., XIX, 46. *See also The Protocol: The Ego and the Id,* Chap. iv, pars. 16-17, p. 227. We were not able to discover why the death instinct does not have an energy as well. For further discussion of this problem, see Chapter Seven, p. 139.

breadwinning. Conflict between man and his environment, between the parts of the psyche, between the instincts and, even between numerous different objects of the same instinct, is for Freud the "normal" state of affairs. It appears that this assumption of a continuous state of conflict is: (a) modeled after the relationship of animals to their environment (Darwin) ; (b) the result of a decision to see man's beginning (individual and racial) as having a continuous effect on the present; (c) the result of beginning with only one of the parts, the id; (d) the result of his extreme beginning-orientation because of which he views later developments, ego and super-ego, as shaky and undependable; (e) the result of viewing all characteristics other than the biological as imported from without. (It is difficult to decide whether Freud's commitment to a dualistic theory of instincts is the necessary result of his view of man in a constant state of conflict, or is a further argument for conflict.) We will discuss Freud's concept of conflict in Chapter Eight. Here we cite some passages that point to its biological character. In dealing with the necessity for a dualistic theory of instincts, Freud asserts: "Our views have from the very first been *dualistic,* and to-day they are even more definitely dualistic than before—now that we describe the opposition as being, not between ego-instincts and sexual instincts but between life instincts and death instincts."[45]

Even when discussing the differentiation of the mental apparatus, Freud found it necessary to point to similar differentiations in simple organisms: "The differentiation between ego and id must be attributed not only to primitive man but even to much simpler organisms, for it is the inevitable expression of the influence of the external world."[46]

And:

This general schematic picture of a psychial apparatus may be supposed to apply as well to the higher animals which resemble man mentally. A super-ego must be presumed to be present wherever, as is the case with man, there is a long period of dependence in childhood. A distinction between ego and id is an unavoidable assump-

[45]*Beyond the Pleasure Principle,* S.E., XVIII, 53.
[46]*The Ego and the Id,* S.E., XIX, 38.

tion. Animal psychology has not yet taken in hand the interesting problem which is here presented.[47]

Freud's description of neurosis is intimately bound up with both the notions of conflict and biology: ". . . and it [neurosis] represents a *conflict* between those portions of the instincts which have been received into the ego after having passed through this development and those portions of them which, springing from the repressed unconscious, strive—as do other, completely repressed, instinctual impulses—to attain direct satisfaction."[48]

B5. Phylogentic Endowment

Freud's beginning-orientation will place special emphasis on the history of the race, phylogeny, as well as the early life of the individual, i.e. infancy and childhood.

It need hardly be said that any emphasis on phylogeny is an emphasis on biology and phylogeny appears and reappears throughout Freud's theory. One of the reasons for the importance of dream analysis in psychoanalytic research is that through the careful analysis of dreams we discover the extent to which man's archaic heritage is operative in contemporary life. Freud will not only claim that an individual's experiences survive in memory but also that memories even of racial and primitive experiences are effective in his present life. Man's archaic heritage or phylogenetic acquisition is transmitted from generation to generation through the acquisition of the ego ideal. And what may appear as manifestations of man's "higher" nature, religion, social feeling and conscience can be traced to earlier or vestigial relationships within the family.

The influence of man's phylogenetic endowment in contemporary life is obvious throughout Freud. In discussing and explaining hypnosis Freud tells us: "Let us recall that hypnosis has something positively uncanny about it; but the characteristic of uncanniness suggests something old and familiar that has under-

---

[47]*An Outline of Psycho-Analysis*, S.E., XXIII, p. 147.
[48]*Group Psychology*, S.E., XVIII, 143.

gone repression.[49] He continues to describe hypnosis in the following manner:

> . . .the hypnotist awakens in the subject a portion of his archaic heritage which had also made him compliant towards his parents and which had experienced an individual re-animation in his relation to his father; what is thus awakened is the idea of a paramount and dangerous personality, towards whom only a passive-masochistic attitude is possible, to whom one's will has to be surrendered, . . . It is only in some such way as this that we can picture the relation of the individual member of the primal horde to the primal father. As we know from other reactions, individuals have preserved a variable degree of personal aptitude for revving old situations of this kind.[50]

So also when Freud discusses ambivalence he sees the archaic as affecting contemporary life. "Marked instinctual ambivalence in a human being living at the present day may be regarded as an archaic inheritance, for we have reason to suppose that the part played in instinctual life by the active impulses in their unmodified form was greater in primeval times than it is on an average to-day."[51] Freud argues that memories of the experiences of primitive man and the primitive group are also effective in the present. "Just as primitive man survives potentially in every individual, so the primal horde may arise once more out of any random collection; in so far as men are habitually under the sway of group formation we recognize in it the survival of the primal horde."[52]

In his theory of dreams, Freud asserts that dreams reveal the importance of the history of mankind in man's contemporary life:

> Furthermore, dreams bring to light material which cannot have originated either from the dreamer's adult life or from his forgotten childhood. We are obliged to regard it as part of the *archaic heritage* which a child brings with him into the world, before any experience of his own, influenced by the experiences of his ancestors. We find the counterpart of this phylogenetic material in the earliest human legends and in surviving customs. Thus dreams constitute a source of human prehistory which is not to be despised.[53]

---

[49]*Group Psychology*, S.E., XVIII, 125.
[50]*Ibid.*, p. 127.
[51]Instincts and their vicissitudes, S.E., XIV, 131.
[52]*Group Psychology*, S.E., XVIII, 123.
[53]*An Outline of Psycho-Analysis*, S.E., XXIII, 166-167.

In Civilization and Its Discontents. Freud claims that the "oceanic feeling" which had been argued for as a primary feeling and as a proof of a primary religious feeling or instinct, represents a vestige of a primitive or infantile state.

> There is nothing strange in such a phenomenon, whether in the mental field or elsewhere. In the animal kingdom we hold to the view that the most highly developed species have proceeded from the lowest; and yet we find all the simple forms still in existence to day. The race of the great saurians is extinct and has made way for the mammals; but a true representative of it, the crocodile, still lives among us. This analogy may be too remote, and it is also weakened by the circumstance that the lower species which survive are for the most part not the true ancestors of the present-day more highly developed species. As a rule the intermediate links have died out and are known to us only through reconstruction. In the realm of the mind, on the other hand, what is primitive is so commonly preserved alongside of the transformed version which has arisen from it that it is unnecessary to give instances as evidence. When this happens it is usually in consequence of a divergence in development: one portion (in the quantitative sense) of an attitude or instinctual impulse has remained unaltered, while another portion has undergone further development.[54]

Freud does, however, distinguish the phylogenesis of the mind from other phylogenesis known to him.

> But here, too, we find the same thing. The earlier phases of development are in no sense still preserved; they have been absorbed into the later phases for which they have supplied the material. The embryo cannot be discovered in the adult. The thymus gland of childhood is replaced after puberty by connective tissue, but is no longer present itself; in the marrow-bones of the grown man I can, it is true, trace the outline of a child's bone, but it itself has disappeared, having lengthened and thickened until it has attained its definitive form. The fact remains that only in the mind is such preservation of all the earlier stages alongside of the final form possible, and that we are not in a position to represent this phenomenon in pictorial terms.[55]

---

[54]*Civilization and Its Discontents*, S.E., XXI, 68-69. *See also The Protocol: Civilization and Its Discontents*, Chap. i, pars. 4-10, pp. 233-234.

[55]*Civilization and Its Discontents*, S.E., XXI, p. 71. It should be pointed out that in one sense Freud liberated himself from the biological here by claiming that the conservation is only mental.

As a consequence of his view that man's archaic heritage is transmitted, Freud emphasizes the contribution even to the ego ideal from the biological content of the id.

> Through the forming of the ideal, what biology and the vicissitudes of the human species have created in the id and left behind in it is taken over by the ego and re-experienced in relation to itself as an individual. Owing to the way in which the ego ideal is formed, it has the most abundant links with the phylogenetic acquisition of each individual—his archaic heritage.[56]

B6. The Role of Infancy and Childhood

Just as phylogeny plays an important role in individual development, so, following a similar biological pattern, Freud sees the child as father to the man. Early experiences are basic and pervasive. An additional reason for Freud's emphasis on dream analysis is that through dreams we can familiarize ourselves with the early life of the patient. In this early period of infancy and childhood, character is formed (through the resolution of Oedipus) and neuroses created (through incomplete resolution of Oedipus). Basic to Freud's theory is the importance of infantile sexuality, both in itself and as operative in the adult life of the individual through object choice, regression, perversion or neurosis. Fear, anxiety and the fear of death, can all be traced to experiences undergone by the individual in the early part of his life.[57]

The relationship of infancy to phylogeny is seen in the following:

> A feebleness of the ego of this sort is to be found in all of us in childhood, and that is why the experience of the earliest years of

---

[56]*The Ego and the Id*, S.E., XIX, 36. *See also The Protocol: The Ego and the Id*, Chap. iii, par. 21, p. 224.

[57]Much of the foregoing has a wholly familiar ring, consisting as it does of the most widely known and the most widely adopted of Freud's views. Its importance to this volume consists in the extent to which Freud's view of the contributions of early life are determined by his conceptual frame and not by empirical data recognized by all. The question of the distribution of the position between these two sources—conceptual frame and data—cannot be resolved in this work. For the wide acceptance of Freud's view in this matter has precluded a concerted search for data which might indicate something less than certainty for Freud's data. Therefore, we shall cite references that appear to emanate only from Freud's conceptual frame.

the child are of such great importance for later life. Under the extraordinary burden of this period of childhood—we have in a few years to cover the enormous developmental distance between stone-age primitive men and the participants in contemporary civilization, and, at the same time, and in particular, we have to fend off the instinctual impulses of the earlier sexual period—under this burden, then, our ego takes refuge in repression and lays itself open to a childhood neurosis, the precipitate of which it carries with it unto maturity as a disposition to a later nervous illness.[58]

For Freud, the child is in more intimate contact with his unconscious or, more specifically, the "primary process."[59] Among the reasons for the importance of dreams is that they give us an insight into the early life of the patient.

> Memory very often reproduces in dreams impressions from the dreamer's early childhood of which we can definitely assert not only that they had been forgotten but that they had become unconscious owing to repression. That explains the help—usually indispensable—given us by dreams in the attempts we make during the analytical treatment of neuroses to reconstruct the dreamer's early life.[60]

Similarly neurosis cannot be understood without reference to the early life of the child. "And secondly, the aetiology of the disorders which we study is to be looked for in the individual's developmental history—that is to say, in his early life."[61]

Freud maintains throughout his works an assertion which is central to his theory of neurosis—the existence of infantile or childhood sexuality. The Oedipal conflict which is a conflict within childhood sexuality is said to be inescapable and its importance is continuous for it represents the conflict of the two basic and early instinctual expressions in the life of the child.[62]

The super-ego (the internalization of the values of society) is not present at the beginning but is the result of the child's response to his parents. " 'Very true,' we can say, 'and here we have

---

[58]*Lay Analysis,* S.E., XX, 241.

[59]See *Beyond the Pleasure Principle,* S.E., XVIII, 34-36, and *The Protocol: Beyond the Pleasure Principle,* Chap. v, pars. 2 and 3, 185-186. For Freud's description of the "primary process," see *The Unconscious,* S.E., XIV, 186.

[60]*An Outline of Psycho-Analysis,* S.E., XXIII, 166.

[61]*Ibid.,* p. 156.

[62]See *The Ego and the Id,* S.E., XIX, 56-57.

that higher nature, in this ego ideal or super-ego, the representative of our relation to our parents. When we were little children we knew these higher natures, we admired them and feared them; and later we took them into ourselves'."[63]

Fear, anxiety and the fear of death all originate in the early life of the child.

> Here, moreover, is once again the same situation as that which underlay the first great anxiety-state of birth and the infantile anxiety of longing—the anxiety due to separation from the protecting mother.
>
> These considerations make it possible to regard the fear of death, like the fear of conscience, as a development of the fear of castration.[64]

Of course, all of the above might have entered into Freud's theory as consequences of his view that childhood is a period of lability. This is improbable, though, in the light of the fact that the lability of childhood does not necessitate Freud's insistence on the durable and consequential character of what occurs in childhood. Rather this insistence upon durability and fatefulness of early experience derives, we believe, from his insistence on interpreting the relation of childhood events to adult events as analogous to the relation of phylogeny to ontogeny. Freud concludes his discussion of the Oedipus complex in *The Ego and the Id:*

> . . . and the fact of his Oedipus complex, the repression of which we have shown to be connected with the interruption of libidinal development by the latency period and so with the diphasic onset of man's sexual life. According to one psycho-analytic hypothesis, the last-mentioned phenomenon, which seems to be peculiar to man, is a heritage of the cultural development necessitated by the glacial epoch. We see, then, that the differentiation of the super-ego from the ego is no matter of chance; it represents the most important characteristics of the development both of the individual and of the species; indeed, by giving permanent expression to the influence of the parents it perpetuates the existence of the factors to which it owes its origin.[65]

---

[63]*The Ego and the Id*, S.E., XIX, 36.
[64]*Ibid.*, p. 58.
[65]*The Ego and the Id*, S.E., XIX, 35.

B7. Psychological Development

In addition to the importance he ascribed to man's beginnings, racial and individual, Freud decided to explain psycho-genesis in biological terms. This can be demonstrated by at least three of his theoretical decisions:

1. The Application of the Principle That Ontogeny Recapitulates Phylogeny

Freud adopts this biological principle to explain psychological development. The concept of an Oedipal conflict presupposes each individual's predisposition to identify with his father and that, in this relationship to his father, the individual undergoes a relationship similar to that of the original band of brothers with the leader or father. Through the resolution of Oedipus, the individual develops values as did the "original" family or group. We shall see that Freud similarly uses a recapitulative ontongeny to explain group psychology, religion, dreams and infantile sexuality.

Freud tells us that primitive man is to be found operative in contemporary man, "Just as primitive man survives potentially in every individual, so the primal horde may arise once more out of any random collection; in so far as men are habitually under the sway of group formation we recognize in it the survival of the primal horde."[66] The concept of Oedipal conflict[67] involves at least the following propositions: (1) every individual has a predisposition to identify with his father; (2) in this relationship to his father, he undergoes an experience similar to that of the original band of brothers in their relationship to the leader or father;[68] (3) as a result of mastering the Oedipal conflict, religion and social feeling were developed.[69]

> If we consider once more the origin of the super-ego as we have described it, we shall recognize that it is the outcome of two highly

[66]*Group Psychology*, S.E., XVIII, 123.

[67]See *The Protocol: The Ego and the Id*, Chap. iii, pars. 11-19, pp. 222-223.

[68]*Ibid.*, Chap. iii, par. 23, p. 224.

[69]See *The Ego and the Id*, S.E., XIX, 37. *The Protocol: The Ego and the Id*, Chap. iii, par. 25, p. 224. Freud roots the replacement of object choice by identification in the memory of the experience of cannibalism. See *The Ego and the Id*, p. 31, n. 1.

important factors, one of a biological and the other of a historical nature; namely, the lengthy duration in man of his childhood helplessness and dependence, and the fact of his Oedipus complex, the repression of which we have shown to be connected with the interruption of libidinal development by the latency period and so with the diphasic onset of man's sexual life. According to one psychoanalytic hypothesis, the last-mentioned phenomenon, which seems to be peculiar to man, is a heritage of the cultural development necessitated by the glacial epoch. We see, then, that the differentiation of the super-ego from the ego is no matter of chance; it represents the most important characteristics of the development both of the individual and of the species; indeed, by giving permanent expression to the influence of the parents it perpetuates the existence of the factors to which it owes its origin.[70]

Similarly, we can demonstrate Freud's use of the recapitulative ontogeny when he deals with such phenomena as the group,[71] religion,[72] dreams.[73] With respect to infantile sexuality Freud tells us: "And here we come upon the fact that the onset of sexual life is *diphasic*, that it occurs in two waves—something that is unknown except in man and evidently has an important bearing on hominization." [74]

In a footnote to the above Freud writes:

. . . the suggestion that man is descended from a mammal which reached sexual maturity at the age of five, but that some major external influence was brought to bear on the species and at that point interrupted the straight course of development of sexuality. Other transformations in the sexual life of man as compared with that of animals might be connected with this—such as the abolition of the periodicity of the libido and the exploitation of the part played by menstruation in the relation between sexes.[75]

---

[70]*The Ego and the Id*, S.E., XIX, 35. Amid all these emphases upon a recapitulative ontogeny, we must not overlook the fact that for once Freud is making a great deal of a species characteristic as against the generic. See Chapter Three, pp. 32-33.

[71]See *The Protocol: Group Psychology and the Analysis of the Ego*, Chap. ix, par. 11, pp. 206-207.

[72]*Totem and Taboo*, S.E., XIII, ix-162.

[73]See this text, p. 63.

[74]*An Outline of Psycho-Analysis*, S.E., XXIII, 153.

[75]*Ibid.*, p. 153, n. 1.

2. *The Use of the Notion of Preformationism*[76]

Freud adopted this principle to explain the instincts and infantile sexuality. The adoption of this principle directs Freud to assert that basic phenomena that appear at a later stage of development must have been present from the very beginning. Freud's beginning-orientation would require that all basic phenomena be present from the very beginning. Thus, the instincts in Freud are not subject to development and even if they are not "visible" they are present but "mute." Similarly with sexuality. If it is to be found after latency, then it must have been present in early childhood and infancy.

Freud handled the difficulty of demonstrating the existence of the death instinct at the early stages of biological development in the following manner:

> It will be seen at once that to concede in this way that higher organisms have a natural death is of very little help to us. For if death is a *late* acquisition of organisms, then there can be no question of there having been death instincts from the very beginning of life on this earth.[77]

Similarly, when arguing for the primary nature of the sexual instincts, Freud asserts: "And even though it is certain that sexuality and the distinction between the sexes did not exist when life began, the possibility remains that the instincts which were later to be described as sexual may have been in operation from the very first, and it may not be true that it was only at a later time that they started upon their work of opposing the activities of the 'ego instincts'."[78] Freud refused to accept the possibility that infantile sexuality be conceived of as organ pleasure. One of the arguments that he presents is performationist:

> And now, for my justification, there are two other considerations which I must ask you to take into account. As you know, we call the dubious and indefinable pleasureable activities of earliest childhood sexual because, in the course of analysis, we arrive at them from the

[76]By "preformationism" we refer to the embryological conception that "parts" or "organs" are present but feeble at the beginning.

[77]*Beyond the Pleasure Principle*, S.E., XVIII, 47. Freud's instincts, as we have indicated earlier, are ultimate, first and are not subject to development.

[78]*Ibid.*, p. 41.

symptoms after passing through indisputably sexual material. They
need not necessarily themselves be sexual on that account—agreed!
But take an analogous case. Suppose we had no means of observing
the development from their seed of two dicotyledonous plants, the
apple-tree and the bean, but that it was possible in both cases for us
to trace their development backwards from the fully developed individual plant to the first seedling with two seed-leaves. The two seed-
leaves have a neutral appearance; they are just alike in both cases. Am
I then to suppose that they are really alike, and that the specific difference between an apple-tree and a bean is only introduced into the
plants later? Or is it biologically more correct to believe that this difference is already there in the seedling, although I cannot observe
any distinction in the seed-leaves? But we are doing the same thing
when we call the pleasure in the activities of an infant-in-arms a sexual one. I cannot discuss here whether each and every organ-pleasure
should be called a sexual one or whether, alongside of the sexual one,
there is another which does not deserve to be so called.[79]

Thus, in the treatment of sexuality he rejects the simple notion
that sex begins at puberty, in favor of a very early beginning, a
period of latency and a resumption of sexuality—the three stages
being based upon a speculation concerning man's evolutionary
origin.[80]

3. Epigenesis

Freud decided to explain psychological development in epi-
genetic terms.[81] His decision to model the psyche on embryological
development in the organism does not involve simply the adoption of a biological model, but will force the ego and the super-
ego to be dependent on the first part, the id, throughout life.[82]
We shall discuss this problem further in Chapter Eight.

B8. Lamarckism

It is well known that Freud accepted Lamarck's theory of
evolution to explain psychological development as well as biological development. The appearance of the life instinct, con-

---

[79]*Introductory Lectures on Psycho-Analysis*, S.E., XVI, 324-325.

[80]See *The Ego and the Id*, S.E., XIX, 35.

[81]See Chapter Three, pp. 34, 38-39. Freud, as we see, makes use of both epigene-
tic and preformationist embryological theories.

[82]Chapter Three, pp. 38-39.

sciousness, the transformation of group psychology to individual psychology, the origin of sexual reproduction, are explained by some special "outside force" which makes possible the development or progress from a lower to a higher stage. Jones brings to our attention an interesting discussion of the extent to which Freud was committed to Lamarckian biology:

> How immovable he was in the matter I discovered during a talk I had with him in the last year of his life over a sentence I wished him to alter in the Moses book in which he expressed the Lamarckian view in universal terms. I told him that he had of course the right to hold any opinion he liked in his own field of psychology, even if it ran counter to all biological principles, but begged him to omit the passage where he applied it to the whole field of biological evolution, since no responsible biologist regarded it as tenable any longer. All he would say was that they were all wrong and the passage must stay. And he documented this recalcitrance in the book with the following words: "This state of affairs is made more difficult, it is true, by the present attitude of biological science, which rejects the idea of acquired qualities being transmitted to descendants. I admit, in all modesty, that in spite of this I can not picture biological development proceeding without taking this factor into account.[83]

In a theoretical discussion concerning the development of instincts, Freud suggests: "Both higher development and involution might well be the consequences of adaptation to the pressure of external forces . . ."[84] In speculating on the origin of the life instincts he claims:[85] "The attributes of life were at some time evoked in inanimate matter by the action of a force of whose nature we can form no conception."[86] And similarly the origin of consciousness is ascribed to an outside force: "It may perhaps have been a process[87] similar in type to that which later caused the development of consciousness in a particular stratum of living matter."[88]

---

[83]Jones, Ernest: *The Life and Works of Sigmund Freud*, 3 vols. New York, Basic Books, 1957, III, 313.

[84]*Beyond the Pleasure Principle*, S.E., XVIII, 41.

[85]Life is a late development for Freud. See our Chapter Three, pp. 32-33.

[86]*Beyond the Pleasure Principle*, S.E. XVIII, 38.

[87]*Process* refers here to the force in the previous quotation.

[88]*Ibid.*, p. 38.

In developing the theory of the "Oedipal conflict," Freud points to the importance of the *first* identification.[89] In his theory of the group, Freud tries to locate the particular event in history which made possible the change from group psychology to individual psychology. After postulating the developmental stages that mankind went through Freud tells us:

> We have said that it would be possible to specify the point in the mental development of mankind at which the advance from group psychology to individual psychology was achieved also by the individual members of the group.
>
> For this purpose we must return for a moment to the scientific myth of the father of the primal horde. He was later on exalted into the creator of the world, and with justice, for he had produced all the sons who composed the first group. He was the ideal of each one of them, at once feared and honoured, a fact which led later to the idea of taboo. These many individuals eventually banded themselves together, killed him and cut him in pieces.[90] None of the group of victors could take his place, or, if one of them did, the battles began afresh, until they understood that they must all renounce their father's heritage. They then formed the totemic community of brothers, all with equal rights and united by the totem prohibitions which were to preserve and to expiate the memory of the murder. But the dissatisfaction with what had been achieved still remained, and it became the source of new developments. The persons who were united in this group of brothers gradually came towards a revival of the old state of things at a new level. The male became once more the chief of a family, and broke down the prerogatives of the gynaecocracy which had become established during the fatherless period. As a compensation for this he may at that time have acknowledged the mother deities, whose priests were castrated for the mother's protection, after the example had been given by the father of the primal horde. And yet the new family was only a shadow of the old one; there were numbers of fathers and each one was limited by the rights of the others.
>
> It was then, perhaps, that some individual, in the exigency of his longing, may have been moved to free himself from the group and take over the father's part. He who did this was the first epic poet; and the advance was achieved in his imagination. This poet disguised the truth with lies in accordance with his longing. He invented the

---

[89]*The Ego and the Id*, S.E., XIX, 31. *See also The Protocol: The Ego and the Id*, Chap. iii, par. 9, p. 221.

[90]Can it be that Freud unknowingly was making room here for a guilt instinct?

heroic myth. The hero was a man who by himself had slain the father —the father who still appeared in the myth as a totemic monster. Just as the father had been the boy's first ideal, so in the hero who aspires to the father's place the poet now created the first ego ideal. The transition to the hero was probably afforded by the youngest son, the mother's favourite, whom she had protected from paternal jealousy, and who, in the era of the primal horde, had been the father's successor. In the lying poetic fancies of prehistoric times the woman, who had been the prize of the battle and the temptation to murder, was probably turned into the active seducer and instigator to the crime.

The hero claims to have acted alone in accomplishing the deed, which certainly only the horde as a whole would have ventured upon. But, as Rank has observed, fairy tales have preserved clear traces of the facts which were disavowed. For we often find in them that the hero who has to carry out some difficult task (usually the youngest son, and not infrequently one who has represented himself to the father-substitute as being stupid, that is to say, harmless)—we often find, then, that this hero can carry out his task only by the help of a crowd of small animals, such as bees or ants. These would be the brothers in the primal horde, just as in the same way in dream symbolism insects or vermin signify brothers and sisters (contemptuously, considered as babies). Moreover every one of the tasks in myths and fairy tales is easily recognizable as a substitute for the heroic deed.

The myth, then, is the step by which the individual emerges from group psychology.[91]

Freud searched for that moment in the history of the individual or the group that made possible the development from one stage to another. Thus, after having located within culture the conflict of Eros versus Death, he states: "And we may probably add more precisely, a struggle for life in the shape it was bound to assume after a *certain event* which still remains to be discovered."[92] The idea of myth as an external force occurs in several other places in Freud.[93] I am not completely able to understand Freud's adoption of myth as a suitable force or source of energy to

[91]*Group Psychology*, S.E., XVIII 135, 136.

[92]*Civilization and Its Discontents*, S.E., XXI, 122, n. 2. Emphasis mine.

[93]As for example *Beyond the Pleasure Principle*, S.E., XVIII, 57-58. See also *Protocol: Beyond the Pleasure Principle*, Chap. vi par. 27-31, p. 190, where Freud attempts to explain the origin of sexual reproduction on the basis of a Platonic myth.

explain the progress from one stage to another. Unless we attribute this force to a "mystical" power.

B9. Determinism

Despite his Lamarckist bent, Freud's theory is terrifyingly deterministic or conservative.

By determinism we are referring to a naive determinism (contrasted to a "naive free will") namely, that the past, biological and psychological, so pre-empts the present that there is little room for reordering the human situation. This determinism is maintained by Freud through his granting importance to phylogeny and to the early life of the child. It appears that Freud's Lamarckism does not involve making the new by reassembling the old. Rather it results in little more than the addition of one edifice to another; the older edifice not only persists but influences the later addition. Thus dreams, slips of tongue, free association are important in Freud's theory and in the practice of therapy in that they are present indicators of all-important past experiences.

As we shall see in Chapter Nine, Freud's determinism, coupled with his beginning orientation, which makes the ego (rationality) and the super-ego (values) shaky and constantly open to regression, present great problems to educators.

Freud's psychological determinism is strictly analogous to his biological determinism. All events and experiences are recorded in the psyche (in the unconscious, and the preconscious), affect contemporary life and can be reproduced under the right conditions. ". . . we have been inclined to take the opposite view, that in mental life nothing which has once been formed can perish—that everything is somehow preserved and that in suitable circumstances (when, for instance, regression goes back far enough) it can once more be brought to light."[94] Regression, temporary or neurotic, is one way in which early experience can be recovered. The non-perishable quality of all experience is also evidenced in normal life by wit and humor, which are taken to be the outlet of the repressed.

In the course of our development we have effected a separation of

---

[94]*Civilization and Its Discontents,* S.E., XXI, 69.

our mental existence into a coherent ego and into an unconscious and repressed portion which is left outside it; and we know that the stability of this new acquisition is exposed to constant shocks. In dreams and in neuroses what is thus excluded knocks for admission at the gates, guarded though they are by resistances; and in our waking health we make use of special artifices for allowing what is repressed to circumvent the resistances and for receiving it temporarily into our ego to the increase of our pleasure. Jokes and humour, and to some extent the comic in general, may be regarded in this light.[95]

Those experiences which have not been repressed are stored up in memory, and are both operative in contemporary life and, under the proper circumstances, can be brought back into consciousness. "These word-presentations are residues of memories; they were at one time perceptions, and like all mnemic residues they can become conscious again. . . . We think of the mnenic residues as being contained in systems which are directly adjacent to the system *Pcpt.-Cs.,* so that the cathexes of those residues can readily extend from within on to the elements of the latter system."[96] That the child is father to the adult[97] and that infantile experience plays an important role throughout life we have already discussed. We cite but one more piece of evidence, this time drawn from Freud's discussion of the super-ego or conscience, in which he claims that the infantile form of conscience continues to be operative despite the fact that the adult super-ego has been formed. "This, however, is easily explained by the original infantile stage of conscience, which, as we see, is not given up after the introjection into the super-ego, but persists alongside of it and behind it."[98]

B10. Regression

A curious incoherence is involved in Freud's use of the Lamarckist view for it clashes with his more conventional biological concept of preformationist or recapitulative ontogeny. When later developments in the individual meet counter pres-

---

[95]*Group Psychology,* S.E., XVIII, 131.

[96]*The Ego and the Id,* S.E., XIX, 20.

[97]See pp. 65-66.

[98]*Civilization and Its Discontents,* S.E., XXI, 126.

sure, there is regression, since the earlier state or stage has remained present and powerful.

Therefore, the basis for neurosis often may be the result of an
incomplete formation of a new stage:

> While the ego goes through its transformation from a *pleasure-
> ego* into a *reality-ego,* the sexual instincts undergo the changes that
> lead them from their original auto-erotism through various intermedi-
> ate phases to object-love in the service of procreation. If we are right
> in thinking that each step in these two courses of development may
> become the site of a disposition to later neurotic illness, it is plausible
> to suppose that the form taken by the subsequent illness (the *choice
> of neurosis*) will depend on the particular phase of the development
> of the ego and of the libido in which the dispositional inhibition of
> development has occurred.[99]

But no matter how complete the development is from stage to
stage, the individual remains threatened by regression. This constant threat of regression is emphasized in Freud's treatment of
group life:

> Human groups exhibit once again the familiar picture of an in-
> dividual of superior strength among a troop of equal companions, a
> picture which is also contained in our idea of the primal horde. The
> psychology of such a group, as we know it from the descriptions to
> which we have so often referred—the dwindling of the conscious indi-
> vidual personality, the focusing of thoughts and feelings into a com-
> mon direction, the predominance of the affective side of the mind and
> of unconscious psychical life, the tendency to the immediate carrying
> out of intentions as they emerge—all this corresponds to a state of re-
> gression to a primitive mental activity, of just such a sort as we should
> be inclined to ascribe to the primal horde.[100]

Regression[101] is explained by Freud as being due to a defusion of
the instincts: ". . . the essence of a regression of libido (e.g. from
the genital to the sadistic-anal phase) lies in a defusion of instincts, just as, conversely, the advance from the earlier phase to
the definitive genital one would be conditioned by an accession
of erotic components."[102]

---

[99]*Formulations on the Two Principles of Mental Functioning,* (hereafter referred
to as *Mental Functioning*), S.E., XII, 224-225.

[100]*Group Psychology,* S.E., XVIII, 122.

[101]Freud does make a distinction between a regression that is temporary and a
more permanent one, such as those involved in the regressions in neurosis.

[102]*The Ego and the Id,* S.E., XIX, 42.

B11. The Derivative Position of Other Human Manifestations

By now it is rather clear that not only the life process itself
and individual development are viewed by Freud with a biological
bias, but for that matter all human manifestations must be viewed
from a biological perspective. Freud refused to recognize any other
instincts besides Eros and Death[103] and definitely refused to consider the possibility of an instinct toward higher development observable in the animal or plant world. ". . . There is unquestion-
ably no universal instinct towards higher development observable
in the animal or plant world, even though it is undeniable that
the development does in fact occur in that direction. . . . Both
higher development and involution might well be the consequences of adaptation to the pressure of external forces . . ."[104]
All human activity which appears to be of a higher nature is explained by Freud in the light of the diversion (sublimation, etc.)
of libidinal energy. Thus, for example, intellectual activity will
be seen to be nothing more than a sublimation of libido. "If
thought-processes in the wider sense are to be included among
these displacements, then the activity of thinking is also supplied
from the sublimation of erotic motive forces."[105]

Art, religion, love and beauty as well are conceived of as displacements of one kind or another of the basic libidinal or sexual
energy.[106] All human values are to be found in the super-ego
which is not only a derivative of the id but in very close contact
with it.

> It is easy to show that the ego ideal answers to everything that is
> expected of the higher nature of man.[107] As a substitute for a long-
> ing for the father, it contains the germ from which all religions have
> evolved. The self-judgement which declares that the ego falls short
> of its ideal produces the religious sense of humility to which the be-
> liever appeals in his longing. As a child grows up, the role of father
> is carried on by teachers and others in authority; their injunctions
> and prohibitions remain powerful in the ego ideal and continue, in

---

[103]See the qualification in our earlier discussion of instinct, pp. 55-56.

[104]*Beyond the Pleasure Principle,* S.E., XVIII, 41.

[105]*The Ego and the Id,* S.E., XIX, 45.

[106]*Civilization and Its Discontents,* S.E., XXI, 79-82.

[107]The relationship of the ego ideal to the super-ego is discussed on p. 146-147,
n. 17.

the form of conscience, to exercise the moral censorship. The tension between the demands of conscience and the actual performances of the ego is experienced as a sense of guilt. Social feelings rest on identifications with other people, on the basis of having the same ego ideal.

Religion, morality, and a social sense—the chief elements in the higher side of man—were originally one and the same thing. According to the hypothesis which I put forward in *Totem and Taboo* they were acquired phylogenetically out of the father-complex: religion and moral restraint through the process of mastering the Oedipus complex itself, and social feeling through the necessity for overcoming the rivalry that then remained between the members of the younger generation. . . . Even today the social feelings arise in the individual as a superstructure built upon impulses of jealous rivalry against his brothers and sisters.[108]

Freud summarized his commitment to the fact that all human experience can be understood in terms of his instinct theory in *An Outline of Psycho-Analysis.* "This concurrent and mutually opposing action of the two basic instincts gives rise to the whole variegation of the phenomena of life."[109]

A NOTE ON FREUD'S METAPSYCHOLOGY

Although we specifically refrain from advancing the following as a thesis, it is worth remarking that much of the foregoing seems to reach its apotheosis in the fundamental terms of Freud's metapsychology. He defines his metapsychology as follows:

In the theory of psycho-analysis we have no hesitation in assuming that the course taken by mental events is automatically regulated by the pleasure principle. . . . In taking that course into account in our consideration of the mental processes which are the subject of our study, we are introducing an 'economic' point of view into our work; and if, in describing those processes, we try to estimate this 'economic' factor in addition to the 'topographical' and 'dynamic' ones, we shall, I think, be giving the most complete description of them of which we can at present conceive, and one which deserves to be distinguished by the term 'metapsychological'.[110]

Thus the terms are pleasure, economics, topography and dynamics. Of pleasure we have said enough. His economics ap-

[108]*The Ego and the Id,* S.E., XIX, 37.
[109]*An Outline of Psycho-Analysis,* S.E., XXIII, 149.
[110]*Beyond the Pleasure Principle,* S.E., XVIII, 7.

pears to be a implified derivation of Claude Bernard's homeo-statics. His dynamics is, for the most part, analogous to the Newtonian resolution of forces, and his topography is derived from neurology. This latter is worth documentation.

In reviewing the distinction, conscious-unconscious, in *Beyond the Pleasure Principle,* Freud assigned a position to consciousness thus: ". . . we have merely adopted the views on localization held by cerebral anatomy, which locates the 'seat' of consciousness in the cerebral cortex—the outermost, enveloping layer of the central organ."[111]

> It is a difficult one because it goes beyond pure psychology and touches on the relations of the mental apparatus to anatomy. We know that in the very roughest sense such relations exist. Research has given irrefutable proof that mental activity is bound up with the function of the brain as it is with no other organ. We are taken a step further—we do not know how much—by the discovery of the unequal importance of the different parts of the brain and their special relations to particular parts of the body and to particular mental activities. But every attempt to go on from there to discover a localization of mental processes, every endeavour to think of ideas as stored up in nerve-cells and of excitations as travelling along nerve-fibres, has miscarried completely. The same fate would await any theory which attempted to recognize, let us say, the anatomical position of the system *Cs.*—conscious mental activity—as being in the cortex, and to localize the unconscious processes in the subcortical parts of the brain. There is a hiatus here which at present cannot be filled, nor is it one of the tasks of psychology to fill it. Our psychical topography has *for the present* nothing to do with anatomy; it has reference not to anatomical localities, but to regions in the mental apparatus, wherever they may be situated in the body. (The Unconscious, S.E., XIV, 174-175.)

Freud saw his work in psychology as offering the rationale for this anatomical structure. "Cerebral anatomy has no need to consider *why*,[112] speaking anatomically, consciousness should be lodged on the surface of the brain. . . . Perhaps *we* shall be more successful in accounting for this situation. . . ."[113]

---

[111]*Beyond the Pleasure Principle,* S.E., XVIII, 24. I am informed by Joseph Schwab that, since the work of Carl Lashley, any notion of fixed and definite localization of function of the brain has had to be abandoned by biologists. It is difficult to understand why Freud in a later work, *Beyond the Pleasure Principle,* localizes a mental process or function, while in an earlier work, *The Unconscious,* he refuses to do so.

[112]Emphasis mine.

[113]*Beyond the Pleasure Principle,* S.E., XVIII, 24.

Freud maintained his commitment to the direct relation between mental topography and anatomical topography in his later writings as well. "We have said that consciousness is the *surface* of the mental apparatus; that is, we have ascribed it as a function to a system which is spatially the first one reached from the external world—and spatially not only in the functional sense but, on this occasion, also in the sense of anatomical dissection."[114]

The id is the embodiment of the biological commonplace, which Freud ranks at the top of the hierarchy of commonplaces. "The power of the id expresses the true purpose of the individual organism's life."[115] From *The New Introductory Lectures* comes this description of the character of the id:

> We approach the id with analogies: we call it a chaos, a cauldron full of seething excitations. We picture it as being open at its end to somatic influences, and as there taking up into itself instinctual needs which find their psychical expression in it, but we cannot say in what substratum. It is filled with energy reaching from the instincts, but it has no organization, produces no collective will, but only a striving to bring about the satisfaction of the instinctual needs subject to the observance of the pleasure principle. The logical laws of thought do not apply in the id, and this is true above all of the law of contradiction . . . Wishful impulses which have never passed beyond the id, but impressions, too, which have been sunk into the id by repression, are virtually immortal; after the passage of decades they behave as though they had just occurred. . .
>
> The id of course knows no judgements of value: no good and evil, no morality. The economic or, if you prefer, the quantitative, factor, which is intimately linked to the pleasure principle, dominates all its processes. Instinctual cathexes seeking discharge—that, in our view, is all there is in the id. It even seems that the energy of these instinctual impulses is in a state different from that in the other regions of the mind, far more mobile and capable of discharge; otherwise the displacements and condensations would not occur which are the characteristic of the id and which so completely disregard the *quality* of what is cathected . . [116]

---

[114]*The Ego and the Id*, S.E., XIX, 19.
[115]*An Outline of Psycho-Analysis*, S.E., XXIII, 148.
[116]*New Introductory Lectures*, S.E., XXII, 73-75.

Chapter Five

□

THE RATIONAL COMMONPLACE

THE SECOND "ORGAN" of Freud's tri-partite psyche is the ego. The ego does not begin its life as an independent part, but rather as a portion of the id that has been modified through the organism's contact with the external world.

The id, driven by the instincts and striving for pleasure, requires an agency that can guide it through a complicated and hostile reality. This is the principal role of the ego. The ego thus strives to substitute the reality principle for the pleasure principle. This does not mean, however, that the ego changes the direction or purpose of the organism. On the contrary, it will be demonstrated that the reality principle is a refinement of the pleasure principle, a guarantee that the organism will attain pleasure without being annihilated.

To carry out this function, the ego will have to manipulate by various and devious means the immediate wishes of the id. To handle this very complicated task which involves "guarding the approaches to motility," "censoring" the demands of the id, assessing the dangers of the external world and compromising the conflicting interests of the other parts of the psyche, Freud grants to the ego a number of ingenious devices such as flights, postponement, renunciation, defence, sublimation, projection, introjection, the manipulation of the signal of anxiety and the other affects.

But ingenious as these devices may be, the ego's power must always be more apparent than real. This is so because the ego develops slowly under the influence of an all powerful id. By the time the ego gains its own strength, much of the pattern of instinctual expression has already been developed. And, since the instincts are conservative and unpliable, changing or redirecting the instincts is not easily achieved. Further, the ego does not possess its own source of energy. It must "capture" energy from the id. (As we shall see, the price of this victory is heavy.) We discussed in Chapter Four two factors which further weaken the ego's power—the force and fatefulness of early experiences (racial and individual) for the contemporary situation, and the ever-present danger of regression. Regression can weaken the ego by robbing it of its hard-earned energy, by loosening its control over the instincts, or by strengthening the demands of the instincts.

The mature ego, with the development Freud assigns it, will find it difficult to fulfill its tasks. Its predicament is further and vastly complicated by the fact that it is not a "policy-maker" but a "politician." It is caught not only between the wishes of the id and the demands of reality, but also between the demands of the super-ego, the needs of the id, and the requirements of the external world.

To summarize, the ego is weak because its development is secondary, because it must work through the "secondary processes," and because it must struggle with the powerful id and super-ego.

It is clear that the ego is Freud's rational commonplace. The ego carries out its task by attempting to introduce rational processes into the life of the irrational id and super-ego. It has capacities for cognition, judgment, memory and perception. But the effective use of its capacities is at the mercy of the constant regression-threatened development pattern which Freud adopts. That is, there are lower and higher, more or less primitive sorts of cognition, judgment, et cetera and the choice between the more and the less does not lie with the ego alone.

However, the ego is a highly organized agency as compared to the unorganized id, and is largely conscious and pre-conscious as compared to the unconscious id. Accordingly, Freud has located it on the periphery of his mental topography, where it can have access both to the outer and inner worlds. Freud's characteristic determinism, like his characteristic regression-threatened development, pervades the rational commonplace as well as the biological commonplace. For it is not only internal and historical experience that persists and continues to influence behavior but all the experiences undergone by the ego as well.

It is difficult to understand (except by reference to his beginning-orientation) why Freud insists upon the ego developing out of the id, not having an intrinsic pleasure or an energy of its own, not possessing any "inner life" of its own and remaining essentially "passive" throughout. This characterization of the ego becomes all the more problematical in the light of Freud's contention that through therapy this situation can be altered.

We shall now demonstrate that Freud conceived of an ego that develops out of the id and we shall discover how the ego serves the needs of the id. Man's mental life at birth is embodied in the id alone. As a result of environmental influences, one portion of the id is modified and thus the second part of the psyche or mental apparatus is developed. "Originally, to be sure, everything was id; the ego was developed out of the id by the continual influence of the external world."[1] The ego is seen as analogous to a cortical layer.

> We need scarcely look for a justification of the view that the ego is that portion of the id which was modified by the proximity and influence of the external world, which is adapted for the reception of stimuli and as a protective shield against stimuli, comparable to the cortical layer by which a small piece of living substance is surrounded.[2]

and:

> . . . I must ask you to picture the ego as a kind of facade of the id, as a frontage, like an external, cortical, layer of it. We can hold on to this last analogy. We know that cortical layers owe their peculiar characteristics to the modifying influence of the external medium on which they abut. Thus we suppose that the ego is the layer of the mental apparatus (of the id) which has been modified by the influence of the external world (of reality).[3]

In fact, there are some passages where Freud appears to refuse to make a real distinction between the ego and the id. "For there is no natural opposition between the ego and the id; they belong together, and under healthy conditions cannot in practice be

[1]*An Outline of Psycho-Analysis*, S.E., XXIII, 163.
[2]*New Introductory Lectures*, S.E., XXII, 75.
[3]*Lay Analysis*, S.E., XX, 195.

distinguished from each other."[4] And, "The ego is not sharply separated from the id; its lower portion merges into it."[5]

We have shown in Chapter Four that the id strives for the satisfaction of instinctual needs in accordance with the pleasure principle. To achieve this satisfaction in a complex and sometimes hostile reality, the id requires the guidance of an apparatus or agency. The ego is this agency and fulfills this role by substituting the reality principle for the pleasure principle.

> The instincts in the id press for immediate satisfaction at all costs, and in that way they achieve nothing or even bring about appreciable damage. It is the task of the ego to guard against such mishaps, to mediate between the claims of the id and the objections of the external world. It carries on its activity in two directions. On the one hand, it observes the external world with the help of its sense-organ, the system of consciousness, so as to catch the favourable moment for harmless satisfaction; and on the other hand it influences the id, bridles its 'passions', induces its instincts to postpone their satisfaction, and indeed, if the necessity is recognized, to modify its aims, or, in return for some compensation, to give them up. In so far as it tames the id's impulses in this way, it replaces the pleasure principle, which was formerly alone decisive, by what is known as the 'reality principle', which, though it pursues the *same ultimate aims,* takes into account the conditions imposed by the real external world.[6]

In the light of this passage (and many others) it is clear that the reality principle does not change the purpose or goal of the organism, but simply refines the pleasure principle so that the organism can achieve pleasure in the light of external reality. Through the substitution of the reality principle for the pleasure principle, the ego guarantees that the organism's life of pleasure will have duration. ". . . it has taken on the task of representing the external world to the id—fortunately for the id, which could not escape destruction, if, in its blind efforts for the satisfaction of its instincts, it disregarded that supreme external power."[7] Freud explains the origin of the reality principle in the following manner:

[4]*Ibid.,* p. 201.
[5]*The Ego and the Id,* S.E., XIX, 24.
[6]*Lay Analysis,* S.E., XX, 201. Emphasis mine.
[7]*New Introductory Lectures,* S.E., XXII, 75.

We have put forward the fiction that we did not always possess this ability and that at the beginning of our mental life we did in fact hallucinate the satisfying object when we felt the need for it. But in such a situation satisfaction did not occur, and this failure must very soon have moved us to create some contrivance with the help of which it was possible to distinguish such wishful perceptions from a real fulfilment and to avoid them for the future. In other words, we gave up hallucinatory satisfaction of our wishes at a very early period and set up a kind of 'reality-testing'.[8]

To summarize, the ego develops as a response to the needs of the id. "If the id's instinctual demands meet with no satisfaction, intolerable conditions arise. Experience soon shows that these situations of satisfaction can only be established with the help of the external world. At that point the portion of the id which is directed towards the extrnal world—the ego—begins to function."[9]

Freud has postulated an ego whose tasks are complicated and he has granted it very subtle methods to accomplish these tasks. Among the ego's tasks are these:

1. The ego must guard the approaches to motility. "It is to this ego that consciousness is attached; the ego controls the approaches to motility—that is, to the discharge of excitations into the external world;"[10] It carries out this function by introducing a rational factor.

The ego controls the approaches to motility under the id's orders; but between a need and an action it has interposed a postponement in the form of the activity of thought, during which it makes use of the mnemic residues of experience. In that way it has dethroned the pleasure principle which dominates the course of events in the id without any restriction and has replaced it by the reality principle, which promises more certainty and greater success.[11]

---

[8]A metapsychological supplement to the theory of dreams (hereafter referred to as Dreams). In *Papers on Metapsychology,* S.E., XIV, 231.

[9]*Lay Aanalysis,* S.E., XX, 200-201. It is important to note that even though, with the establishment of the ego, the reality principle begins to function, the organism (man) remains under the dominion of the pleasure-principle (as we shall show on pp. 91-97). In Chapter Three, we argued that as a result of Freud's emphasis on the generic over the specific, man would necessarily be characterized primarily in terms of his needs and the machinery (the other parts—ego and super-ego) to satisfy these needs.

[10]*The Ego and the Id,* S.E., XIX, 17.

[11]*New Introductory Lectures,* S.E., XXII, 75-76.

2. The ego censors the demands or wishes of the id.

> The ego develops from perceiving the instincts to controlling them; but this last is only achieved by the (psychical) representative of the instinct being allotted its proper place in a considerable assemblage, by its being taken up into a coherent context. To adopt a popular mode of speaking, we might say that the ego stands for reason and good sense while the id stands for the untamed passions.[12]

And the following, "We shall place reality-testing among the major *institutions of the ego,* alongside the *censorships* which we have come to recognize between the psychical systems, . . ."[13]

3. The ego will have to develop a "sharp eye for assessing the outside world," and will have to make decisions involving the censorship of wishes as well as decisions concerning those excitations that are to be permitted to enter the organism.

> We need scarcely look for a justification of the view that the ego is that portion of the id which was modified by the proximity and influence of the external world, which is adapted for the reception of stimuli and as a protective shield against stimuli, . . . The relation to the external world has become the decisive factor for the ego; . . .
> In accomplishing this function, the ego must observe the external world, must lay down an accurate picture of it in the memory-traces of its perceptions, and by its exercise of the function of 'reality-testing' must put aside whatever in this picture of the external world is an addition derived from the internal sources of excitation.[14]

4. The ego has the complicated task of compromising and mediating among conflicting demands: censorship conflicting with the wishies of the id, excitations from without conflcting with the internal structure of the organism, and demands of the various parts of the psyche with each other.

> When we follow the ego's efforts to satisfy them simultaneously—or rather, to obey them simultaneously—we cannot feel any regret at having personified this ego and having set it up as a separate organism. . . . In its attempts to mediate between the id and reality, it is often obliged to cloak the *Ucs.* commands of the id with its own *Pcs.* rationalizations, to conceal the id's conflicts with reality, to pro-

---

[12]*Ibid.,* p. 76. Regression, as we shall see on pp. 98-100, will destroy or weaken this organization and coherent unity.

[13]Dreams, S.E., XIV, 233.

[14]*New Introductory Lectures,* S.E., XXII, 75.

fess, with diplomatic disingenuousness, to be taking notice of reality even when the id has remained rigid and unyielding.[15]

Or consider the following:

> Whenever possible, it tries to remain on good terms with the id; it clothes the id's *Ucs.* commands with its *Pcs.* rationalizations; it pretends that the id is showing obedience to the admonitions of reality, even when in fact it is remaining obstinate and unyielding; it disguises the id's conflict with reality and, if possible, its conflicts with the super-ego too. In its position midway between the id and reality, it only too often yields to the temptation to become sycophantic, opportunist and lying, like a politician who sees the truth but wants to keep his place in popular favour.[16]

As we have stated, Freud makes it possible for the ego to carry out its tasks by granting to it a set of ingenious devices or subterfuges. We shall discuss some of them below.

(1) Renunciation—The ego does not require the id to renounce its functions, it restricts its own.

> The ego renounces these functions, which are within its sphere, in order not to have to undertake fresh measures of repression—*in order to avoid a conflict with the id.* . . . The ego is not allowed to carry on those (professional) activities because they would bring success and gain, and these are things which the severe super-ego has forbidden. So the ego gives them up too, *in order to avoid coming into conflict with the super-ego.*[17]

(2) Postponement—Temporarily, the ego manages to postpone the demands of the id, by introducing an apparent modification. "In the course of development and original pleasure principle undergoes a modification with reference to the external world, giving place to the *'reality principle'*, in accordance with which the mental apparatus learns to postpone the pleasure of satisfaction and to tolerate temporarily feelings of unpleasure."[18]

(3) Sublimation—The deflection of the original aim or goal of an instinct by the ego.[19] "Sublimation is a process that concerns

---

[15]*Ibid.*, pp. 77-78.
[16]*The Ego and the Id*, S.E., XIX, 56.
[17]*Anxiety*, S.E., XX. 90.
[18]*Psycho-Analysis*, S.E., XX, 266.
[19]We shall discuss this method further in Chapter Seven.

object-libido and consists in the instinct's directing itself towards an aim other than, and remote from, that of sexual satisfaction; in this process the accent falls upon deflection from sexuality."[20]

(4) Projection—The ability to handle a troublesome internal demand by transferring it to the outside where it now can be manipulated by the ego.

> It is of value to the individual to possess a means such as this of recognizing reality, which at the same time helps him to deal with it, and he would be glad to be equipped with a similar power against the often merciless claims of his instincts. That is why he takes such pains to transpose outwards what becomes troublesome to him from within—that is, to *project* it.[21]

Or the following:

> A dream is, therefore, among other things, a *projection:* an external-ization of an internal process. We may recall that we have already met with projection elsewhere among the means adopted for defence.[22]

(5) Introjection (Identification) —The ability to give up a desired object by internalizing it and then identifying with it. The ego suffers by use of this device as well, and weakens itself in its relationship to the id.

> When it happens that a person has to give up a sexual object, there quite often ensues an alteration of his ego which can only be described as a setting up of the object inside the ego, as it occurs in melancholia; the exact nature of this substitution is as yet unknown to us. It may be that by this introjection, which is a kind of regres-sion to the mechanism of the oral phase, the ego makes it easier for the object to be given up or renders that process possible. It may be that this identification is the sole condition under which the id can give up its objects.[23]

(6) Anxiety—The ego, recognizing the power of the pleasure principle over the entire organism, uses the signal of anxiety to help control the direction of the organism. "An increase in un-

---

[20]*Narcissism*, S.E., XIV, 94.

[21]Dreams, S.E., XIV, 232-233.

[22]*Ibid.*, pp. 223-224.

[23]*The Ego and the Id*, S.E., XIX, 29. Freud compared introjection to the can-nibalism characteristic of the oral stage in the history of the individual and race (see the footnote, *The Ego and the Id*, p. 29). Again we see how his phylogenetic conceptions pervaded his conception of psychological development. See our Chap-ter Four, pp. 62-65.

pleasure that is expected and foreseen is met by a *signal of anxiety;*"[24] or "The ego has set itself the task of self-preservation which the id appears to neglect. It (the ego) makes use of the sensations of anxiety as a signal to give a warning of dangers that threaten its integrity."[25]

(7) Flight—When the ego perceives a problem in reality, it arranges for the avoidance by an escape from the situation.

> In the case of external danger the organism has recourse to attempts at flight. The first thing it does is to withdraw cathexis from the perception of the dangerous object; later on as it discovers it is a better plan to perform muscular movements of such a sort that will render perception of the dangerous object impossible even in the absence of any refusal to perceive it—that it is a better plan, that is, to remove itself from the sphere of danger.[26]

(8) Repression—A different version of flight. "Repression is an equivalent of this attempt at flight. The ego withdraws its (preconscious) cathexis from the instinctual representative that is to be repressed and uses that cathexis for the purpose of releasing unpleasure (anxiety) ."[27]

Our description of the role and function of the ego might lead us to believe that Freud conferred upon it considerable strength. There are passages in several of Freud's works that might lend credence to such a view.

> At the same time this view implies a concession to the ego that it can exert a very extensive influence over processes in the id, and we shall have to find out in what way it is able to develop such surprising powers.
>
> It seems to me that the ego obtains this influence in virtue of its intimate connections with the perceptual system—connections which, as we know, constitute its essence and provide the basis of its differentiation from the id. The function of this system, which we have called *Pcpt.-Cs.*, is bound up with the phenomenon of consciousness. It receives excitations not only from outside but from within, and endeavours, by means of the sensations of pleasure and unpleasure which reach it from these quarters, to direct the course of mental events in accordance with the pleasure principle. We are very apt to think of

[24]*An Outline of Psycho-Analysis*, S.E., XXIII, 146.
[25]*Ibid.*, p. 199.
[26]*Anxiety*, S.E. XX, 92.
[27]*Ibid.*, pp. 92-93.

the ego as powerless against the id; but when it is opposed to an instinctual process in the id it has only to give a *'signal of unpleasure'* in order to attain its object with the aid of that almost omnipotent institution, the pleasure principle.[28]

There are other works in which Freud speaks of the ego having the strength to suppress completely the demands of the id. For example: "As regards *internal* events, in relation to the id, it performs that task by gaining control over the demands of the instincts, by deciding whether they are to be allowed satisfaction, by postponing that satisfaction to times and circumstances favourable in the external world or by *suppressing their excitations entirely.*"[29] There is the well known, often quoted, reference which points to the possibility of the id being conquered by the ego.

Nevertheless it may be admitted that the therapeutic efforts of psychoanalysis have chosen a similar line of approach. Its intention [psychotherapy] is, indeed, to strengthen the ego, to make it more independent of the super-ego, to widen its field of perception and enlarge its organization, so that it can appropriate fresh portions of the id. Where id was, there ego shall be.[30]

Were it not for the principle which rules explication of text we would assert that these statements of Freud are inconsistent with the remaining and overwhelmingly larger body of his theory.

Schwab phrases the principle thus: "The appeal to incoherence in a text is to abort the effort to understand the text when it departs from one's own notion of the coherence to be expected. Thus it is to be undertaken only as a last resort."[31]

We feel we have exhaustively tried to understand these passages as offering novel communications but have found the weight of textual evidence to be against the "appeal to incoherence" on two grounds: first, because the content of these passages is qualified or more fully explicated in the same work or in other works of Freud; and second, because the contraries and contradictions of these passages far outweigh their seemingly novel content in fre-

---

[28]*Ibid.*, pp. 91-92.
[29]*An Outline of Psycho-Analysis*, S.E., XXIII, 145-146. Emphasis on last four words is mine.
[30]*New Introductory Lectures*, S.E., XXII, 80.
[31]Oral communication.

quency, length and in centrality to Freud's doctrine.

In the first passage, from *Anxiety*, the ego does not dominate the id. Its seeming success in opposing an instinctual process is acquired by signaling "unpleasure" or invoking the pleasure principle by which the id is directed. That is, the ego manages the id, it does not control it.

The second passage, from *An Outline of Psycho-Analysis*, although it cannot be explained away, should be seen in terms of the rest of that work, in which many passages can be cited to contradict this one.[32]

The third passage refers to the strength the ego is to acquire as a result of therapy. We have discussed in Chapter Three, and shall further demonstrate in Chapter Eight, that through the importance Freud grants to transference, the success of therapy itself may be said to depend upon a relationship emanating from the needs of the id and not from the ego.

We shall now examine some of the contraries of these passages to be found in Freud's works.

It is our contention that the ego will have to play a secondary role in Freud's theory for several reasons. The first is that, as we have documented in Chapter Four, the id and its demands represent the basic nature of the organism. The ego, on the other hand, attempts to direct this basic nature in the light of conflicting external and secondary demands. Freud claims that the ego can never really attain mastery over the inner demands.

We have pointed out how the living vesicle is provided with a shield against stimuli from the external world; and we have previously shown that the cortical layer next to that shield must be differentiated as an organ for receiving stimuli from without. This sensitive cortex, however, which is later to become the system *Cs.*, also receives excitations from *within*. The situation of the system between the outside and the inside and the difference between the conditions governing the reception of excitations in the two cases have a decisive effect on the functioning of the system and of the whole mental apparatus. Towards the outside it is shielded against stimuli, and the amounts of excitation impinging on it have only a reduced effect. Towards the inside there can be no such shield; the excitations in

[32]See *An Outline of Psycho-Analysis,* S.E., XXIII, 200, n. 2.

the deeper layers extend into the system directly and in undiminished amount, in so far as certain of their characteristics give rise to feelings in the pleasure-unpleasure series. The excitations coming from within are, however, in their intensity and in other, qualitative, respects—in their amplitude, perhaps—more commensurate with the system's method of working than the stimuli which stream in from the external world. This state of things produces two definite results. First, the feelings of pleasure and unpleasure (which are an index to what is happening in the interior of the apparatus) predominate over all external stimuli. And secondly, a particular way is adopted of dealing with any internal excitations which produce too great an increase of unpleasure: there is a tendency to treat them as though they were acting, not from the inside, but from the outside, so that it may be possible to bring the shield against stimuli into operation as a means of defence against them. This is the origin of *projection,* which is destined to play such a large part in the causation of pathological processes.

I have an impression that these last considerations have brought us to a better understanding of the dominance of the pleasure principle; . . .[33]

Freud maintained his commitment to the dominance of the pleasure principle, despite the apparent competence of the ego to attain a primary position by virtue of its ability to "censor" the demands of the id. The ego's influence is temporary, gained by renouncing a portion of future control over the id.

The ego, as we put it, institutes a *repression* of these instinctual impulses. For the moment this has the effect of fending off the danger; but one cannot confuse the inside and the outside with impunity. One cannot run away from oneself. In repression the ego is following the pleasure principle, which it is usually in the habit of correcting; and it is bound to suffer damage in revenge. This lies in the ego's having permanently narrowed its sphere of influence. The repressed instinctual impulse is now isolated, left to itself, inaccessible, but also uninfluenceable. It goes its own way. Even later, as a rule, when the ego has grown stronger, it still cannot lift the repression; its synthesis is impaired, a part of the id remains forbidden ground to the ego. Nor does the isolated instinctual impulse remain idle; it understands how to make up for being denied normal satisfaction; it produces psychical derivatives which take its place; it links itself to other processes which by its influence it likewise tears away from the ego; and finally it breaks through into the ego and into consciousness in the

---

[33]*Beyond the Pleasure Principle*, S.E., XVIII, 28-29.

form of an unrecognizable distorted substitute, and creates what we call a symptom.[34]

In Chapter Three, we claimed that Freud's beginning orientation will pervade his entire theoretical structure. We shall now consider the implications of beginning orientation for the ego. The ego, being a later development, will of necessity be weak, reflecting the great importance Freud granted to beginnings. First, phylogenetic influences leave their mark on the ego: "Nor should we forget the phylogenetic influences, which are represented in some way in the id in forms that we are not yet able to grasp, and which must certainly act upon the ego more powerfully in that early period than later."[35] Then there is the importance granted to infantile sexuality.

> If this is so, it would have to be said from a biological standpoint that the ego comes to grief over the task of mastering the excitations of the early sexual period, at a time when its immaturity makes it incompetent to do so. It is in this lagging of ego development behind libidinal development that we see the essential precondition of neurosis; and we cannot escape the conclusion that neuroses could be avoided if the childish ego were spared this task—if, that is to say, the child's sexual life were allowed free play, as happens among many primitive peoples.[36]

The ego, not existing at the very beginning and developing under the influence of strong and healthy instincts, finds itself at a distinct disadvantage. "The ego, which to begin with is still feeble, becomes aware of the object-cathexes, and either acquiesces in them or tries to fend them off by the process of repression."[37]

The implications of determinism for the ego are similar. As we mentioned,[38] Freud claims that in addition to the experiences of the race and those of childhood, all recent experience continues to affect contemporary and future situations. Thus Freud will

---

[34]*Lay Analysis*, S.E., XX, 203. It is true that this passage describes the early life of the individual. However, we shall cite other references in this chapter to show that the ego gains its apparent power at its own expense. This abiding life situation finds only one exception—in the successful culmination of therapy.

[35]*An Outline of Psycho-Analysis*, S.E., XXIII, 201.

[36]*Ibid.*, p. 200.

[37]*The Ego and the Id*, S.E., XIX, 29.

[38]Chapter 4, pp. 75-76?

explain the "oceanic feeling" in the following manner. "Thus the part played by the oceanic feeling, which might seek something like the restoration of limitless narcissism, is ousted from a place in the foreground. The origin of the religious attitude can be traced back in clear outlines as far as the feeling of infantile helplessness."[39] Dream interpretation is based on the assumption that the previous day's experience is absorbed into the personality and thus can be reproduced in the dream.

> It is best to begin by pointing out that the formation of a dream can be provoked in two different ways. Either, on the one hand, an instinctual impulse which is ordinarily suppressed (an unconscious wish) finds enough strength during sleep to make itself felt by the ego, or, on the other hand, an urge left over from waking life, a preconscious train of thought with all the conflicting impulses attached to it, finds reinforcement during sleep from an unconscious element.[40]

This assumption of the force of all prior experience (racial, individual, past and recent) places memory in a central role in Freud's system.[41]

The ego's secondary position in Freud's theory is underscored by virtue of its being not a "policy maker" but a "politician." The ego must show allegiance to *three* competing masters.

> From the other point of view, however, we see this same ego as a poor creature owing service to three masters and consequently menaced by three dangers: from the external world, from the libido of the id, and from the severity of the super-ego. Three kinds of anxiety correspond to these there dangers, since anxiety is the expression of a retreat from danger. As a frontier-creature, the ego tries to mediate between the world and the id, to make the id pliable to the world and, by means of its muscular activity, to make the world fall in with the wishes of the id. In point of fact it behaves like the physician during an analytic treatment: it offers itself, with the attention it pays to the real world, as a libidinal object to the id, and aims at attaching the id's libido to itself. It is not only a helper to the id; it is also a submissive slave who courts his master's love. Whenever possible, it tries to remain on good terms with the id; it clothes the id's

[39]*Civilization and Its Discontents*, S.E., XXI, 72.

[40]*An Outline of Psycho-Analysis*, S.E., XXIII, 166.

[41]See *The Protocol: The Ego and the Id*, Chapter ii, par. 9, 217. Here Freud missed the opportunity (despite his determinism) of introducing inherited categories of thought (as we find, for example, in Kant).

Ucs. commands with its *Pcs.* rationalizations; it pretends that the id is showing obedience to the admonitions of reality, even when in fact it is remaining obstinate and unyielding; it disguises the id's conflicts with reality and, if possible, its conflicts with the super-ego too. In its position midway between the id and reality, it only too often yields to the temptation to become sycophantic, opportunist and lying, like a politician who sees the truth but wants to keep his place in popular favour.[42]

Or the following:

We are warned by a proverb against serving two masters at the same time. The poor ego has things even worse: it serves three severe masters and does what it can to bring their claims and demands into harmony with one another. These claims are always divergent and often seem incompatible. No wonder that the ego so often fails in its task. Its three tyrannical masters are the external world, the super-ego and the id. When we follow the ego's efforts to satisfy them simultaneously—or rather, to obey them simultaneously—we cannot feel any regret at having personified this ego and having set it up as a separate organism.[43]

Because of its late arrival on the scene and the demanding and tyrannical masters it must serve, the ego's power, not surprisingly, is more apparent than real. "This last power is, to be sure, a question more of form than of fact; in the matter of action the ego's position is like that of a constitutional monarch, without whose sanction no law can be passed but who hesitates long before imposing his veto on any measure put forward by Parliament."[44] Or the following:

The ego's relation to the id might be compared with that of a rider to his horse. The horse supplies the locomotive energy, while the rider has the privilege of deciding on the goal and of guiding the powerful animal's movement. But only too often there arises between the ego and the id the not precisely ideal situation of the rider being obliged to guide the horse along the path by which it itself wants to go.[45]

---

[42]*The Ego and the Id,* S.E., XIX, 56.

[43]*New Introductory Lectures,* S.E., XXII, 77.

[44]*The Ego and the Id,* S.E., XIX, 55.

[45]*New Introductory Lectures,* S.E. XXII, 77. Freud's use of Plato's horse-horseman image (Phaedrus) further supports our interpretation of the power relationship between id and ego.

Freud stresses the permanent liability of the ego's "late" development.

> We have heard how the weak and immature ego of the first period of childhood is permanently damaged by the stresses put upon it in its efforts to fend off the dangers that are peculiar to that period of life. Children are protected against the dangers that threaten them from the external world by the solicitude of their parents; they pay for this security by a fear of *loss of love* which would deliver them over helpless to the dangers of the external world. This factor exerts a decisive influence on the outcome of the conflict when a boy finds himself in the situation of the Oedipus complex, in which the threat to his narcissism by the danger of castration, reinforced from the primaeval sources, takes possession of him. Driven by the combined operation of these two influences, the contemporary real danger and the remembered one with its phylogenetic basis, the child embarks on his attempts at defence—repressions—which are effective for the moment but nevertheless turn out to be psychologically inadequate when the later re-animation of sexual life brings a reinforcement to the instinctual demands which have been repudiated in the past.[46]

The discussion of energy in Chapter Four, as well as the fuller treatment of it in Chapter Seven, will demonstrate that for Freud there is only one original source of energy, id energy which he calls libido. For the ego to do its work it must capture its energy from the id and desexualize it.[47] The price for attaining this energy is heavy. For the ego must force itself upon the id as an object choice.

> From another point of view it may be said that this transformation of an erotic object-choice into an alteration of the ego is also a method by which the ego can obtain control over the id and deepen its relations with it—at the cost, it is true, of acquiescing to a large extent in the id's experiences. When the ego assumes the features of the object, it is forcing itself, so to speak, upon the id as a love-object and is trying to make good the id's loss by saying: 'Look, you can love me too—I am so like the object.'[48]

To obtain energy the ego will have to change the direction of the libido or sublimate it. "The transformation [of erotic libido] into ego-libido of course involves an abandonment of sexual aims,

---

[46]*An Outline of Psycho-Analysis*, S.E., XXIII, 200.
[47]See Chapter Four, pp. 59-60.
[48]*The Ego and the Id*, S.E., XIX, 30.

a desexualiation."[49] This process and its results do not represent the organism's method of operation in its original or primary state.

> At the very beginning, all the libido is accumulated in the id, while the ego is still in process of formation or is still feeble. The id sends part of this libido out into erotic object-cathexes, whereupon the ego, now grown stronger, tries to get hold of this object-libido and to force itself on the id as a love-object. The narcissism of the ego is thus a secondary one, which has been withdrawn from objects.[50]

It is with this acquired energy that the ego is to do its work such as the thinking that is required to assess reality. "If thought-processes in the wider sense are to be included among these displacements, then the activity of thinking is also supplied from the sublimation of erotic motive forces."[51]

The functions of the ego as stated by Freud and discussed previously leave little room for any conception of an ego with its own inner life.[52] All of the rational processes that are developed by the ego are developed in order to handle the needs of the id. The ego, in itself, has no inner life to begin with, for as we have stated above, it is but a modified portion of the id. Freud further emphasizes his conception of an ego that is influenced by the biological: "This general schematic picture of a psychical apparatus may be supposed to apply as well to the higher animals which resemble man mentally . . . A distinction between ego and id is an unavoidable assumption. Animal psychology has not yet taken in hand the interesting problem which is here presented."[53]

The fact that the ego is constantly open to the danger of regression will further emphasize its unreliability. First there is the fact that the ego itself must regress if it is to make use of the mechanism of introjection. "It may be that by this introjection, which is a kind of regression to the mechanism of the oral phase, the ego makes it easier for the object to be given up or renders

---

[49]*Ibid.*, p. 46.

[50]*Ibid.*

[51]*Ibid.*, p. 45, as we indicated in Chapter Four, pp. 78-79, so for all other (non-biological) activity such as art, values, work.

[52]See *The Protocol: The Ego and the Id.*, Chapter i par. 8, p. 215.

[53]*An Outline of Psycho-Analysis*, S.E., XXIII, 147.

that process possible."[54] The ego constantly uses regression as one way of handling the demands of the id. "If it succeeds in making an instinct regress, it will actually have done it more injury than it could have by repressing it. Sometimes, indeed, after forcing an instinct to regress in this way, it goes on to repress it."[55] But in causing regression the ego forces the organism to adopt a more primitive organization or method of handling situations. "In the first place, an excessive strength of instinct can damage the ego in a similar way to an excessive 'stimulus' from the external world. It is true that the former cannot destroy it: but it *can destroy its characteristic dynamic organization and change the ego back into a portion of the id.*"[56] In fact, it is precisely a regression that often characterizes a neurosis. "The genital organization of the libido turns out to be feeble and insufficiently resistant, so that when the ego begins its defensive efforts the first thing it succeeds in doing is to throw back the genital organization (of the phallic phase), in whole or in part, to the earlier sadistic-anal level. This fact of regression is decisive for all that follows."[57]

Neurosis is sometimes described as a form of regression in which the ego loses its hard earned strength and capacities.

> Thereupon the ego breaks off its relation to reality; it withdraws the cathexis from the system of perception, *Cs.*—or rather, perhaps, it withdraws *a* cathexis, the special nature of which may be the subject of further enquiry. With this turning away from reality, reality-testing is got rid of, the (unrepressed, completely conscious) wishful phantasies are able to press forward into the system, and they are there regarded as a better reality.[58]

Furthermore the enfeeblement of the ego strengthens the demands of instinct.

> But if the relative feebleness of the ego is the decisivise factor for the genesis of a neurosis, it must also be possible for a later physical illness to produce a neurosis, provided that it can bring about an enfeeblement of the ego. And that, once again, is very frequently found. A physical disorder of this kind can affect the instinctual life in the

[54]*The Ego and the Id,* S.E., XIX, 29.
[55]*Anxiety,* S.E., XX, 105.
[56]*An Outline of Psycho-Analysis,* S.E., XXIII, 199. Emphasis mine.
[57]*Anxiety,* S.E., XX, 113.
[58]Dreams, S.E., XIV, 233.

id and increase the strength of the instincts beyond the limit up to which the ego is capable of coping with them. The normal model of such processes is perhaps the alteration in women caused by the disturbances of menstruation and menopause. Or again, a general somatic illness, indeed an organic disease of the nervous central organ may attack the nutritional conditions of the mental apparatus and compel it to reduce its functioning and to bring to a halt its more delicate workings, one of which is the maintenance of the ego organization.[59]

In several of his works in which Freud sketches a primitive to a more advanced kind of rationality, regression is often viewed as a movement backwards from a higher level of thinking to a lower level or more primitive form of thinking.

We call this kind of regression a *topographical* one, to distinguish it from the previously mentioned *temporal* or developmental regression. The two do not necessarily always coincide, but they do so in the particular example before us. The reversal of the course of the excitation from the *Pcs.* through the *Ucs.* to perception is at the same time a return to the early stage of hallucinatory wish-fulfilment.[60]

The regression then would not only bring forth a more primitive state of libidinal organization but a more primitive state of rationality as well. Not possessing its own energy, and being vulnerable to attacks of regression only accentuates the secondary position of Freud's ego.

The ego, with all its limitations, represents Freud's treatment of the rational commonplace.[61] "To adopt a popular mode of speaking, we might say that the ego stands for reason and good sense while the id stands for the untamed passions."[62] However reason itself is of a circumscribed nature. The ego has no inner life of its own as we indicated previously,[63] and develops essentially from the importations of perceptions from without that are

---

[59]*Lay Analysis*, S.E., XX, 242. Note the extent to which in this passage Freud makes the ego dependent on its biological predispositions.

[60]Dreams, S.E., XIV, 227.

[61]We do not intend to present an analysis of rationality in Freud. Here we intend only to show that Freud did develop the rational commonplace and that it is destined to play a secondary role in his theory of personality.

[62]*New Introductory Lectures*, S.E., XXII, 76.

[63]p. 98.

stored up in memory. "We have also already concluded . . . that the ego is especially under the influence of perception, and that, speaking broadly, perceptions may be said to have the same significance for the ego as instincts have for the id."[64]

It appears that Freud himself wanted to emphasize the ego's lack of an internal rational structure when he describes its relation to two kinds of perception.

> Our ideas about the ego are beginning to clear, and its various relationships are gaining distinctness. We now see the ego in its strength and in its weaknesses. It is entrusted with important functions. By virtue of its relation to the perceptual system it gives mental processes an order in time and submits them to 'reality-testing' . . . All the experiences of life that originate from without enrich the ego; the id, however, is its second external world, which it strives to bring into subjection to itself.[65]

For Freud, there is no rational factor or virtue to be found internally or as part of man's basic or constitutional nature.

In Freud's view, the first and conditioning function of the ego is to discriminate between perceptions from within and those from without. The initial process of discrimination is described as follows:

> Let us imagine ourselves in the situation of an almost entirely helpless living organism, as yet unoriented in the world, which is receiving stimuli in its nervous substance. This organism will very soon be in a position to make a first distinction and a first orientation. On the one hand, it will be aware of stimuli which can be avoided by muscular action (flight); these it ascribes to an external world. On the other hand, it will also be aware of stimuli against which such action is of no avail and whose character of constant pressure persists in spite of it; these stimuli are the signs of an internal world, the evidence of instinctual needs. The perceptual substance of the living organism will thus have found in the efficacy of its muscular activity a basis for distinguishing between an 'outside' and an 'inside.'[66]

And since beginnings are determining, the role of the rational factor is to mediate the wishes of the id or to steer a course for the

---

[64] *The Ego and the Id*, S.E., XIX, 40.

[65] *Ibid.*, p. 55.

[66] Instincts and their vicissitudes, S.E., XIV, 119.

id. Schwab points out[67] that it is the dominating role of beginnings that leads Freud to develop his empirically oriented rationality by moving from things, not to ideas, but to the third of this famous trilogy, words.

> The system *Ucs.* contains the thing-cathexes of the objects, the first and true object-cathexes; the system *Pcs.* comes about by this thing-presentation being hypercathected through being linked with the word-presentations corresponding to it. It is these hypercathexes, we may suppose, that bring about a higher psychical organization and make it possible for the primary process to be succeeded by the secondary process which is dominant in the *Pcs.*[68]

And:

> . . . those acts of cathexis which are comparatively remote from perception, are in themselves without quality and unconscious, and that they attain their capacity to become conscious only through being linked with the residues of perceptions of *words*. But word-presentations, for their part too, are derived from sense-perceptions, in the same way as thing-presentations are; the question might therefore be raised why presentations of objects cannot become conscious through the medium of their *own* perceptual residues. Probably, however, thought proceeds in systems so far remote from the original perceptual residues that they have no longer retained anything of the qualities of those residues, and, in order to become conscious, need to be reinforced by new qualities. Moreover, by being linked with words, cathexes can be provided with quality even when they represent only *relations* between presentations of objects and are thus unable to derive any quality from perceptions. Such relations, which become comprehensible only through words, form a major part of our thought-processes.[69]

These word-perceptions are stored up in memory.

> These word-presentations are residues of memories; they were at one time perceptions, and like all mnemonic residues they can become conscious again. Before we concern ourselves further with their nature, it dawns upon us like a new discovery that only something which has once been a *Cs.* perception can become conscious, and that anything arising from within (apart from feelings) that seeks to become conscious must try to transform itself into external perceptions: this becomes possible by means of memory-traces.[70]

---

[67]Oral communication.
[68]The Unconscious, S.E., XIV, 201-202.
[69]*Ibid.*, p. 202.
[70]*The Ego and the Id*, S.E., XIX, 20.

To distinguish realities from ideas and wishes, Freud introduces the notion of judgment. ". . . for, as we know, our judgment is very well able to distinguish realities from ideas and wishes, however intense they may be."[71] Since judgment and other characteristics of rationality were developed under the influence of the id, or to serve its needs, there always is the danger that the capacity of judgment will be impaired, failing to distinguish between internal and external perceptions.

> Let us, furthermore, bear in mind the great practical importance of distinguishing perceptions from ideas, however intensely recalled. Our whole relation to the external world, to reality, depends on our ability to do so. We have put forward the fiction that we did not always possess this ability and that at the beginning of our mental life we did in fact hallucinate the satisfying object when we felt the need for it. But in such a situation satisfaction did not occur, and this failure must very soon have moved us to create some contrivance with the help of which it was possible to distinguish such wishful perceptions from a real fulfilment and to avoid them for the future. In other words, we gave up hallucinatory satisfaction of our wishes at a very early period and set up a kind of 'reality-testing'. The question now arises in what this reality-testing consisted, and how the hallucinatory wishful psychosis of dreams and amentia and similar conditions succeeds in abolishing it and in re-establishing the old mode of satisfaction.[72]

The ego is so intimately tied to and dependent upon the id and open to the danger of regression that it is not surprising that rational powers and organization can easily be undermined. "On the other hand, we can already learn from pathology the way in which reality-testing may be done away with or put out of action. We shall see this more clearly in the wishful psychosis of amentia than in that of dreams."[73]

In summary, it is clear that rationality serves the purpose of helping the "basic" nature of man express itself. There is no *basic* rational characteristic of man. It is an importation and this importation makes it possible for man to live with pleasure in his environment.

---

[71]Dreams, S.E., XIV, 230.
[72]*Ibid.*, p. 231.
[73]*Ibid.*, p. 233.

Freud has characterized the id as a cauldron of seething passions; he will describe the ego as an organized entity tending toward higher and higher organization.

> In the id there are no conflicts; contradictions and antitheses persist side by side in it unconcernedly, and are often adjusted by the formation of compromises. In similar circumstances the ego feels a conflict which must be decided; and the decision lies in one urge being abandoned in favour of the other. The ego is an organization characterized by a very remarkable trend towards unification, towards synthesis. This characteristic is lacking in the id; it is, as we might say, 'all to pieces'; its different urges pursue their own purposes independently and regardless of one another.[74]

And the following:

> But what distinguishes the ego from the id quite especially is a tendency to synthesis in its contents, to a combination and unification in its mental processes which are totally lacking in the id. When presently we come to deal with the instincts in mental life we shall, I hope, succeed in tracing this essential characteristic of the ego back to its source. It alone produces the high degree of organization which the ego needs for its best achievements.[75]

The location of the ego in the Freud's topography is best seen in a diagram Freud has made of the anatomy of the mental apparatus.[76] It is clear that the ego is that part of the personality that abuts on the external world and that its nucleus is the system perception-consciousness. Thus we see that the ego is the most external of the parts in the mental anatomy. However, it would be a mistake to conceive of the ego as being only conscious and preconscious for there are parts of the ego that are unconscious as well.

> The inside of the ego, which comprises above all the thought-processes, has the quality of being preconscious. This is characteristic of the ego and belongs to it alone. . . . The preconscious state, cahracterized on the one hand by having access to consciousness and on the other hand by its connection with the speech-residues, is nevertheless something peculiar, the nature of which is not exhausted by these two characteristics. The evidence for this is the fact that large portions of

---

[74]*Lay Analysis*, S.E., XX, 196.

[75]*New Introductory Lectures*, S.E., XXII, 76.

[76]See the diagram on p. 78 of *New Introductory Lectures as well as the diagram* on p. 27 of *The Ego and the Id*.

the ego, and particularly of the super-ego, which cannot be denied the characteristic of preconsciousness, none the less remain for the most part unconscious in the phenomenological sense of the word.[77]

As we indicated[78] the ego in Freud does not possess the power to stimulate or instigate. It can guide and direct the id but itself cannot aspire to any kind of important change or self-direction.

The antithesis ego—non-ego (external), i.e. subject—object, is, as we have already said . . . ., thrust upon the individual organism at an early stage, by the experience that it can silence *external* stimuli by means of muscular action but is defenceless against *instinctual* stimuli. This antithesis remains, above all, sovereign in our intellectual activity and creates for research the basic situation which no efforts can alter. The polarity of pleasure—unpleasure is attached to a scale of feelings, whose paramount importance in determining our actions (our will) has already been emphasized . . . . The antithesis active—passive must not be confused with the antithesis ego-subject—external world-object. The relation of the ego to the external world is passive in so far as it receives stimuli from it and active when it reacts to these. It is forced by its instincts into a quite special degree of activity towards the external world, so that we might bring out the essential point if we say that the ego-subject is passive in respect of external stimuli but active through its own instincts. The antithesis active—passive coalesces later with the antithesis masculine—feminine, which, until this has taken place, has no psychological meaning. The coupling of activity with masculinity and of passivity with femininity meets us, indeed, as a biological fact; but it is by no means so invariably complete and exclusive as we are inclined to assume.[79]

Hence we see that only the instincts supply the active components of the organism's life, while the ego is essentially passive. The one exception appears to be the individual who has undergone successful therapy. However, theoretically even in therapy the ego is held to be passive. According to Freud the redirection of the ego will require a libidinal or erotic component—the transference to the physician.[80] The ego, if it is to become "more mature," will require help from the outside.

It is easy now to describe our therapeutic aim. We try to restore the

[77]*An Outline of Psycho-Analysis*, S.E., XXIII, 162.
[78]p. 92-93.
[79]Instincts and their vicissitudes, S.E., XIV, 134.
[80]See Chapter Three, p. 43.

ego, to free it from its restrictions, and to give it back the command over the id which it has lost owing to its early repressions. It is for this one purpose that we carry out analysis, our whole technique is directed to this aim. We have to seek out the repressions which have been set up and to urge the ego to correct them with our help and to deal with conflicts better than by an attempt at flight. Since these repressions belong to the very early years of childhood, the work of analysis leads us, too, back to that period. Our path to these situations of conflict, which have for the most part been forgotten and which we try to revive in the patient's memory, is pointed out to us by his symptoms, dreams and free associations. These must, however, first be interpreted—translated—for, under the influence of the psychology of the id, they have assumed forms of expression that are strange to our comprehension. We may assume that whatever associations, thoughts and memories the patient is unable to communicate to us without internal struggles are in some way connected with the repressed material or are its derivatives. By encouraging the patient to disregard his resistances to telling us these things, we are educating his ego to overcome its inclination towards attempts at flight and to tolerate an approach to what is repressed. In the end, if the situation of the repression can be successfully reproduced in his memory, his compliance will be brilliantly rewarded. The whole difference between his age then and now works in his favour; and the thing from which his childish ego fled in terror will often seem to his adult and strengthened ego no more than child's play.[81]

As we have pointed out, it is difficult to understand why Freud did not conceive of man's possessing an ego at birth—if not an "actual" ego then at least one in potential. By this we do not mean an ego that is derived from the id but rather a separate and distinct part. It would be interesting to speculate upon the consequences of such a reformulation for Freud's theory and conception of therapy.

---

[81]*Lay Analysis*, S.E., XX, 205. Freud in his essay, *Analysis Terminable and Interminable*, S.E., XXIII, 211-253 points to the difficulty, after completing an analysis, of being assured of a "dependable" ego or an "obedient" id.

Chapter Six

□

THE SOCIAL COMMONPLACE

As we stated in Chapter Four, for Freud, conflict represents the normal state of affairs. One of the basic conflicts throughout life is that between free instinctual expression and society's opposition to such expression. Out of this conflict there develops the inhibitional system, which Freud assigns to his third organ, the super-ego. The super-ego is a precipitate of the ego, and thus a secondary offspring of the id. The super-ego is the repository of self-observation, "conscience" and a "holding up" of ideals. These functions, Freud claims, develop as the reactions of the amoral child to the restrictions imposed by living in a family-society.

Since the child is not born with these inhibitions but is born with an id, some momentous act must occur for values and prohibitions to be introjected into the mental apparatus. In the myth of Oedipus, Freud is able to locate the point, both in the history of the individual and in the history of the race, at which society's prohibitions are introjected. The Oedipal conflict proves to be a formulation that is responsive to several of Freud's principles.

1. Infantile sexuality—If there is infantile sexuality then toward whom should this sexuality be expressed if not those close to the child, i.e. mother, father and siblings.

2. The recapitulation of phylogenesis—Every individual lives through the history of the race as a result of the Oedipal conflict.

3. The vitality of man's archaic heritage—By establishing the super-ego, the racial heritage is transmitted.

4. The child as father to the man—The Oedipal conflict is the "seat" of all neurosis and a source of constant danger throughout life.

5. Lamarckism—Not only the individual but the "societal"

super-ego arises as a result of a "momentous" occasion.

Oedipus itself illustrates the importance of conflict in Freud, for it is the result of a conflict of two opposing instinctual wishes, an object cathexis toward the mother and an identification with the father. The super-ego will play a powerful role throughout the life of the individual since it represents this early and basic experience, is so closely related to the id and emerges when the ego is not as yet fully developed. Because it involves such basic instinctual expressions, the super-ego will not be amenable to change.

We shall discover that socialization or the development of civilization requires the renunciation of a good deal of man's instinctual nature.

Since the super-ego is the precipitate of the Oedipal conflict, the threatening father image is internalized as well, and thus there develops for Freud a harsh and severe super-ego. As the super-ego develops, other figures, who replace the parents and who serve as models, influence its development. As we will indicate, Freud found difficulty in precisely locating the super-ego on his topography. He finally decides to place it in intimate relationship to the id and further from the perceptual system than the ego. Like the ego, it must obtain its energy from the id and is under the domination of the pleasure principle. The super-ego, by virtue of its dominion over the ego, will be ranked second in the Freudian hierarchy. It will add to the burdens of the ego, for now the ego will often have to repress instincts at the behest of the super-ego.

For Freud the super-ego is the social commonplace. He saw the group, by and large, as an over-sized individual. He certainly did not admit to a group instinct. Thus the social factor in Freud emerges essentially as the way instinctual nature is molded in the early and basic group, the family. It is here that values are instilled and inhibitions developed. Future group participation will depend very much on the experiences in the first group—the family.

It is obvious that there are other ways of conceiving of the development of inhibitions and of granting a different and more central role to the social commonplace than we find in Freud's theory.

We shall now follow Freud's decision to construct a third part that will serve as the inhibitional system for the organism. Freud found the division of the mental apparatus into an id and an ego insufficient. "The considerations that led us to assume the existence of a grade in the ego, a differentiation within the ego, which may be called the 'ego ideal' or 'super-ego', have been stated elsewhere. They still hold good."[1] Freud decided that this third part should be a precipitate of the ego, that is, a part that split off from the ego.

> The long period of childhood, during which the growing human being lives in dependence on his parents, leaves behind it as a precipitate the formation in his ego of a special agency in which this parental influence is prolonged. It has received the name of *super-ego*. In so far as this super-ego is differentiated from the ego or is opposed to it, it constitutes a third power which the ego must take into account.[2]

Since all there is of human personality at birth is an id, Freud will have to introduce an inhibitional system at some point during the child's development.

> Even the conscience is something 'within us', yet it is not so from the first. In this it is a real contrast to sexual life, which is in fact there from the beginning of life and not only a later addition. But, as is well known, young children are amoral and possess no internal inhibitions against their impulses striving for pleasure.[3]

Also:

> The picture of an ego which mediates between the id and the external world, which takes over the instinctual demands of the former in order to lead them to satisfaction, which derives perceptions from the latter and uses them as memories, which, intent on its self-preservation, puts itself in defence against excessively strong claims from both sides and which, at the same time, is guided in all its decisions by the injunctions of a modified pleasure principle—this picture in fact applies to the ego only up to the end of the first period of childhood,

---

[1]*The Ego and the Id*, S.E., XIX, 28. *See also The Protocol: The Ego and the Id*, chap. iii, pars. 1 and 2, p. 220.

[2]*An Outline of Psycho-Analysis*, S.E., XXIII, 146. The super-ego will be shown to be separated off from the ego; it is this separation that causes the feeling of guilt.

[3]*New Introductory Lectures*, S.E., XXII, 61-62.

till about the age of five. At about that time an important change has taken place. A portion of the external world has, at least partially, been abandoned as an object and has instead, by identification, been taken into the ego and thus become an integral part of the internal world. This new psychical agency continues to carry on the functions which have hitherto been performed by the people [the abandoned objects] in the external world: it observes the ego, gives it orders, judges it and threatens it with punishments, exactly like the parents whose place it has taken.[4]

Freud describes the content of this new agency. "We have allotted it the functions of self-observation, of conscience and of (maintaining) the ideal. . . . The super-ego is the representative for us of every moral restriction, the advocate of a striving towards perfection—it is, in short, as much as we have been able to grasp psychologically of what is described as the higher side of human life."[5] Or the following: "It is easy to show that the ego ideal answers to everything that is expected of the higher nature of man."[6]

Freud's adoption of the principle of conflict in the relationship of the parts of the psyche to each other as well as in the relationship of the instincts to each other is nowhere better observed than in the development of the super-ego.

Freud adopts the myth of Oedipus to explain the development of the super-ego—man's inhibitional system.[7]

In working with melancholia Freud felt that he had discovered a fundamental process that consists of the replacement of an object cathexis by an identification. He saw in this process the basis for character formation as well, therefore, a stage in the development of the super-ego.[8]

We succeeded in explaining the painful disorder of melancholia by supposing that (in those suffering from it) an object which was lost has been set up again inside the ego—that is, that an object-cathexis has been replaced by an identification. At that time, however, we

[4]*An Outline of Psycho-Analysis*, S.E., XXIII, 205.

[5]*New Introductory Lectures*, S.E., XXII, 66-67.

[6]*The Ego and the Id*, S.E., XIX, 37.

[7]See *Lay Analysis*, S.E., XX, 211-217.

[8]The discussion in this section is based almost entirely on *The Protocol: The Ego and the Id*, chap. iii, pp. 214-232.

did not appreciate the full significance of this process and did not know how common and how typical it is. Since then we have come to understand that this kind of substitution has a great share in determining the form taken by the ego and that it makes an essential contribution towards building up what is called its 'character'.[9]

Freud saw the super-ego as developing through the following stages:

1. Stage one—In the very early life of the child there is little distinction between an object cathexis and an identification, for the ego and the id have not as yet separated.

2. Stage two[10]—As the child develops and grows, object cathexis relates itself to the needs of the id and the developing ego becomes aware of it.[11] The identification with the father[12] and the object cathexis to the mother conflict, for they cannot co-exist. As the child continues to develop conflict grows more intense. That is, the father is seen as an obstacle to the child's attaining the mother. From this point on the identification with the father takes on a "hostile coloring" for the child now wants to eliminate the father so that he can take the father's place.

Thereafter we notice a distinct ambivalence in the child's relationship to his father.

At a very early age the little boy develops an object-cathexis for his mother, which originally related to the mother's breast and as the prototype of an object-choice on the anaclitic model; the boy deals with his father by identifying himself with him. For a time these two relationships proceed side by side, until the boy's sexual wishes in regard to his mother become more intense and his father is perceived as an obstacle to them; from this the Oedipus complex originates. His

---

[9]*The Ego and the Id*, S.E., XIX, 28.

[10]This is the description of the simple Oedipal conflict. Freud goes on to describe a more complex Oedipal conflict, but this description will not add to our discussion. See *The Ego and the Id*, S.E., XIX, 31-33.

[11]We are now following Freud's description of the Oedipus complex from the standpoint of the male child. For the female child Oedipus is more complex.

[12]For Freud, this first identification is of vast importance. "This leads us back to the origin of the ego ideal; for behind it there lies hidden an individual's first and most important identification, his identification with the father in his own personal history." (*The Ego and the Id*, S.E., XIX, 31). Thus we see again the importance of man's archic inheritance and the initial or first identification. This notion of a prehistory shows a Lamarckian influence.

identification with his father then takes on a hostile colouring and changes into a wish to get rid of his father in order to take his place with his mother. Henceforward his relation to his father is ambivalent; it seems as if the ambivalence inherent in the identification from the beginning had become manifest. An ambivalent attitude to his father and an object-relation of a solely affectionate kind to his mother make up the content of the simple positive Oedipus complex in a boy.[13]

3. Stage three—Since the id must be satisfied and cannot be, Freud makes the ego regress to a mechanism of the oral phase, the introjection of the object.[14] By this introjection, the ego does indeed gain some control over the id but at the price of later subservience.

> From another point of view it may be said that this transformation of an erotic object-choice into an alteration of the ego is also a method by which the ego can obtain control over the id and deepen its relations with it—at the cost, it is true, of acquiescing to a large extent in the id's experiences. When the ego assumes the features of the object, it is forcing itself, so to speak, upon the id as a love-object and is trying to make good the id's loss by saying: 'Look you can love me too—I am so like the object.'[15]

4. Stage four—The resolution of Oedipus. The Oedipus complex or conflict can be resolved by virtue of the child giving up the object cathexis to his mother and replacing it either by an

---

[13]*The Ego and the Id*, S.E., XIX, 31-32.

[14]Freud interprets this phenomenon which accompanies the giving up of a sexual object, as similar to the process in melancholia, i.e. the reinstatement of the object into the ego (identification). See *The Protocol: The Ego and the Id*, chap. iii, par. 6., 221. The extent to which Freud's stages (oral, anal and genital) are based on Freud's phylogenetic commitment can be observed in many passages and especially in the following:

An interesting parallel to the replacement of object-choice by identification is to be found in the belief of primitive peoples, and in the prohibitions based upon it, that the attributes of animals which are incorporated as nourishment persist as part of the character of those who eat them. As is well known, this belief is one of the roots of cannibalism and its effects have continued through the series of usages of the totem meal down to Holy Communion. [Cf. *Totem and Taboo* (1912-13), *Standard Ed.*, 13, 82, 142, 154-5, etc.] The consequences ascribed to this belief to oral mastery of the object do in fact follow in the case of the later sexual object-choice. (*The Ego and the Id*, S.E., XIX, 29, n. 2.)

[15]*The Ego and the Id*, S.E., XIX, 30.

identification with his mother or an identification with the father. The identification with the father, which is the more common outcome, will permit an affectionate relationship to be continued with the mother, while an identification with the mother often is the cause of homosexuality.

> Along with the demolition of the Oedipus complex, the boy's object-cathexis of his mother must be given up. Its place may be filled by one of two things: either an identification with his mother or an intensification of his identification with his father. We are accustomed to regard the latter outcome as the more normal; it permits the affectionate relation to the mother to be in a measure retained.[16]

The "resolution" of the Oedipal conflict marks the end of the phase of childhood sexuality and the beginning of the period of latency, and forms a precipitate in the ego.

> *The broad general outcome of the sexual phase dominated by the Oedipus complex may, therefore, be taken to be the forming of a precipitate in the ego, consisting of these two identifications in some way united with each other. This modification of the ego retains its special position; it confronts the other contents of the ego as an ego ideal or super-ego.*[17]

The Oedipal conflict will prove to be a formulation that conforms to several of Freud's biological principles.

1. Infantile sexuality—It is clear that the Oedipus complex assumes that the child has a sexual desire for his mother.

> A child's first erotic object is the mother's breast that nourishes it; love has its origin in attachment to the satisfied need for nourishment. . . . By her care of the child's body she becomes its first seducer. In these two relations lies the root of a mother's importance, unique, without parallel, established unalterably for a whole lifetime as the first and strongest love-object and as the prototype of all later love-relations—for both sexes.[18]

If there is infantile sexuality then one would expect this sexuality to be expressed in relation to those close to the child, i.e. mother, father and siblings.

---

[16]*The Ego and the Id*, S.E., XIX, 32.

[17]*Ibid.*, p. 34.

[18]*An Outline of Psycho-Analysis*, S.E., XXIII, 188.

So let us turn to our chief witness in matters concerning primaeval times—mythology. It informs us that the myths of every people, and not only of the Greeks, are filled with examples of love-affairs between fathers and daughters and even between mothers and sons. Cosmology, no less than the genealogy of royal races, is founded upon incest. For what purpose do you suppose these legends were created? To brand gods and kings as criminals? To fasten on them the abhorrence of the human race? Rather, surely, because incestuous wishes are a primordial human heritage and have never fully been overcome, so that their fulfilment was still granted to gods and their descendants when the majority of common humans were already obliged to renounce them. It is in complete harmony with these lessons of history and mythology that we find incestuous wishes still present and operative in the childhood of the individual.[19]

2. The recapitulation of phylogenesis—Every individual lives through the history of the race as a result of the Oedipal conflict.

According to one psycho-analytic hypothesis, the last-mentioned phenomenon, which seems to be peculiar to man, is a heritage of the cultural development necessitated by the glacial epoch. We see, then, that the differentiation of the super-ego from the ego is no matter of chance; it represents the most important characteristics of the development both of the individual and of the species; indeed, by giving permanent expression to the influence of the parents it perpetuates the existence of the factors to which it owes its origin.[20]

And the following:

Religion, morality, and a social sense—the chief elements in the higher side of man—were originally one and the same thing. According to the hypothesis which I put forward in *Totem and Taboo* they were acquired phylogenetically out of the father-complex: religion and moral restraint through the process of mastering the Oedipus complex itself, and social feeling through the necessity for overcoming the rivalry that then remained between the members of the younger generation. . . . Even to-day the social feelings arise in the individual as a superstructure built upon impulses of jealous rivalry against his brothers and sisters.[21]

---

[19]*Lay Analysis*, S.E., XX, 214. We have a clear manifestation here of Freud's extreme beginning orientation. This citation should be noted by those who believe Freud uses myth allegorically. See *On the History of the Psycho-Analytic Movement*, S.E., XIV, 3-66.

[20]*The Ego and the Id*, S.E., XIX, 35.

[21]*Ibid.*, p. 37.

After having argued for the importance of infantile sexuality in the Oedipal conflict, Freud has the following to say about the importance of recapitulation. "In all this the phylogenetic foundation has so much the upper hand over personal accidental experience that it makes no difference whether a child has really sucked at the breast or has been brought up on the bottle and never enjoyed the tenderness of a mother's care."[22]

3. The vitality of man's archaic heritage—Through the resolution of Oedipus and the development of the super-ego, the racial heritage is transmitted.

> Through the forming of the ideal, what biology and the vicissitudes of the human species have created in the id and left behind in it is taken over by the ego and re-experienced in relation to itself as an individual. Owing to the way in which the ego ideal is formed, it has the most abundant links with the phylogenetic acquisition of each individual—his archaic heritage.[23]

4. The child as father to the man—The impact of the Oedipal conflict is one that will be felt throughout the life of man. It is Oedipus which demonstrates very forcibly the importance of the early period of life upon all that is to take place in later life. In prefatory remarks to a description of the Oedipus complex, Freud states the following: "Analytic experience has convinced us of the complete truth of the assertion so often to be heard that the child is psychologically father to the adult and that the events in his first years are of paramount importance for his whole later life. It will thus be of special interest to us if there is something that may be described as the central experience of this period of childhood."[24] And the following:

> The most important conflict with which a small child is faced is his relation to his parents, the *'Oedipus Complex'* it is in attempting to grapple with this problem that those destined to suffer from a neurosis habitually come to grief. The reactions against the instinctual

---

[22]*An Outline of Psycho-Analysis*, S.E., XXIII, 188. It is interesting to note the manifold complications that can arise in any individual life due to discrepancy between Oedipus as transmitted to that individual phylogenetically, and Oedipus as relived in his actual family.

[23]*The Ego and the Id*, S.E., XIX, 36.

[24]*An Outline of Psycho-Analysis*, S.E., XXIII, 187.

demands of the Oedipus complex are the source of the most precious and socially important achievements of the human mind; and this holds true not only in the life of individuals but probably also in the history of the human species as a whole. The super-ego, too, the moral agency which dominates the ego, has its origin in the process of over-coming the Oedipus complex.[25]

5. Freud's Lamarckism—This is reflected in his commitment to the importance of the first identification as compared to all other identifications. The insistence that it is an identification *de novo* emphasizes his adoption of the Lamarckian princi-ple.[26] Freud locates the "momentous occasion" in the history of the race—the murder of the father—when the super-ego was estab-lished.[27] He also postulates a moment in history that brought about the development of civilization. "This struggle is what all life essentially consists of, and the evolution of civilization may therefore be simply described as the struggle for life of the human species."[28] Freud footnotes this statement: "And we may probably add more precisely, a struggle for life in the shape it was bound to assume after a certain event which still remains to be discovered."[29]

The super-ego[30] will prove to be a very powerful agency in the Freudian mental apparatus, which accounts for its occupying sec-ond place in the Freudian trinity, since it results from instinctual renunciation. It will maintain a close relationship with the id.

> For we have been obliged to assume that within the ego itself a par-ticular agency has become differentiated, which we name the super-ego. This super-ego occupies a special position between the ego and the id. It belongs to the ego and shares its high degree of psycho-

---

[25]*Psycho-Analysis*, S.E., XX, 268.

[26]The importance of the first identification only further emphasizes Freud's com-mitment to the importance of the beginning of human life.

[27]See pp. 71-75.

[28]*Civilization and Its Discontents*, S.E., XXI, 122.

[29]*Ibid.*, p. 122, n. 2.

[30]Freud claims that the content of the child's super-ego need not resemble the actual experience in the family (i.e. parental prohibitions and threats) but that it is modeled on the super-ego of the parents. Further, there is great variation in the kind of super-ego developed. "What it amounts to is that in the formation of the super-ego and the emergence of a conscience innate constitutional factors and influences from the real environment act in combination. This is not at all surprising; on the contrary, it is a universal aetiological condition for all such processes." (*Civilization and Its Discontents*, S.E., XXI, 130.)

logical organization; but it has a particularly intimate connection with the id. It is in fact a precipitate of the first object-cathexes of the id and is the heir to the Oedipus complex after its demise. This super-ego can confront the ego and treat it like an object; and it often treats it very harshly.[31]

In addition to its intimate relationship to the id, the super-ego carries with it the power of the archaic or phylogenetic heritage. "The past, the tradition of the race and of the people, lives on in the ideologies of the super-ego, and yields only slowly to the influences of the present and to new changes; and so long as it operates through the super-ego it plays a powerful part in human life. . ."[32] Consequently the super-ego is destined to rule over the ego throughout life, to be conservative, and not easily amenable to change.

Although it is accessible to all later influences, it nevertheless pre-serves throughout life the character given to it by its derivation from the father-complex—namely, the capacity to stand apart from the ego and to master it. It is a memorial of the former weakness and depend-ence of the ego, and the mature ego remains subject to its domina-tion. As the child was once under a compulsion to obey its parents, so the ego submits to the categorical imperative of its super-ego.

But the derivation of the super-ego from the first object-cathexes of the id, from the Oedipus complex, signifies even more for it. This derivation, as we have already shown . . . brings it into rela-tion with the phylogenetic acquisitions of the id and makes it a re-incarnation of former ego-structures which have left their precipitates behind in the id. Thus the super-ego is always close to the id and can act as its representative vis-á-vis the ego. It reaches deep down into the id and for that reason is farther from consciousness than the ego is.[33]

The super-ego will not only rule over the ego but it will rule over it harshly.[34] "The torments caused by the reproaches of con-science correspond precisely to a child's fear of loss of love, a fear the place of which has been taken by the moral agency."[35] And the

---

[31]*Lay Analysis,* S.E., XX, 223.

[32]*New Introductory Lectures,* S.E., XXII, 67.

[33]*The Ego and the Id,* S.E., XIX, 48-49.

[34]For further discussion of the severity or harshness of the super-ego see *The Protocol: Civilization and Its Discontents,* Chap. viii, pp. 246-249.

[35]*An Outline of Psycho-Analysis,* S.E., XXIII, 206.

following: "But even ordinary normal morality has a harshly restraining, cruelly prohibiting quality. It is from this, indeed, that
the conception arises of a higher being who deals out punishment inexorably."[36]

When the child has liberated himself from the family, the
super-ego continues to develop by virtue of the influence of other
important figures in the society.

> This parental influence of course includes in its operation not only
> the personalities of the actual parents but also the family, racial and
> national traditions handed on through them, as well as the demands
> of the immediate social *milieu* which they represent. In the same way,
> the super-ego, in the course of an individual's development, receives
> contributions from later successors and substitutes of his parents,
> such as teachers and models in public life of admired social ideals.[37]

The super-ego, as we demonstrated, functions to restrain instinctual needs. After the super-ego is formed, the "forbid-
dings" of the father continue to exert this restraining influence.
The super-ego is further developed through identifications with
other "parent-figures" in the society at large, and therefore is
sometimes referred to as the "dread of society."[38] The conflict that
Freud establishes between the parts of the psyche is based on his
view that conflict is inherent in the relationship of the individual
to his society.

> A good part of the struggle of mankind centres round the single task
> of finding an expedient accommodation—one, that is, that will bring
> happiness—between this claim of the individual and the cultural
> claims of the group; and one of the problems that touches the fate
> of humanity is whether such accommodation can be reached by means
> of some particular form of civilization or whether this conflict is ir-
> reconcilable.[39]

---

[36]*The Ego and the Id*, S.E., XIX, 54.

[37]*An Outline of Psycho-Analysis*, S.E., XXIII, 146. Freud grants an overbearing
role to the relationships that have been formed in the first group, the family. See
our pp. 127-128.

[38]We shall discuss Freud's conception of guilt (ego vs. ego ideal) in Chapter
Eight, pp. 146, 146, n. 17.

[39]*Civilization and Its Discontents*, S.E., XXI, 96. Freud sees the conflict between
the individual and his society as both an historical and a contemporary condition
of life. "It seems certain that we do not feel comfortable in our present-day civilization, but it is very difficult to form an opinion whether and in what degree

$\longrightarrow$

Freud brings the data of clinical experience to support his conception of the impact of societal restraint imposed upon the individual.

It arose when people came to know about the mechanism of the neuroses, which threaten to undermine the modicum of happiness enjoyed by civilized men. It was discovered that a person becomes neurotic because he cannot tolerate the amount of frustration which society imposes on him in the service of its cultural ideals, and it was inferred from this that the abolition or reduction of those demands would result in a return to possibilities of happiness.[40]

We discover conflict not only within the individual, and between the individual and society, but also within society. That is so, because Freud views the society as an individual "writ large." He therefore located within society the conflict between the instincts and the conflict between the parts of the psyche. As to the instincts:

. . . .I was led to the idea that civilization was a special process which mankind undergoes, and I am still under the influence of that idea. I may now add that civilization is a process in the service of Eros, whose purpose is to combine single human individuals, and after that families, then races, peoples and nations, into one great unity, the unity of mankind. Why this has to happen, we do not know; the work of Eros is precisely this. These collections of men to be libidinally bound to one another. Necessity alone, the advantages of work in common, will not hold them together. But man's natural aggressive instinct, the hostility of each against all and of all against each, opposes this programme of civilization. This aggressive instinct is the derivative and the main representative of the death instinct which we have found alongside of Eros and which shares world-dominion with it. And now, I think, the meaning of the evolution of civilizations is no longer obscure to us. It must present the struggle between Eros and Death, between the instinct of life and the instinct of destruction, as it works itself out in the human species.[41]

---

men of an earlier age felt happier and what part their cultural conditions played in the matter." *(Ibid, p. 89)*.

[40]*Civilization and Its Discontents*, S.E., XXI, 87.

[41]*Ibid.*, p. 122. We see here one of the rare instances of Freud's emphasis on the specific rather than the generic. This passage seems to suggest that even work, i.e. breadwinning, is *qua* work, a response to an instinctual need and not a means to

→

Freud's commitment to cultural struggle as a universal phenomenon made it necessary for him to explain the lack of cultural struggle in animal life.

> Why do our relatives, the animals, not exhibit any such cultural struggle? We do not know. Very probably some of them—the bees, the ants, the termites—strove for thousands of years before they arrived at the State institutions, the distribution of functions and the restrictions on the individual, for which we admire them to-day. . . . In the case of other animal species it may be that a temporary balance has been reached between the influences of their environment and the mutually contending instincts within them, and that thus a cessation of development has come about. It may be that in primitive man a fresh access of libido kindled a renewed burst of activity on the part of the destructive instinct.[42]

As to the parts of the psyche, Freud introduces the concept of a societal super-ego.

> The analogy between the process of civilization and the path of individual development may be extended in an important respect. It

---

a bread and butter end.

Freud further develops the connection between the primitive as he imagines it to have existed and the present or more specifically, between the biological and the sublimation of the biological.

> Psycho-analytic material, incomplete as it is and not susceptible to clear interpretation, nevertheless admits of a conjecture—a fantastic-sounding one —about the origin of this human feat. It is as though primal man had the habit, when he came in contact with fire, of satisfying an infantile desire connected with it, by putting it out with a stream of his urine. The legends that we possess leave no doubt about the originally phallic view taken of tongues of flame as they shoot upwards. Putting out fire by micturating —a theme to which modern giants, Gulliver in Lilliput and Rabelais' Gargantua, still hark back—was therefore a kind of sexual act with a male, an enjoyment of sexual potency in a homosexual competition. The first person to renounce this desire and spare the fire was able to carry it off with him and subdue it to his own use. By damping down the fire of his own sexual excitation, he had tamed the natural force of fire. This great cultural conquest was thus the reward for his renunciation of instinct. Further, it is as though woman had been appointed guardian of the fire which was held captive on the domestic hearth, because her anatomy made it impossible for her to yield to the temptation of this desire. It is remarkable too, how regularly analytic experience testifies to the connection between ambition, fire and urethral erotism. (*Ibid.*, p. 90, n. 1.)

[42]*Ibid.*, p. 123.

can be asserted that the community, too, evolves a super-ego under whose influence cultural development proceeds. It would be a tempting task for anyone who has a knowledge of human civilizations to follow out this analogy in detail. I will confine myself to bringing forward a few striking points. The super-ego of an epoch of civilization has an origin similar to that of an individual. It is based on the impression left behind by the personalities of great leaders—men of overwhelming force of mind or men in whom one of the human impulses has found its strongest and purest, and therefore often its most one-sided, expression.[43] In many instances the analogy goes still further, in that during their lifetime these figures were—often enough, even if not always—mocked and maltreated by others and even dispatched in a cruel fashion. In the same way, indeed, the primal father did not attain divinity until long after he had met his death by violence.[44]

Freud points to the super-ego functions in society:

Sublimation of instinct is an especially conspicuous feature of cultural development; it is what makes it possible for higher psychical activities, scientific, artistic or ideological, to play such an important part in civilized life. . . . In the third place, finally, and this seems the most important of all, it is impossible to overlook the extent to which civilization is built up upon a renunciation of instinct, how much it presupposes precisely the non-satisfaction (by suppression, repression or some other means?) of powerful instincts. This 'cultural frustration' dominates the large field of social relationships between human beings. As we already know, it is the cause of the hostility against which all civilizations have to struggle.[45]

Freud speculates about the possibility of the erosion of instinct resulting from the long history (individual and racial) of instinctual renunciation, i.e. of a Lamarckian effect even on the instincts.

The sexual life of civilized men is notwithstanding severely impaired; it sometimes gives the impression of being in process of involution as a function, just as our teeth and hair seem to be as organs. One is probably justified in assuming that its importance as a source of feelings of happiness, and therefore in the fulfilment of our aim in life, has sensibly diminished. Sometimes one seems to perceive that it is not only the pressure of civilization but something in the nature of

---

[43]Note the Lamarckian influence in this section as well.
[44]*Civilization and Its Discontents*, S.E., XXI, 141-142.
[45]*Ibid.*, p. 97.

the function itself which denies us full satisfaction and urges us along other paths. This may be wrong; it is hard to decide.[46]

Freud footnotes this passage with a discussion that evinces the dual roots of his theory: biology and psychology.

The view expressed above is supported by the following considerations. Man is an animal organism with (like others) an unmistakably bisexual disposition. The individual corresponds to a fusion of two symmetrical halves, of which, according to some investigators, one is purely male and the other female. It is equally possible that each half was originally hermaphrodite. Sex is a biological fact which, although it is of extraordinary importance in mental life, is hard to grasp psychologically. We are accustomed to say that every human being displays both male and female instinctual impulses, needs and attributes; but though anatomy, it is true, can point out the characteristic of maleness and femaleness, psychology cannot. For psychology the contrast between the sexes fades away into one between activity and passivity, in which we far too readily identify activity with maleness and passivity with femaleness, a view which is by no means universally confirmed in the animal kingdom. The theory of bisexuality is still surrounded by many obscurities and we cannot but feel it as a serious impediment in psycho-analysis that it has not yet found any link with the theory of the instincts. However this may be, if we assume it as a fact that each individual seeks to satisfy both male and female wishes in his sexual life, we are prepared for the possibility that those (two sets of) demands are not fulfiled by the same object, and that they interfere with each other unless they can be kept apart and each impulse guided into a particular channel that is suited to it.[47]Another difficulty arises from the circumstance that there is so often associated with the erotic relationship, over and above its own sadistic components, a quota of plain inclination to aggression. The love-object will not always view these complications with the degree of understanding and tolerance shown by the peasant woman who complained that her husband did not love her any more, since he had not beaten her for a week.

The conjecture which goes deepest, however, is the one which takes its start from what I have said above in my footnote on p.99f. It is to the affect that, with the assumption of an erect posture by man and with the depreciation of his sense of smell, it was not only his anal erotism which threatened to fall a victim to organic repres-

---

[46]*Ibid.*, p. 105.

[47]Notice the extent to which Freud introduces the concept of conflict within an instinct itself.

sion, but the whole of his sexuality; so that since this, the sexual function has been accompanied by a repugnance which cannot further be accounted for, and which prevents its complete satisfaction and forces it away from the sexual aim into sublimations and libidinal displacements. I know that Bleuler (1913) once pointed to the existence of a primary repelling attitude like this toward sexual life. All neurotics, and many others besides, take exception to the fact that '*inter urinas et faeces nascimur* (we are born between urine and faeces)'. The genitals, too, give rise to strong sensations of smell which many people cannot tolerate and which spoil sexual intercourse for them. Thus we should find that the deepest root of the sexual repression which advances along with civilization is the organic defence of the new form of life achieved with man's erect gait against his earlier animal existence. This result of scientific research coincides in a remarkable way with commonplace prejudices that have often made themselves heard. Nevertheless, these things are at present no more than unconfirmed possibilities which have not been substantiated by science. Nor should we forget that, in spite of the undeniable depreciation of olfactory stimuli, there exist even in Europe peoples among whom the strong genital odours which are so repellent to us are highly prized as sexual stimulants and who refuse to give them up.[48]

Because of the super-ego's intimate relationship with the id, Freud assigns it an intermediate position between the ego (the outside world) and the id. In the diagram of the anatomy of the mental personality in *New Introductory Lectures*,[49] the super-ego is found dipping further into the id than the ego and not extending as far out to the external world as the ego. The super-ego can be conscious, preconscious or unconscious, as demonstrated by Freud's discussion of both normal and pathological mental states. "Thus the super-ego takes up a kind of intermediate position be-

---

[48]*Civilization and Its Discontents*, S.E., XXI, 105-106, n. 3. It is important to know that Freud did conceive of the possibility of ameliorating the conflict between the individual and society.

But this struggle between the individual and society is not a derivative of the contradiction—probably an irreconcilable one—between the primal instincts of Eros and death. It is a dispute within the economics of the libido, comparable to the contest concerning the distribution of libido between ego and objects; and it does admit of an eventual accommodation in the individual, as, it may be hoped, it will also do in the future of civilization, however much that civilization may oppress the life of the individual today. (*Ibid.*, p. 141).

[49]S.E., XXII, 78.

tween the id and the external world; it unites in itself the influences of the present and the past."[50]

The super-ego's function forces it into conflict with the pleasure principle. "In order for these aims to be fulfilled, a restriction upon sexual life is unavoidable. But we are unable to understand what the necessity is which forces civilization along this path and which causes its antagonism to sexuality."[51] Freud continues to explain this antagonism as resulting from society's need to sublimate sexuality in order to develop the homophyllous relations necessary to society.[52] Freud warns that human beings can undertake a limited number of sublimations, and therefore an overly demanding super-ego (or the impact of civilization or society) is often the cause of neurosis.

> In our research into, and therapy of, a neurosis, we are led to make two reproaches against the super-ego of the individual. In the severity of its commands and prohibitions it troubles itself too little about the happiness of the ego, in that it takes insufficient account of the resistances against obeying them—of the instinctual strength of the id (in the first place), and of the difficulties presented by the real external environment (in the second). Consequently we are very often obliged, for therapeutic purposes, to oppose the super-ego, and we endeavour to lower its demands. Exactly the same objections can be made against the ethical demands of the cultural super-ego. It, too, does not trouble itself enough about the facts of the mental constitution of human beings. It issues a command and does not ask whether it is possible for people to obey it. On the contrary, it assumes that a man's ego is psychologically capable of anything that is required of it, that his ego has unlimited mastery over his id. This is a mistake; and even in what are known as normal people the id cannot be controlled beyond certain limits.[53]

---

[50]*An Outline of Psycho-Analysis*, S.E., XXIII, 207. See also *Ibid.*, 160-164.

[51]*Civilization and Its Discontents*, S.E., XXI, 109.

[52]See *The Protocol: Civilization and Its Discontents*, Chap. v, par. 9, p. 241.

[53]*Civilization and Its Discontents*, S.E., XXI, 142-143. Freud is willing to admit the possibility of neurotic societies. "If the development of civilization has such a far-reaching similarity to the development of the individual and if it employs the same methods, may we not be justified in reaching the diagnosis that, under the influence of cultural urges, some civilizations, or some epochs of civilization—possibly the whole of mankind—have become 'neurotic'?" (*Ibid.*, p. 144.) This conjecture may be the point of departure for the work of Fromm and other neo-Freudians as well as those who have struck out in other radical directions.

The super-ego as well as the ego derives its energy from the id. We remember that both the super-ego and the ego are heavily dependent on auditory perceptions.[54] This might lead us to believe that its energy source is therefore external and not derived from the id. Freud prevents this possible misunderstanding, claiming that though the accoustical sense organ is of prime importance for the super-ego, there remains but one source of energy for the entire organism, the id.

> Our tentative answer will be that it is as impossible for the super-ego as for the ego to disclaim its origin from things heard; for it is a part of the ego and remains accessible to consciousness by way of these word-presentations (concepts, abstractions). But the *cathectic energy* does not reach these contents of the super-ego from auditory perception (instruction or reading) but from sources in the id.[55]

The super-ego is assigned second rank in the Freudian hierarchy because of its intimate relationship with the ruling id.

> The ego ideal is therefore the heir of the Oedipus complex, and thus it is also the expression of the most powerful impulses and most important libidinal vicissitudes of the id. By setting up this ego ideal, the ego has mastered the Oedipus complex and at the same time placed itself in subjection to the id. Whereas the ego is essentially the representative of the external world, of reality, the super-ego stands in contrast to it as the representative of the internal world, of the id. Conflicts between the ego and the ideal will, as we are now prepared to find, ultimately reflect the contrast between what is real and what is psychical, between the external world and the internal world.[56]

THE SOCIAL COMMONPLACE—THE SUPER-EGO

That the super-ego represents the fate of society for Freud should be clear from the preceding discussion. The super-ego arises out of a social relationship (the family), further properties accrue to it from other relationships and the memory of culture becomes part of it via the super-ego of the parents. It is, in short, the inverse of the Platonic state.

In *The Republic,* Book Four, Plato's state is the entire individu-

[54]See *The Ego and the Id*, S.E., XIX, Chap. II, pp. 19-27.
[55]*Ibid.*, pp. 52-53.
[56]*Ibid.*, p. 36.

al writ large. In Freud, a portion of the individual is the state writ small.

Of course, the incorporation of society as one portion of the individual psyche does not mean that society as such is not an object of attention for Freud.

It is within the social commonplace, the super-ego, that Freud locates the individual's values and ideals. As a consequence of their derivation from conflicts with society, values for Freud are (1) an importation; (2) a limitation upon the basic instinctual nature of man (and therefore the source of a great deal of pain, anxiety, and neurosis).

> It is easy to show that the ego ideal answers to everything that is expected of the higher nature of man. As a substitute for a longing for the father, it contains the germ from which all religions have evolved. The self-judgement which declares that the ego falls short of its ideal produces the religious sense of humility to which the believer appeals in his longing. As a child grows up, the role of father is carried on by teachers and others in authority; their injunctions and prohibitions remain powerful in the ego ideal and continue, in the form of conscience, to exercise the moral censorship. The tension between the demands of conscience and the actual performances of the ego is experienced as a sense of guilt. Social feelings rest on identifications with other people, on the basis of having the same ego ideal.
>
> Religion, morality, and a social sense—the chief elements in the higher side of man—were originally one and the same thing. According to the hypothesis which I put forward in *Totem and Taboo* they were acquired phylogenetically out of the father-complex: religion and moral restraint through the process of mastering the Oedipus complex itself, and social feeling through the necessity for overcoming the rivalry that then remained between the members of the younger generation. . . . Even today the social feelings arise in the individual as a superstructure built upon impulses of jealous rivalry against his brothers and sisters. Since the hostility cannot be satisfied, an identification with the former rival develops.[57]

We introduce here a few comments on Freud's view of the group, a matter which becomes significant to the thesis developed in Part III of this volume, which deals with the relationship of Freud's theory of personality to education.

---

[57]*The Ego and the Id*, S.E., XIX, 37.

Freud's refusal to recognize a group instinct makes him view group psychology in terms of individual psychology.[58]

> When once natural continuity has been severed in this way, if a breach is thus made between things which are by nature interconnected, it is easy to regard the phenomena that appear under these special conditions as being expressions of a special instinct that is not further reducible—the social instinct ('herd instinct', 'group mind'), which does not come to light in any other situations. But we may perhaps venture to object that it seems difficult to attribute to the factor of number a significance so great as to make it capable by itself of arousing in our mental life a new instinct that is otherwise not brought into play. Our expectation is therefore directed towards two other possibilities: that the social instinct may not be a primitive one and insusceptible of dissection, and that it may be possible to discover the beginnings of its development in a narrower circle, such as that of the family.[59]

It is in the first group, the family, that relationships and patterns are developed that will affect all future group participation. This is so because the relationship to the parents is basic to the outcome of the Oedipal conflict, which, in turn, makes the major contribution to the creation of character. The resolution of the Oedipal conflict establishes a pattern or relationship to authority figures and peers. Furthermore, since group relationships are viewed as analogous to family relationships, then this early relationship within the family will play a lasting and determinative role.

Freud adopts the following formula to describe the relationships within a group.

> But after the preceding discussions we are quite in a position to give the formula for the libidinal constitution of groups, or at least of such groups as we here hitherto considered—namely, those that have a leader and have not been able by means of too much 'organization' to acquire secondarily the characteristics of an individual. *A primary group of this kind is a number of individuals who have put one and the same object in the place of their ego ideal and have consequently identified themselves with one another in their ego.*[60]

[58]See *The Protocol: Group Psychology and the Analysis of the Ego*, chap. I, par. 1, p. 192, as well as chap. vi, pars, 2 and 3, pp. 199-200 and chap. viii, par. 14, pp. 204-205.

[60]*Group Psychology*, S.E., XVIII, p. 70.

[60]*Ibid.*, p. 116.

Clearly this formula is reminiscent of the relationship of children to their parents and to each other. Consequently Freud sees all identifications (to leaders and ideals) as parent substitutes.

> This parental influence of course includes in its operation not only the personalities of the actual parents but also the family, racial and national traditions handed on through them, as well as the demands of the immediate social *milieu* which they represent. In the same way, the super-ego, in the course of an individual's development, receives contributions from later successors and substitutes of his parents, such as teachers and models in public life of admired social ideals.[61]

As in the case of his treatment of the ego it is not easy to understand why Freud (again, apart from reference to his beginning-orientation) did not organize his mental apparatus with a super-ego (his social commonplace) present from the beginning. The importance that he attributes to the cultural heritage, the centrality of guilt, the decision to adopt the primal myth of Oedipus and to establish a super-ego, all point to the reasonableness of a very early beginning for the social commonplace. If so, why was Freud not willing to grant it original or early status?

Finally, as in the case of the ego and the id, we point out that the social commonplace could have taken on many other aspects and occupied a different position in a hierarchy. Even a cursory examination of theoretical positions in psychology, and especially in social psychology, reveals a diversity of possible locations of the social commonplace. For example, there are views which see the individual as essentially a "group animal," a member of several simultaneous and sometimes competing groups.[62] There is the view that would assign to group participation a pleasure of its own that is basic to living.

By contrast, there are those views which praise the private man and make of society a mere backdrop for his enjoyment of himself and his property.

---

[61]*An Outline of Psycho-Analysis,* S.E., XXIII, 146.

[62]In such a view the social commonplace would occupy the ruling position.

Chapter Seven

□

PLEASURE AND ENERGY

PLEASURE

THE FACTOR OF PLEASURE achieves great clarity and distinctness in Freud by virtue of its simplicity. There is only one pleasure; it is biological and undifferentiated.

Following his biological model, Freud refuses to define pleasure in other than quantitative terms. There is no diversity of pleasure, such as the pleasure of friendship or of creating, but only more or less pleasure. Further, pleasure is a positive name for a quiescient state. Pleasure is the diminution of the needs derived from the instincts and displeasure is a heightening of these needs. Freud points to the relationship between death and the highest, i.e. most acutely pleasurable form of pleasure. Thus, in achieving pleasure, the organism strives for a return to that state which reflects Freud's supra-generic emphasis, the inorganic, the origin and goal of the organic.

Pleasure is primary in several senses of the word. First, it is entirely biological; thus it partakes of the leading position of the biological commonplace. Second, it obeys the primary processes. Third, its reservoir is the id and its centers are to be found in the various erotogenic zones. Consequently, it is coherent with Freud's generic emphasis and further emphasizes the importance he ascribes to what is animal in man.

There are no direct feelings admitted to Freud's theory other than those in the pleasure-pain series. This is because only pleasure-pain feelings are considered primary, being moved to expression by the force of the two basic instincts. This conception of a few basic instincts impelling a few basic expressions of emotion, other qualities or states of feeling being considered epi-phenomenal, is in line with Freud's biologism. In fact, he is more often concerned with the causes of pleasure, the reduction of need tension, than with the expression of it. One apparent exception to his preference for explanation by reference to biology we have already cited—namely, Freud's conjecture that the sensation of pleasure has been blunted as a result of the long history of the race in civilization. But it turns out that the primacy of the phylogentic is here invoked as explanatory principle, i.e. the history of the race is seen to take its toll even on the expression of pleasure.

Just as civilization has taken this toll on the racial scale, growing up in the physical and social environment limits the individual's expression of pleasure. Thus conflict between the individual's need to express pleasure and the opposition to it of historical and contemporary environmental forces may result in an over-restriction of pleasure expression, or possible neurosis. The process of therapy in this view, then, is to help the individual achieve a life style that permits him to attain a greater quantity of pleasure.

Although in the developmental process, the expression of pleasure is further restricted and its intensity reduced, to attain his measure of pleasure an individual may from time to time resort to earlier and more primitive forms of pleasure. In the state of regression he does so resort, and in general he can so resort because later developments and secondary processes are relatively weak.

Pleasure requires the expression and satisfaction of the erotic instincts and, as the organism matures, concentrates on adult sexual pleasure.

Here again, Freud could have organized his theory differently. One striking alternative to his organization is the Platonic conception of pleasure, as being of several kinds, each appropriate to an organ or part. It need hardly be pointed out that a concept of a diversity of pleasures and of pleasure which is active instead of quiescent might take account of facts as richly and diversely as the Freudian conception.

ENERGY

The energy factor in Freud is also biological. Energy is energy of the instincts and thus has somatic sources. (These sources are somatic "tensions" which become instincts only as they enter secondarily into mental life.) The energy of Eros is libido. Freud rarely discusses the energy of the Death instinct.

At first, libido works exclusively according to the regulations of the primary process. It is then that it possesses its greatest thrust, is free of the very notion of contradiction: it can be fickle; it can love and hate simultaneously and remain untroubled by these contraries. This is because libido is non-rational and completely biological.

Later, the ego, in the course of its development, must capture some portion of the previously free and fickle libido, if it is to do its work. The ego captures energy by desexualizing the libido and appropriating it unto itself. It is this desexualized, sublimated or secondary energy that serves the purpose of all non-instinctual activities, such as rationality, work, art and the "striving for perfection." One of the problems introduced into life as a result of this formulation is that an individual can absorb only a limited number of sublimations without a break-down. Thus, an economic limit is set for the energy potential of the ego and its activities.

Freud thought of libido as developing in stages—oral, anal and genital. These stages are another instance of his use of the phylogenetic principle and are clearly demarcated chronological stages through which the individual must grow and to which he may regress.

As in the case of pleasure, Freud could have assumed other theoretical postures, energy could have been assigned to other parts of the psyche as well.

We shall now return to follow Freud's treatment of his concept of pleasure. Freud defines pleasure in terms of stability and quiescence. He refuses to define pleasure in any other than quantitative terms and it appears that his concept of pleasure is entirely biological.

Are we to suppose that the different instincts which originate in the body and operate on the mind are also distinguished by the different *qualities,* and that that is why they behave in qualitatively different ways in mental life? This supposition does not seem to be justified; we are much more likely to find the simpler assumption sufficient— that the instincts are all qualitatively alike and owe the effect they make only to the amount of excitation they carry, or perhaps, in addition, to certain functions of that quantity. What distinguishes from one another the mental effects produced by the various instincts may be traced to the difference in their sources.[1]

Freud will offer only a quantitative definition of pleasure: "We have decided to relate pleasure and unpleasure to the quantity of excitation that is present in the mind but is not in any way 'bound'; and to relate them in such a manner that unpleasure corresponds to an *increase* in the quantity of excitation and pleasure to a diminution."[2] Therefore, a state of pleasure would be one in which there would be little or no motive for change or action. "Sensations of a pleasurable nature have not anything inherently impelling about them, whereas unpleasurable ones have it in the highest degree. The latter impel towards change, towards discharge, and that is why we interpret unpleasure as implying a heightening and pleasure a lowering of energic cathexis."[3] In some passages Freud carries this formulation to its logical conclusion: the highest form of pleasure is death.

But it does so in a far more comprehensive fashion in relation to one particular form of satisfaction in which all component demands converge—by discharge of the sexual substances, which are saturated vehicles, so to speak, of the erotic tensions. The ejection of the sexual substances in the sexual act corresponds in a sense to the separation of soma and germ-plasm. This accounts for the likeness of the condition that follows complete sexual satisfaction to dying, and for the fact that death coincides with the act of copulation in some of the lower animals. These creatures die in the act of reproduction because, after Eros has been eliminated through the process of satisfaction, the death instinct has a free hand for accomplishing its purposes.[4]

---

[1]Instincts and their vicissitudes, S.E., XIV, 123.
For a discussion of the problem of the "source" of an instinct, see pp. 54-55.
[2]*Beyond the Pleasure Principle*, S.E., XVIII, 7-8.
[3]*The Ego and the Id*, S.E., XIX, 22. Satisfaction for Freud is the *extinction* of need. See Chapter Eight p. 145.
[4]*Ibid.,* p. 47. See also *The Protocol: The Ego and the Id,* chap. iv, par. 18, pp. 227-228.

In the light of these passages, we can conclude that pleasure is only biological and that the source of the excitations is somatic. "By the source *(Quelle)* of an instinct is meant the somatic process which occurs in an organ or part of the body and whose stimulus is represented in mental life by an instinct. . . . The study of the source of instincts lies outside the scope of psychology. Although instincts are wholly determined by their origin in a somatic source, in mental life we know them only by their aims."[5] We have previously demonstrated that Freud openly borrowed his concept of pleasure from biology.

> We have already alluded to the most important of these, and all we need now do is to state it expressly. This postulate is of a biological nature, and makes use of the concept of 'purpose' (or perhaps of expediency) and runs as follows: the nervous system is an apparatus which has the function of getting rid of the stimuli that reach it, or of reducing them to the lowest possible level; or which, if it were feasible, would maintain itself in an altogether unstimulated condition.[6]

In adopting this definition of pleasure, Freud remains consistent with his generic emphasis, and with his emphasis upon the suprageneric factor (expressed as the paradox of life's purpose being death).[7] Thus, death would be the doorway of return to the original state of things—the inorganic.

Freud's concept of pleasure is consistent with his generic emphasis in another sense as well. Pleasure exists from the beginning and represents the organism's primary and basic work-style.

> We consider these to be the older, primary processes, the residues of a phase of development in which they were the only kind of mental process. The governing purpose obeyed by these primary processes is easy to recognize; it is described as the pleasure-unpleasure (Lust-Unlust) principle, or more shortly the pleasure principle. . . . Our dreams at night and our waking tendency to tear ourselves away from distressing impressions are remnants of the dominance of this principle and proofs of its power.[8]

Instincts as they strive for pleasure are obeying the primary

---

[5]Instincts and their vicissitudes, S.E., XIV, 123.
[6]*Ibid.*, p. 120.
[7]See Chapter Three, pp. 32-33.
[8]*Mental Functioning*, S.E., XII, 219.

process. That is, they strive only for the diminution of excitation. "It will perhaps not be thought too rash to suppose that the impulses arising from the instincts do not belong to the type of *bound* nervous processes but of *freely mobile* processes which press towards discharge."[9] This primary process is characteristic of the unconscious system, it is free of contradiction and possesses great force.

> The nucleus of the *Ucs.* consists of instinctual representatives which seek to discharge their cathexis; that is to say, it consists of wishful impulses. These instinctual impulses are co-ordinate with one another, exist side by side without being influenced by one another, and are exempt from mutual contradiction. When two wishful impulses whose aims must appear to us incompatible become simultaneously active, the two impulses do not diminish each other or cancel each other out, but combine to form an intermediate aim, a compromise . . . . I have proposed to regard these two processes as distinguishing marks of the so-called *primary psychical process.*[10]

Since the source of the striving for pleasure is an instinct, Freud will locate this striving in the id. Pleasure ultimately consolidates itself in the striving for sexual pleasure. Freud organizes this consolidation in stages related to the body's erotogenic zones.

> What distinguishes the instincts from one another and endows them with specific qualities is their relation to their somatic sources and to their aims. The source of an instinct is a process of excitation occurring in an organ and the immediate aim of the instinct lies in the removal of this organic stimulus.
> There is a further provisional assumption that we cannot escape in the theory of the instincts. It is to the effect that excitations of two kinds arise from the somatic organs, based upon differences of a chemical nature. One of these kinds of excitation we describe as being specifically sexual, and we speak of the organ concerned as the 'erotogenic zone' of the sexual component instinct arising from it.[11]

Freud identifies these zones: "Among them we find occurring with particular frequency those in which the mucous membrane of the mouth and anus are assigned the role of genitals."[12]

---

[9] *Beyond the Pleasure Principle,* S.E., XVIII, 34.

[10] *The Unconscious,* S.E., XIV, 186.

[11] The sexual aberrations, in *Three Essays on the Theory of Sexuality,* S.E., VII, 168.

[12] *Ibid.,* p. 166.

In our Protocol to the essay *Beyond the Pleasure Principle*,[13] we follow Freud's argument that there is no "beyond the pleasure principle." He explained all cases that appear to be beyond the pleasure principle as prior to it and not yet in the service of the pleasure principle. Freud begins *Beyond the Pleasure Principle* in the following manner: "In the theory of psycho-analysis we have no hesitation in assuming that the course taken by mental events is automatically regulated by the pleasure principle."[14] In his summary chapter, Chapter Seven, Freud maintains the dominance of the pleasure principle and explains the cases that appear to contradict it as only apparently contradictory.

When we discussed the ego, in Chapter Five, we attempted to demonstrate that the introduction of the reality principle does not result in a change of goal on the part of the organism. On the contrary, it simply is the organism's method of attaining the maximum pleasure in the light of the external reality. Stated another way, the reality principle is but a refinement of the pleasure principle.[15] "Actually the substitution of the reality principle for the pleasure principle implies no deposing of the pleasure principle, but only a safeguarding of it. A momentary pleasure, uncertain in its results, is given up, but only in order to gain along the new path an assured pleasure at a later time."[16] Because of the centrality of pleasure (unpleasure) in Freud's theory, we have no instance of an immediate feeling except in the pleasure-pain series. Thus, all other feelings and activities are explained as either related to or derived from pleasure or pain.

We have discussed the problems of renunciation, or restraint imposed upon the expression of pleasure, in Chapter Six. Though Freud sees intellectual activity, art and work as sublimations of libidinal energy, he does set a limit as to how many sublimations an individual can undergo without risking neurosis or regression.[17] Moreover, the cause of neurosis is often found to be a harsh super-ego and the role of therapy is to reduce the impact of this

[13]pp. 181-191.

[14]*Beyond the Pleasure Principle,* S.E., XVIII, 7.

[15]It should be noted that the transition from the pleasure principle to the reality principle does involve the "dulling" of pleasure. See Chapter Six, pp. 121-123.

[16]*Mental Functioning,* S.E., XII, 223.

[17]See p. 124.

super-ego on the ego.

When the organism finds that it cannot attain pleasure by one means (normally a more mature means), it may find it necessary to regress to an earlier stage so that it can attain pleasure. Thus, Freud tells us that the neurotic will strive for pleasure even if the satisfaction attained is different from the satisfaction that was aspired to.

> When it happens that a person has to give up a sexual object, there quite often ensues an alteration of his ego which can only be described as a setting up of the object inside the ego, as it occurs in melancholia; the exact nature of this substitution is as yet unknown to us. It may be that by this introjection, which is a kind of regression to the mechanism of the oral phase, the ego makes it easier for the object to be given up or renders that process possible. It may be that this identification is the sole condition under which the id can give up its objects.[18]

Freud hoped that through psychoanalytic therapy the ego would obtain a larger measure of control over the organism. We know that the ego directs the means by which the individual achieves pleasure. Therefore, through therapy Freud hoped to make it possible for the individual to achieve a greater degree of pleasure. "Its intention is, indeed, to strengthen the ego, to make it more independent of the super-ego, to widen its field of perception and enlarge its organization, so that it can appropriate fresh portions of the id. Where id was, there ego shall be."[19] And,

> It was discovered that a person becomes neurotic because he cannot tolerate the amount of frustration which society imposes on him in the service of its cultural ideals, and it was inferred from this that the abolition or reduction of those demands would result in a return to possibilities of happiness.[20]

THE COMMONPLACE PLEASURE

The data with which Freud worked forced him to admit that pleasure could be other than sexual.[21] Even granting Freud's

---

[18]*The Ego and the Id*, S.E., XIX, 29. Also see *The Protocol: The Ego and the Id*, chap. iii, par. 5, pp. 220-221.

[19]*New Introductory Lectures*, S.E., XXII, 80. For further discussion of this point see our pp. 162-163.

[20]*Civilization and Its Discontents*, S.E., XXI, 87.

[21]*Ibid.*, pp. 81-83.

biological emphasis and the supremacy of the id, one could question the necessity of his introducing pleasure into only one of his organ parts. He could have avoided the paradox of the purpose of life being death had he been willing to introduce other pleasures appropriate to the activities of the other organs. Thus, he could have introduced pleasures appropriate to the ego and pleasures appropriate to the super-ego. These part pleasures could have been viewed as competing and could have been rank-ordered with biological pleasure retaining its supremacy. One wonders why Freud never proposed such an alternative, for it might have offered a very rich theoretical and practical yield.

ENERGY

Since energy is the force of instinct and we have demonstrated in Chapter Four that the instincts have somatic sources and are biological, it is clear that energy will also be biological. "By the pressure *(Drang)* of an instinct we understand its motor factor, the amount of force or the measure of the demand for work which it represents."[22] Or the following: "Well, these instincts fill the id: all the energy in the id, as we may put it briefly, originates from them. Nor have the forces in the ego any other origin; they are derived from those in the id."[23]

Freud names the energy that represents Eros *libido.* "We may picture an initial state as one in which the total available energy of Eros, which henceforward we shall speak of as 'libido,' is present in the still undifferentiated ego-id and serves to neutralize the destructive tendencies which are simultaneously present."[24] In this initial state the libido possesses its greatest thrust. This is so for it (the libido) is working exclusively according to the regulations of the "primary process."

> As a new factor we have taken into consideration Breuer's hypothesis that charges of energy occur in two forms . . .; so that we have to distinguish between two kinds of cathexis of the psychical systems or their elements—a freely flowing cathexis that presses on towards discharge and a quiescent cathexis. We may perhaps suspect that

[22]Instincts and their vicissitudes, S.E., XIV, 122.
[23]*Lay Analysis,* S.E., XX, 200.
[24]*An Outline of Psycho-Analysis,* S.E., XXIII, 149-150.

the binding of the energy that streams into the mental apparatus consists in its change from a freely flowing into a quiescent state.[25]

And:

I described the type of process found in the unconscious as the 'primary' psychical process, in contradistinction to the 'secondary' process which is the one obtaining in our normal waking life. Since all instinctual impulses have the unconscious systems as their point of impact, it is hardly an innovation to say that they obey the primary process.[26]

One of the characteristics of the "primary process" is that its demands are free of contradiction and can be fickle.

There are in this system no negation, no doubt, no degrees of certainty: all this is only introduced by the work of the censorship between the *Ucs.* and the *Pcs.* Negation is a substitute, at a higher level, for repression. In the *Ucs.* there are only contents, cathected with greater or lesser strength.

The processes of the system *Ucs.* are *timeless;* i.e. they are not ordered temporally, are not altered by the passage of time; they have no reference to time at all. . . .

The *Ucs.* processes pay just as little regard to *reality.* They are subject to the pleasure principle; their fate depends only on how strong they are and on whether they fulfill the demands of the pleasure-unpleasure regulation.

To sum up: *exemption from mutual contradiction, primary process* (mobility of cathexes), *timelessness,* and *replacement of external by psychical reality*—these are the characteristics which we may expect to find in processes belonging to the system *Ucs.*[27]

We see the fickle nature of the demands of the primary process very nicely in the following:

We see, for instance, that some degree of communication exists between the component instincts, that an instinct deriving from one particular erotogenic source can make over its intensity to reinforce another component instinct originating from another source, that the satisfaction of one instinct can take the place of the satisfaction of another, and more facts of the same nature—. . .

. . . In this connection it is easy to observe a certain *indifference* as to the path along which the discharge takes place, so long as it takes

---

[25]*Beyond the Pleasure Principle*, S.E., XVIII, 31.
[26]*Ibid.*, p. 34.
[27]*The Unconscious*, S.E., XIV, 186-187.

place somehow. We know this trait; it is characteristic of the cathectic processes in the id. It is found in erotic cathexes, where a peculiar indifference in regard to the object displays itself; and it is especially evident in the transferences arising in analysis, which develop inevitably, irrespective of the persons who are their object. Not long ago Rank (1913) published some good examples of the way in which neurotic acts of revenge can be directed against the wrong people.[28]

If energy is the force of the instincts then there should be an energy that represents the death instinct. Throughout most of his writings, Freud refused to assign an energy to death. "(We are without a term analogous to 'libido' for describing the energy of the destructive instinct.)"[29] However, there are some passages in Freud's works which point to his realization that there should be an expression of the death instinct in the form of energy.

> The name 'libido' can once more be used to denote the manifestations of the power of Eros in order to distinguish them from the energy of the death instinct. It must be confessed that we have much greater difficulty in grasping that instinct; we can only suspect it, as it were, as something in the background behind Eros, and it escapes detection unless its presence is betrayed by its being alloyed with Eros.[30]

We have indicated that at first all of the energy is id energy and the ego must capture energy in order to do its work.[31] The ego obtains its energy by desexualizing or sublimating the id energy.

> The transformation of object-libido into narcissistic libido which thus takes place obviously implies an abandonment of sexual aims, a desexualization—a kind of sublimation, therefore. Indeed, the question arises, and deserves careful consideration, whether this is not the universal road to sublimation, whether all sublimation does not take place through the mediation of the ego, which begins by changing sexual object-libido into narcissistic libido and then, perhaps, goes

---

[28]*The Ego and the Id*, S.E., XIX, 44-45. Emphasis mine.

[29]*An Outline of Psycho-Analysis*, S.E., XXIII, 150.

[30]*Civilization and Its Discontents*, S.E., XXI, 121. *Beyond the Pleasure Principle*, S.E., XVIII, 62-64. Here Freud alludes to the possibility that death and its energy may be working unobtrusively. It may be that the energy of death would be the conservative nature of the instincts and their desire to return to the inorganic, the prior state of things.

[31]See our Chapter Five, pp. 97-98.

on to give it another aim.[32]

Freud's decision to begin with only one kind of energy (libidinal energy) made necessary the assumption of the "secondary energy," ego energy. It is this desexualized, sublimated or secondary energy that serves the purposes of all non-instinctual activity, i.e. rationality, work, art, the striving for perfection.

> Another technique for fending off suffering is the employment of the displacements of libido which our mental apparatus permits of and through which its function gains so much in flexibility. The task here is that of shifting the instinctual aims in such a way that they cannot come up against frustration from the external world. In this, sublimation of the instincts lends its assistance. One gains the most if one can sufficiently heighten the yield of pleasure from the sources of psychical and intellectual work. When that is so, fate can do little against one. A satisfaction of this kind, such as an artist's joy in creating, in giving his phantasies body, or a scientist's in solving problems or discovering truths, has a special quality which we shall certainly one day be able to characterize in metapsychological terms. At present we can only say figuratively that such satisfactions seem 'finer and higher'.[33]

We have previously discussed Freud's assertion that the human being can undergo a limited number of sublimations.[34] This is consistent with Freud's biological emphasis and with his commitment to the primacy of man's biological nature.

> Sublimation of instinct is an especially conspicuous feature of cultural development; it is what makes it possible for higher psychical activities, scientific, artistic or ideological, to play such an important part in civilized life. . . . This 'cultural frustration' dominates the large field of social relationships between human beings. As we already know, it is the cause of the hostility against which all civilizations have to struggle. It will also make severe demands on our scientific work, and we shall have much to explain here. It is not easy to understand how it can become possible to deprive an instinct of satisfaction. Nor is doing so without danger. If the loss is not compensated

---

[32]*The Ego and the Id*, S.E., XIX, 30. See also *The Protocol: The Ego and the Id,* chap. iii, par. 7, p. 221 and Ibid., chap. iv. pars. 13-14, pp. 226-227.

[33]*Civilization and Its Discontents*, S.E., XXI, 79. Freud discusses how all the higher activities can be viewed in the light of sublimated energy. See especially the discussion, *Ibid.*, pp. 78-82.

[34]See Chapter Six, p. 124.

for economically, one can be certain that serious disorders will en-sue.[35]

Freud describes the development of the libido in stages re-lated to the erotogenic zones of the body. Neurosis can be traced to fixations, i.e. of energy that has been unable to liberate itself from an investment in an earlier stage. It is to these earlier stages that the individual is most likely to regress under the pressure of en-feeblement of the ego, or the renewed strength of an instinct.

> The sexual instinct, the dynamic manifestation of which in mental life we shall call '*libido*', is made up of component instincts into which it may once more break up and which are only gradually united into well-defined organizations. The sources of these compon-ent instincts are the organs of the body and in particular certain spe-cially marked *erotogenic zones;* but contributions are made to libido from every important functional process in the body. At first the in-dividual component instincts strive for satisfaction independently of one another, but in the course of development they become more and more convergent and concentrated. The first (pregenital) stage of or-ganization to be discerned is the *oral* one, in which—in conformity with the suckling's predominant interest—the oral zone plays the lead-ing part. This is followed by the *sadistic-anal* organization, in which the *anal* zone and the component instinct of *sadism* are particularly prominent; at this stage the difference between the sexes is repre-sented by the contrast between active and passive. The third and final stage of organization is that in which the majority of the com-ponent instincts converge under the *primacy of the genital zones.* As a rule this development is passed through swiftly and unobtru-sively; but some individual portions of the instincts remain behind at the prodromal stages of the process and thus give rise to *fixations* of libido, which are important as constituting predispositions for sub-sequent irruptions of repressed impulses and which stand in a definite relation to the later development of neuroses and perversions.[36]

THE COMMONPLACE ENERGY

As we have previously indicated Freud could have introduced the factor of energy into each of his psychical organs. This would have eliminated the necessity for introducing the concept of "sec-ondary" energy and of sublimation. It also would have made un-

---

[35]*Civilization and Its Discontents*, S.E., XXI, 97.
[36]*Psycho-Analysis*, S.E., XVIII, 244-245.

necessary the assumption of a movable energy which Freud finds necessary to assume though the assumption causes him great difficulty.[37] As in the case of pleasure, we find it difficult to understand what data Freud could not have explained were he to have assumed that each of the psychical organs possesses its own energy.

---

[37]See *The Ego and the Id*, S.E., XIX, 44.

Chapter Eight

☐

THE RELATIONSHIP
OF THE COMMONPLACES
TO EACH OTHER

W E HAVE LOCATED ALL[1] of the commonplaces in Freud: the biological—id, the rational—ego, the social—super-ego, pleasure—a
diminution of need, and energy—libido. In this chapter we will
show how Freud relates the commonplaces to each other and
through this relationship we will examine Freud's treatment of
affect.

Because of his biological emphasis and his beginning-orientation (the importance of that which is early, the emphasis on the
generic and the supra-generic), Freud grants the id a central and
all powerful position. All of the other organs of the psyche are derivatives. That is because of his embryogenesis (epi-genesis), the
ego and the super-ego develop from the id and bear the stigma of
this development throughout life.[2] The id is basic and inflexible
and the ego and super-ego are dependent on it for energy and
pleasure.

However, it would be a mistake to suppose that because of the
all powerful role of the biological commonplace, all parts or commonplaces relate to each other in an accommodating or harmoni-
ous way dictated by the id. On the contrary, the manner in which
Freud relates the commonplaces to each other reflects his decision
to impose an equilibrium of conflict upon the diversity he believed

[1]But see page 28, note 13, and pages 164-165, note 28.
[2]We have mentioned an alternative with regard to embryogenesis (pp. 70-71)—
preformationism: all the parts can be present at birth, formed but feeble. Freud
himself may be suggesting such a possibility. See *Analysis, Terminable and Interminable*, S.E., XXIII, 240-241.

to be inherent to life.[3]

Because of his biological emphasis, Freud saw the organism locked in a never-ending conflict with its environment.[4] But as his beginning-orientation would lead us to suspect, he uses the principle of conflict to characterize much earlier events, even to explain the origin of life.[5] Freud speculates on the origin of the life instinct and suggests that a force disturbed the inanimate and so created the life instinct.[6]

The first conflict is to be found, then, between the organic and the inorganic, between life and death.[7] Conflict as such, arises because Freud's beginning-orientation now requires the notion of a constant retrogressive pull to the original condition, death, or the inorganic. This expression of beginning-orientation is then extended to apply to the relation between the life instinct and all that comes after it. Thus all the instincts are conservative. In brief, the basic clay from which things develop exerts its influence as a counter-force, a polarity, to development. With this view, a Lamarckist evolutionary theory is consistent. For how else can development or new tensions be introduced than by a force, a momentous occasion that bombards or traumatizes and thus upsets the ex-

---

[3]We have here without question an instance of Freud's use of the principle of the whole, as determiner of the character assigned to parts. See Chapter Two, pp. 22-23. Does this subordination of all other aspects of human existence to that of conflict represent the earliest application of his conflict principle, or does it represent, perhaps, the origin of this principle for him? We shall never know.

[4]See Chapter Six, pp. 110-112. See *The Ego and the Id*, S.E., XIX, 38, where he attributes an ego to animals, and *Civilization and Its Discontents*, S.E., XXI, 123, where he explains the apparent lack of a cultural struggle in animal life. Freud's "hydrostatics" (dynamics and economics) of libido follows as a consequence of his conflict principle. That is, having adopted conflict as a principle, he introduces the idea of an economics of available libido. This is so, for in the contrary view, the postulate of an indefinitely large quantity of libido would remove a fundamental source of conflict.

[5]See *Beyond the Pleasure Principle*, S.E., XVIII, 37-39.

[6]Conflict there means the tension that arises when life is being evoked out of inanimate matter, i.e. the tension within the substance between the inanimate and the animate.

[7]Freud defines the life instinct as the guarantee that the organism shall die according to its pattern and not according to some other or novel pattern. See *Beyond the Pleasure Principle*, *Ibid.*, p. 39 and *The Protocol: Beyond the Pleasure Principle*, chap. v, pars. 7, 8, 9, pp. 186-187.

isting equilibrium of conflict? But the new forces are never granted equal status with what is prior and therefore regression (victory of the more ancient force) ever threatens the organism. As the forces of the life instinct increase, the demands made by it upon the organism must be met. If there were no opposition, if the movement required for the life instinct were free to express itself, there would be no pleasure or displeasure, only satisfaction. Thus Freud states:

> What, then, do these instincts want? Satisfaction—that is, the establishment of situations in which the bodily needs can be extinguished. A lowering of the tension of need is felt by our organ of consciousness as pleasurable; an increase of it is soon felt as unpleasure. From these oscillations arises the series of feelings of pleasure-unpleasure, in accordance with which the whole mental apparatus regulates its activity.[8]

However, even the organism itself is viewed as having layers, a mental antomy, through which a need must travel.[9] Therefore there is blockage, both inside the organism (competing and contradictory needs) and between the organism and the environment. Pleasure-unpleasure for Freud represents the conflict between the pure needs of the id (i.e. instinct) and its environment (internal and external).[10]

The character of the conflict which relates all of the commonplaces to one another is most easily seen through an examination of Freud's treatment of affect. For the affects, such as pleasure-unpleasure, represent this conflict. Freud defines affect as the expression of the conflict or tension between derivatives of an instinct (love and hate) as well as between the parts of the psyche.[11] Thus, love arises

---

[8]*Lay Analysis*, S.E., XX, 200.

[9]See the discussion of thought processes in *The Ego and the Id*, S.E., XIX, 19-27.

[10]In the light of the above, it is not surprising that Freud struggled to keep his instincts limited but dualistic. See his debate with Jung in *Beyond the Pleasure Principle*, S.E., XVIII, 52-53.

[11]Freud claims that the affects are the results of early traumas, thus lending support to our interpretation of affects as expressions of conflict, i.e. that new tensions are introduced as a result of traumas: "Affective states have become incorporated in the mind as precipitates of primaeval traumatic experiences, and when a similar situation occurs they are revived like mnemic symbols." (*Anxiety*, S.E., XX, 93.) Similarly the ego (consciousness) is developed as a result of the "bombardment" of the external world (see *Beyond the Pleasure Principle*, p. 38), and the super-ego is the result of a childhood trauma. Apart from the point made here ────────→

for Freud as libido that is not expressed in its pure form, but alloyed with sublimation, such as tenderness and idealization.[12] If the
directly sexual were "regularly and uninhibitedly" expressed, then
there would be no love.

> It is interesting to see that it is precisely those sexual impulses
> that are inhibited in their aims which achieve such lasting ties be-
> tween people. But this can easily be understood from the fact that
> they are not capable of complete satisfaction, while sexual impul-
> sions which are uninhibited in their aims suffer an extraordinary
> reduction through the discharge of energy every time the sexual aim is
> attained.[13]

Similarly, with hate, if aggression were not checked we would have
no hate.[14] Anxiety is explained as the tension of the ego versus the
id or as the tension of the ego versus the super-ego,[15] which is the
signal for external danger.[16] Guilt is explained as the tension of the
super-ego versus the ego, more correctly, of the ego ideal versus the
ego.[17]

---

that affects express conflicts, it is doubtful whether a justifiable explanation can
be given of what affects are to Freud. Freud's statements about affect are nearly
always provisional. He remarks, for example, "So little is known about the psychology of emotional processes that the tentative remarks I am about to make on
the subject may claim a very lenient judgement." (*Anxiety*, p. 169.) Throughout
his volume Freud uses affect and emotion as synonyms. The affects most frequently
mentioned by Freud are love, hate, dread, disgust, mourning, melancholia, guilt,
pain, fear and helplessness.

[12]See the discussion in *Group Psychology*, S.E., XVIII, 142-143.
[13]*Ibid.*, p. 115.
[14]This provides a further reason to question Freud's insistence on late super-ego
development. For do we not have a nascent super-ego in the notion of love and
hate (the derivatives of instinct) that implies restraint of instinct?
[15]If the anxiety represents the ego versus the super-ego, Freud considers this
social anxiety.
[16]It is not surprising in the light of the above, that Freud had difficulty relating
such concepts as pleasure, anxiety and libido. See *Anxiety*, S.E., XX, especially the
addenda, pp. 157-172.
[17]Thus the possibilities for neurosis are almost limitless. Any one of the forces
in a conflict that gains sufficient strength so as to create an imbalance represents
the potential for neurosis.
There is a considerable literature that discusses Freud's interchangeable use of
the super-ego and ego-ideal. It appears in the light of the above (namely the possibility of a "social anxiety," i.e. super-ego versus ego) that the ego ideal is a

--→

This discussion of conflict points to the kind of relationship that Freud establishes among the commonplaces. It is one of check and balance, one in which the parts are in constant tension with each other with only rare moments of equilibrium.[18] The ego tries to mediate for the id and super-ego and inevitably must conflict with them. The super-ego by its very nature conflicts with the id and the ego.

Amidst these conflicts, the rank order of the parts emerges. The id is at the top of the hierarchy for it is closest to the beginning and contains the instincts. The super-ego is second, for it is a result of instinctual restraint. The ego is at the bottom for it is servant to the other two.

As we have indicated in Chapter Two, other hierarchies could be used to interpret the data of existence. In Plato, the rational has the first rank, an instinctual affect for the "right" (spirit) has second rank and the biological the third. There is no social part. Further, there is a pleasure and an energy appropriate to each part. Harry Stack Sullivan ranks the social commonplace at the top, the rational second and the biological third. He assigns to the social commonplace a basic affect—anxiety.[19]

Freud's topography reflects his rank order of parts. The id is to be found in the deepest layer of the mental anatomy the super-ego in the next layer and the ego at the periphery. For Freud, we remember, what is deeper is earlier!

---

qualification within the super-ego and that guilt is a tension between the ego ideal and the ego. A conjecture: in anxiety the force of the "subject matter," i.e. the undifferentiated immediately experienced in human life, asserts itself and insists on an ego energy that is not derivative. Similarly, conflict (tension) is a basic component of the other affects, e.g. mourning (see Mourning and melancholia, S.E., XIV, 237-258), and pain *(Anxiety,* S.E., XX, 170-172.)

[18]It may be that even sensation would be viewed by Freud as a conflict (tension). See *Beyond the Pleasure Principle,* S.E., XVIII, 63-64.

[19]The relationship among the commonplaces in Freud is almost the opposite, if not the opposite, of the Platonic conception of the "ideal" relationship between the parts, i.e. harmony.

Schwab and I have been working out the consequences of a coordinate relationship among the commonplaces. Should this prove feasible, it would offer rich possibilities for educational research. Schwab alludes to this effort in, Schwab, Joseph J.: On the corruption of education by psychology. *School Review,* 66:171-172, 1958.

Because of Freud's imposition of an equilibrium of conflict on the diversity required for living, and also because of the supremacy he grants to beginnings, there is little room in Freud for change and development. The basically conservative nature of the instincts, the check and balance system that he introduces in the relationship between the parts of the psyche, his determinism and the passivity that he assigns to the ego all but eliminate the possibility of change. It is therefore not surprising that Freud viewed therapy as the righting of imbalance in the conflict between the ego and id. In this effort one ego alone cannot prevail. Ego is a late-comer, and the instincts are early and primary. Therefore, the therapist adds the weight of his ego to the patient's weak ego and then we have a conflict of equals. "Thus psycho-analytic treatment acts as a second education of the adult, as a corrective to his education as a child."[20] And the following: "As is well known, the analytic situation consists in our allying ourselves with the ego of the person under treatment, in order to subdue portions of his id which are uncontrolled—that is to say to include them in the synthesis of his ego."[21] In describing neurosis, Freud tells us, "For that reason the conflict cannot be brought to an issue; the disputants can no more come to grips than, in the familiar simile, a polar bear and a whale. A true decision can only be reached when they both meet on the same ground. To make this possible is, I think, the sole task of our therapy."[22] The development from "normal" (tyranny of the id) to "healthy" (controlled by the ego) requires the outside help of the therapist. Thus the therapeutic relationship stands as an exception to the secondary role of the social in Freud. For only in therapy can the social commonplace attain mastery over the biological commonplace.

[20]*Psycho-Analysis,* S.E., XX, 268.

[21]*Analysis, Terminable and Interminable,* S.E., XXIII, 235.

[22]*Introductory Lectures on Psycho-Analysis,* S.E., XVI, 433. See also Preface to Aichhorn's *Wayward Youth,* S.E., XIX, 273-275.

PART III

FREUD'S PERSONALITY THEORY AND EDUCATION

Chapter Nine

☐

FREUD'S PERSONALITY
THEORY AND EDUCATION

IN THIS CHAPTER, we offer one possible translation of Freud's theory for education. Freud himself did not address the problems of educational theory and practice, but he believed that the insights of psychoanalysis could greatly benefit education.

> None of the applications of psycho-analysis has excited so much interest and aroused so many hopes, and none, consequently, has attracted so many capable workers, as its use in the theory and practice of education. It is easy to understand why; for children have become the main subject of psycho-analytic research and have thus replaced in importance the neurotics on whom its studies began. Analysis has shown how the child lives on, almost unchanged, in the sick man as well as in the dreamer and the artist; it has thrown light on the motive forces and trends which set its characteristic stamp upon the childish nature; and it has traced the stages through which a child grows to maturity. No wonder, therefore, if an expectation has arisen that psycho-analytic concern with children will benefit the work of education, whose aim it is to guide and assist children on their forward path and to shield them from going astray.[1]

However, Freud saw therapy as a kind of second education for neurotics, not to be confused with the process of education.

> The second lesson has a somewhat conservative ring. It is to the effect that the work of education is something *sui generis:* it is not to be confused with psycho-analytic influence and cannot be replaced by it.

---

[1]Preface to Aichhorn's *Wayward Youth* (hereafter referred to as *Wayward Youth*), S.E., XIX, 273. See also *Psycho-Analysis and Faith,* where Freud, in his letters to Pfister, encourages Pfister's translation of psycho-analytic theory for educational purposes. (Freud, Sigmund and Pfister, Oskar: *Psycho-Analysis and Faith.* [Meng, Henrich, and Freud, Ernst L. (Eds.); Mosbacher, Eric (Tran.).] New York, Basic, 1963).

Psycho-analysis can be called in by education as an auxiliary means of dealing with a child; but it is not a suitable substitute for education. Not only is such a substitution impossible on practical grounds but it is also to be disrecommended for theoretical reasons. The relation between education and psycho-analytic treatment will probably before long be the subject of a detailed investigation.[2] Here I will only give a few hints. One should not be misled by the statement —incidentally a perfectly true one—that the psycho-analysis of an adult neurotic is equivalent to an after-education. A child, even a wayward and delinquent child, is still not a neurotic; and after-education is something quite different from the education of the immature. The possibility of analytic influence rests on quite definite preconditions which can be summed up under the term 'analytic situation'; it requires the development of certain psychical structures and a particular attitude to the analyst. Where these are lacking—as in the case of children, of juvenile delinquents, and, as a rule, of impulsive criminals—something other than analysis must be employed, though something which will be at one with analysis in its *purpose*.[3]

It is unfortunate that Freud's admonition was generally disregarded and conclusions appropriate to the therapeutic situation were indiscriminately applied to education. Freud was clearly sensitive to the complexity of applying the insights and conclusions of psychoanalysis to the field of education.

Since Freud did not undertake such a translation, we must derive, as best we can, a conception of education consistent with Freud's frame of reference and especially with his view of the developing child, of the relation of society and knowledge to the individual and of the nature of the teacher. The teacher, is, of all of these, the most polyvalent and will appear as (a) the significant adult (surrogate parent or supplement to parents) ; (b) the representative of society; (c) the representative of society as seen by the child; (d) the source of knowledge.[4]

---

[2]We do not know what work Freud refers to unless it is the introduction to Pfister's *Psychoanalytic Method*.

[3]*Wayward Youth*, S.E., XIX, 274. The problem of mistaking education and therapy for analogous processes becomes especially poignant with respect to the teacher's roles in the classroom. See pp. 164-165, n. 28.

[4]In this chapter, education is narrowly conceived as that body of experiences taking place in the "milieu" of formal schooling. By this we mean experiences (a) initiated in and by the school and (b) initiated by parents acting to educate. We do not include the natural education which occurs as parents and children normally interact.

THE CHILD (STUDENT)

We have decided to divide the topic into three parts: (1) the child as he enters the school; (2) the child's life in the school; (3) the child as affected by education: the aims of education.[5]

The Child as He Enters the School

Freud's beginning-orientation, his biological emphasis, his view of life as continuous conflict and his Lamarckist evolutionary stance, all conspire to emphasize the importance of the period of early childhood. The early experiences of the child, the organizational pattern that he develops for his libido, the ego strength that he possesses constitutionally,[6] the manner in which the ego responds to the traumata of life, the resolution of the Oedipal conflict, the pattern of relationships[7] and the specific equilibrium of conflict that he develops out of conflicts among the emerging psychical organs—all of these present problems for education, some surmountable and some insurmountable.

The child entering the school will already have established much of his instinctual pattern,[8] and thus have available larger or smaller quantities of ego energy. It is this ego energy which is required for education. The ego will have developed through the experiences (traumata) encountered in its contact with the external world. Therefore, the ego, too, will already have developed a characteristic, though not entirely fixed, pattern of responses. The style

---

[5]Of necessity we treat the first two parts of the topic sketchily. There is already a large literature devoted to what the child knows as he enters school and to his life in school, including works by such masters as August Aichhorn, Bruno Bettelheim and Fritz Redl. We shall refer to their work without presenting their conclusions. For although some of their conclusions agree with ours, they follow from very different interpretations of Freud.

[6]Freud must face the ineluctable fact of individual differences. He does so by assuming genetic differences in potential ego strength and strength of instincts. Super-ego, of course, enters into *genetic* variability only insofar as it derives from the ego. In addition, super-ego exhibits differences in the "Lamarckian heredity" of different social histories. Over and above these genetic differences there are, of course, individual differences due to differing social environments.

[7]This is not, of course, the Sullivanian "pattern" of relationship.

[8]This should lead educators to place special emphasis on nursery and early childhood education.

of inhibition, the repressions and sublimations are also well established at this period of life.

In the light of Freud's determinism, both racial and individual,[9] and his beginning-orientation, it is clear that the child entering school has, from this standpoint, a character that is in large measure already formed.

The Child's Life in the School

A theory and practice of education that bases itself on Freud's conception of the child must plan for as much instinctual gratification as is possible and appropriate for the child at each specific age.[10] We refer not only to the expression of Eros and its derivatives, but also to the expression of the Death Instinct and especially its derivative, aggression. The further sublimations required by the new experience of education, e.g. new group membership, long periods of concentration, the anxiety that is evoked by the competition involved in learning, will only intensify the strength of the death instinct, i.e. aggression. The extremes of discipline—permissiveness and the blockage of instinctual expression—are not strategies consistent with Freud's view. The concept of necessary conflict among the parts of the psyche requires that the ego and super-ego be developed and assume their appropriate roles in mental life. Consequently, an over-permissive school environment would be detrimental to the child's proper growth.

> *Education* can be described without more ado as an incitement to the conquest of the pleasure principle, and to its replacement by the reality principle; it seeks, that is, to lend its help to the developmental process which affects the ego. To this end it makes use of an offer of love as a reward from the educators; and it therefore fails if a spoilt

[9]Freud discusses the importance of the contribution of the racial super-ego in terms of the responses of different races to such matters as psycho-analysis, etc. See *Analysis, Terminable and Interminable,* S.E., XXIII, 240-241.

[10]In the last analysis, formal education for a Freudian can be at most only a rehearsal for the dramas which will have the profound and enduring educational effects. The two profound dramas are (1) the vicissitudes of living; (2) a psychoanalysis which is didactic in the highest sense. Nevertheless, the overture or rehearsal can, either by being appropriate or inappropriate, lay a good or bad foundation for the educationl profit to be derived from the vicissitudes of living and (for the elect who deserve it) the vicissitudes of a didactic analysis.

child thinks that it possesses that love in any case and cannot lose it whatever happens.[11]

And the following:

> Thus education has to find its way between the Scylla of non-interference and the Charybdis of frustration. Unless this problem is entirely insoluble, an optimum must be discovered which will enable education to achieve the most and damage the least. It will therefore be a matter of deciding how much to forbid, at what times and by what means.[12]

As to blockage of instinctual expression, we have cited in Chapter Six Freud's view of the relationship between neurosis and a strict super-ego. From this view we infer that the school must not contribute further to the development of an over-strict super-ego. However, as we shall indicate, there is another kind of super-ego education which *is* to be undertaken by the school. If the school permits reasonable gratification of the instincts then it will support the mediating effort of the ego (between id and super-ego) and help protect the ego from the danger of regression.

MEANS FOR THE GRATIFICATION OF THE INSTINCTS

In planning effectively for reasonable expression of instincts, the following must be involved:

A. The Physical Environment of the School

The works of Bruno Bettelheim and Fritz Redl are replete with examples of classrooms and work space with designated areas for free activity and for controlled activity. Similarly, the time schedule must be planned to make room for proper transitions between highly structured and less structured activity. In both cases the limits or rules must be clearly presented to the child.[13]

B. The Teacher as an Object of Aggression and Love

The teacher is an object of identification, for he serves as leader and as parent-surrogate. This identification may either be positive

[11]*Mental Functioning*, S.E., XII, 224.

[12]*New Introductory Lectures*, S.E., XXII, 149.

[13]See Bettelheim, Bruno: *Love Is Not Enough*. Glencoe, Free Press, 1950, Chapter V; and Redl, Fritz, and Wineman, David: *The Aggressive Child*. Glencoe, Free Press, 1957.

through love, or negative through aggression. The school must ensure that the child has sufficent opportunities for positive identifications that are appropriate to his stage of development, i.e. age. Because of the fairly similar sequence of libidinal stages that children
undergo, one criterion for teacher selection and assignment of children to a teacher would be the kind of identification with the
teacher that is desirable at a specific age or grade level. The personality of the teacher must be one that permits and encourages the
investment of the child's libidinal energy at every stage of development—pre-latency or post-latency, and the onset of puberty or post-
puberty, to mention only the grosser developmental distinctions. By offering the child opportunities for negative identification, we mean that some teachers should be the object for the expression of hostility. It may be that the school should "institutional-
ize" negative identification by making such teachers the school dis-
ciplinarians.

C. Group Loyalties and Aggressions

The relationships of the children to each other and to peer
leaders involve erotic ties.[14] The educator must be sensitive to the
kind of leader (oppressive, seductive, etc.) that emerges in the
group. If the peer leader intensifies conflict or inhibits the development of some or all of the members of the group, the teacher will
have to pit his authority against that of the peer leader. However, if
the leader serves a positive function by reducing conflict in the
group and in the individual, the teacher must support the peer
leader and exploit the peer leader's roll in the group.

Any functioning group will have to express aggression. The
teacher must channel this expression of aggression constructively.
Physical work, athletics, competitive sports (which combine the
physical and the "dislike" of the outsider) , arts and crafts and, on a
more sophisticated level, dramatics and dance are among the means
available for this purpose. Competitiveness among groups in the
school, though desirable in itself, can undermine the feeling for
the school as a whole. We shall discuss later a possibility for devel-

---

[14]In Freud's theory of group relations, "excesses" such as clannishness would be
considered necessary in the school. See *Protocol: Group Psychology and the Analysis of the Ego.* Chapter v, par. 10, pp. 198-199. See also Chapter vi, pp. 199-201.

oping a feeling for the school as an over-arching group encompassing the various smaller groups.

D. Control and Non-Control of Individual Relations

The teacher must guide the relationships between individuals,
encouraging and supporting varieties of "homosexual" and "hetero-
sexual" relationships among children. There may be types of relationships that the teacher should help arrange so that the child
develops an ability to relate to diverse persons, situations and
groups. Thus the teacher might arrange partnerships among members of the same sex or of opposite sexes, or teams for class projects,
and alternate these with individual work. There may even be
a proper sequencing of experiences, e.g. a proper order and development (less complex to more complex) implicit in the diversity of relationships that children should be exposed to in the school.

The Ego

One of the educational objectives of the school is to lend
strength to the ego in its development but there is as well another
important role that the school (educator) plays in respect to the
ego: the educator must diagnose the child's ego strength. This information is especially important in understanding the child's social
adjustment, e.g. the child as a result of an ego weakness may be pro-
voking his peers when in essence he is attempting to make contact.
In this case the school can demonstrate to the child that his actions
are inappropriate by offering other models, by adult intervention
and interpretation. Similarly the teacher must be able to diagnose
and distinguish between those learning difficulties that are due to
instinctual interference as contrasted to those due to ego malfunction. If the cause of difficulty is in ego malfunction, the school
should provide remedial exercises to correct the situation. The
child's ego must be taught to recognize the dangers of the
physical reality of the school (rehearsal for recognition of the
realities of successive outer worlds). In the same way he must be
given training to deal with the social reality, the peer group and
school society as a whole. The school should introduce exercise in
practical problem solving, e.g. ethical decision making, based upon

and aimed toward greater hedonistic expression. The ego should be guided in its relations to parents, adults and strangers. In planning such exercises, the educator must never lose sight of the essential limits placed on the strength and capacity of the ego, i.e. Freud's limitation on the ego's potential for control over the organism. The educator must be concerned with supporting the ego during periods of stress, e.g. disappointment, personal or social, and stressful transition periods such as the onset of puberty.

The Super-Ego

As in the case of the ego, the educator should attempt to ascertain the content and strength of the super-ego in each child. Pending more extensive modifications of the super-ego which the school will undertake as one of its educational objectives, there is one duty it has with respect to the child's life in the school. The domination of a harsh super-ego is to be ameliorated somewhat by the very careful exposure to personality models that differ from those of parents but whose differences are not perceived by the child as offering sharp contrasts.

Energy

Although energy of the ego will later be required for the work of education the first investment of ego energy must be in the function of mediation between id and super-ego. The school must be sure that it does not add to the conflict between the parts of the psyche, that it permits instinctual gratification, and does reduce the "normal" anxieties aroused by schooling (competition, support of proper group feeling). Stated another way, the school should arrange for a reasonable expression of instinct and offer "effective" sublimations immediately accessible to the child, so as to make possible the maximum investment of energy in education.

Pleasure

By introducing activities that make possible appropriate sublimations, the school can help the child find ways of attaining new pleasures in different forms. The discovery of new pleasures will in turn maximize the efficiency of the psychological apparatus and thus grant additional possibilities for education. There might also be room for some direct expression of instinct, such as in physical work.

THE CHILD AS AFFECTED BY EDUCATION: THE AIMS OF EDUCATION

We have argued that Freud assigned importance to genetic differences of constitution (strength of instinct, potential ego strength, the inheritance of the super-ego) as well as to the impact of the environment upon the life of the child. It should follow that there would be significant differences among individuals in their potential for education.

One instance of the innate and ineradicable inequality of men is their tendency to fall into the two classes of leaders and followers. The latter constitute the vast majority; they stand in need of an authority which will make decisions for them and to which they for the most part offer an unqualified submission. This suggests that more care should be taken than hitherto to educate an upper stratum of men with independent minds, not open to intimidation and eager in the pursuit of truth, whose business it would be to give direction to the dependent masses. It goes without saying that the encroachments made by the executive power of the State and the prohibition laid by the Church upon freedom of thought are far from propitious for the production of a class of this kind. The ideal condition of things would of course be a community of men who had subordinated their instinctual life to the dictatorship of reason. Nothing else could unite men so completely and so tenaciously, even if there were no emotional ties between them. But in all probability that is a Utopian expectation.[15]

---

[15]*Why War.* S.E., XXII, 212-213. Ernest Jones, in his life of Freud, reports on a meeting of psychoanalysts in which Freud agreed with a suggestion that psychoanalysis should develop its own elite:

Freud had for some time been occupied with the idea of bringing together analysts in a closer bond, and he had charged Ferenczi with the task of making the necessary proposals at the forthcoming Congress. After the scientific program Ferenczi addressed the meeting on the future organization of analysts and their work. There was at once a storm of protest. In his speech he had made some very derogatory remarks about the quality of Viennese analysts and suggested that the center of the future administration could only be Zurich, with Jung as President. Moreover, Ferenczi with all his personal charm, had a decidedly dictatorial side to him, and some of the pro-

———————————→

This distinction between the masses and the elite is maintained in the following:

> We know that in the mass of mankind there is a powerful need for an authority who can be admired, before whom one bows down, by whom one is ruled and perhaps even ill-treated. We have learnt from the psychology of individual men what the origin is of this need of the masses. It is a longing for the father felt by everyone from his childhood onwards, for the same father whom the hero of legend boasts he has overcome.[16]

If the classification of children according to their potential for education appears to follow from the passages cited, then we should go on to attempt a description, consistent with Freud's theory, of what some common and differing aims of education might be for the elite and for the masses.[17]

The Ego

Common to the Masses and the Elite

Education would be concerned primarily with developing the ego of the child so that he could gain greater mastery over his physical and social environment. Through the subject matter of education the child should master those facts (information) and skills that would help him avoid dangers and minimize anxiety. For threats of this kind delay, interfere with or retard the development of the ego. Education should also contribute, however, to the student's ability to attain pleasures more directly and systematically

---

posals went far beyond what is customary in scientific circles. Before the Congress he had already informed Freud that 'the psychoanalytical outlook does not lead to democratic equalizing: there should be an élite rather on the lines of Plato's rule of philosophers.' In his reply Freud said he had already had the same idea. (*The Life and Work of Sigmund Freud.* 3 vols. New York, Basic, 1953-1957, Vol. II, 69.)

Freud's discussion of the role of early childhood in the development of intellectual curiosity would bear on the question of the early selection of those who could serve as leaders and whose reason might control instinct. See *Leonardo da Vinci and a Memory of His Childhood,* S.E., XI, 77-81.

[16]*Moses and Monotheism,* S.E., XXIII, 109.

[17]Only two sections follow—on the ego and super-ego—for we know no way to affect the id except via the ego and super-ego.

since this would make more energy available to the ego for intellectual activities. It should also contribute to the development of "habits," meaning hobbies, that offer constructive sublimations.

Education must then teach the child to recognize the social realities, to recognize "real" authority figures, and social anxieties which are legitimate, because they are realistic. In this way, unnecessary conflict between ego and super-ego will be eliminated.

Finally, the school should help the child attain a proper perspective regarding the limitations of his ego, i.e. his abilities and aspirations. Consequently it is important to train the child for a work-responsibility (vocational training) that he can assume as an adult, in order that he may discover his competencies and in order to provide him with a socially recognized role for these competencies.

The Elite

The passages quoted tend to give the impression that "elite" means potential political leadership. Freud corrects this emphasis when he discusses science, art and work. He means by "the elite" the men of "independent mind" who contribute to art, the sciences, social and political policy and belief.

Because of the important role that members of the elite are to assume in society, they should undergo psychoanalytic therapy. If they are to attain mastery over the environment, or lead the society they must develop an exceptionally dependable and strong ego. The only way to "ensure" such an ego, that will not regress under stress, is to fortify it through therapy.[18]

The school should prepare these "gifted" children for a life of leadership in the professions, the arts, and politics.[19] They should be taught how to assume and maintain leadership and experience its rewards.[20]

---

[18]Chapter Eight, p. 148. Freud did not claim that for leaders or geniuses psychoanalysis is a prerequisite for leadership, but rather that successful psychoanalytic therapy is the only "available assurance" that the characteristics of leadership or creativity will endure. See *Leonardo da Vinci*, especially Chapter VI, S.E., XI, 130-137.

[19]Freud suggests how we might help children decide what profession they are most suited for. See pp. 171-173.

[20]Training in the behavioral sciences will prepare them to assume leadership, see p. 171. And they will desire leadership as a result of the natural inclination to rule. See pp. 162-163.

However, even members of an elite (especially in the light of their having undergone psychoanalytic therapy) must be made to feel and understand the limits of their ego strength. For though Freud recognizes the importance of the artistic life and the role of work, especially of scientific work,[21] he nevertheless maintains that the power of the ego remains limited.[22]

The Super-Ego

The Masses

Education attempts, limited as its impact would be upon the implacable super-ego, to reduce the strictness and harshness of the super-ego. Simultaneously, it would inculcate habits of obedience, via identification, to the proper ego-ideals.[23]

The Elite

As a result of therapy the members of the elite will have had the harshness of their super-ego reduced. Furthermore, since the ego will have attained greater strength through therapy and greater versatility through education, these elite individuals will have learned how to live in the society without necessarily adopting its values, nor having to make energy-wasting gestures of rebellion or offense.[24]

As a result of the proper education guilt feelings will also have been reduced in frequency and intensity, for the teachers will have taken heed of Freud's admonition:

> That the education of young people at the present day conceals from them the part which sexuality will play in their lives is not the only reproach which we are obliged to make against it. Its other sin is that it does not prepare them for the aggressiveness of which they are

---

[21]"It is science which comes nearest to succeeding in this conquest; science, however, also offers intellectual pleasure during its work and promises practical gain at the end." (*Mental Functioning*, S.E., XII, 223-224.)

[22]See Chapter 5, as well as Freud's treatment of this problem in *Analysis Terminable and Interminable*, S.E., XXIII.

[23]Freud does not tell us how this obedience is developed. Plato on the other hand introduces a psychic organ, "spirit," which would ensure (given the proper education) that the masses would follow the elite.

[24]In his Introduction to Pfister's *The Psychoanalytic Method*, S.E., XII, 330-331, Freud appeals for education that responds to the child's constitution and is not directed by the values of the teacher.

destined to become the objects. In sending the young into life with such a false psychological orientation, education is behaving as though one were to equip people starting on a Polar expedition with summer clothing and maps of the Italian Lakes. In this it becomes evident that a certain misuse is being made of ethical demands. The strictness of those demands would not do so much harm if education were to say: 'This is how men ought to be, in order to be happy and to make others happy; but you have to reckon on their not being like that.' Instead of this the young are made to believe that everyone else fulfils those ethical demands—that is, that everyone else is virtuous. It is on this that the demand is based that the young, too, shall become virtuous.[25]

They will learn how to exercise the charm which enlists followers and they will be willing to assume leadership. This is possible, for men identify with their parents' super-ego (and not with their parents)[26] and thus the elite will want to rule.

Pleasure and Energy

Here educators can treat the masses and the elite alike. The aim of education is to maximize both pleasure and energy insofar as the two are commensurate with one another. Immediate, instinctual pleasure will be maximized for the elite by their relative freedom from the domineering super-ego. For the masses, greater pleasure accrues from *permitted* instinctual acts. For both, however, a large proportion of the increase of pleasure must arise from the greater variety of sublimations they can undertake since energy would be depleted by too much immediate instinctual satisfaction. Indeed, for the elite, sublimated pleasures must exceed the directly instinctual by a wide margin, otherwise they would not possess the energy required for their leadership roles.

THE TEACHER

As indicated previously, the teacher is polyvalent. He is simultaneously significant adult, representative of society, representative of society as seen by the child, and source of knowledge. Each of these aspects is treated separately below.

---

[25]*Civilization and Its Discontents*, S.E., XXI, 134, n. 1.
[26]See p. 118.

The Teacher as Significant Adult

The teacher must understand two children: the child he confronts in the classroom and the vestigial child within himself. To help him understand his pupils, Freud explicitly suggests psychoanalysis:

> . . . every such person [educator] should receive a psycho-analytic training, since without it children, the object of his endeavours, must remain an inaccessible problem to him. A training of this kind is best carried out if such a person himself undergoes analysis and experiences it on himself: theoretical instruction in analysis fails to penetrate deep enough and carries no conviction.[27]

Of course this analysis will also render accessible the vestigial child in himself.

Effective response to the child will not only require that the teacher be sensitized to children and their biological nature, but that he be aware of his inhibitional system and possess a fair degree of control over his own instinctual expressions.

In describing the corresponding relation in therapy—the analyst-patient relationship—Freud stresses the need for psychoanalysts to have achieved a "healthy" life style.

> . . .whereas the special conditions of analytic work do actually cause the analyst's own defects to interfere with his making a correct assessment of the state of things in his patient and reacting to them in a useful way. It is therefore reasonable to expect of an analyst, as a part of his qualifications, a considerable degree of mental normality and correctness. In addition, he must possess some kind of superiority, so that in certain analytic situations he can act as a model for his patient and in others as a teacher.[28]

---

[27]Preface to Aichhorn's *Wayward Youth*, S.E., XIX, 274. See also *New Introductory Lectures*, S.E., XXII, 149-150.

[28]*Analysis Terminable and Interminable*, S.E. XXIII, 248. The therapist-teacher analogy will prove a mistaken one. On the one hand, the teacher is a likely object for the investment of the child's libido. There are probably many ways in which a version of transference does take place or could take place, creating a problematic situation when education involves the changing of attitudes and values. The concept of identification — first to people and through people to ideas — emerges as the key concept for this issue. On closer look, there is little likeness between the therapeutic and educational situations, even in this respect. For transference in therapy must occur in a one-to-one relation, within the context and style of the therapeutic encounter. The teacher, on the other hand, faces many pupils at

---→

Even more than the analyst, the teacher serves as an overt model, for super-ego development: "In the same way, the super-ego, in the course of an individual's development, receives contributions from later successors and substitutes of his parents, such as teachers and models in public life of admired social ideals."[29] Therefore, the teacher both in his own person and as midwife to the heroes of the society (past and present) continues the work of the parents. The child may identify with him and thus the teacher's values would be introjected as additions to those already in the super-ego.

The Teacher as Representative of Society

As the representative of society the teacher can shrewdly minimize its harmful effects. The environment of the school and the classroom are under the control of the teacher and therefore the oppressive environment of the society (at large, the family, or peer group) can be mitigated by experience that allows the safe expression of aggression and constructive sublimation of Eros.

The Teacher as Representative of Society as Seen by the Child

Because the child sees him as representative of society, the teacher would frequently and systematically ally himself with the children against society. Thus, he would gain the confidence of the child and also mediate (control) a "healthy" expression of adolescent revolt. In his role of ally to the student in his revolt against society, the teacher could conceivably solicit and obtain parental support. He could argue that, because the only alternatives are revolt or guided revolt, it would prove profitable to join in supporting these efforts of the school.

To the extent that the teacher is conscious of the bonds established between himself and the children, and also of the bonds es-

---

once and, even if psychoanalyzed, he would be untrained in techniques to cope with transferences. No educational system can permit the teacher to assume the role of therapist, and the teacher could cause immeasurable harm should he attempt to assume this role. Freud's concept of the therapist and its implications for education is clearly an important topic to treat, and one deserving of its own volume.

[29]*An Outline of Psycho-Analysis*, S.E., XXIII, 146.

tablished among the children themselves, the teacher can utilize his power for educational purposes.[30] However, the difference in background and experience of teacher and student may complicate identifications in various ways. The children may identify with an "apparent" teacher and not the "real" teacher. The teacher may inflict upon the children his prejudices concerning teacher-student or peer relationships. This problem takes on special significance in a Freudian theory of education since the teacher-student relationship tends to arouse vestigial erotic feelings.

The Teacher as Source of Knowledge

The teacher as source of knowledge should serve first as a model to demonstrate that knowledge leads to mastery, pleasure and profit.[31] To do this, his training will have to emphasize careful study of the child with special emphasis on such matters as libidinal development, ego strength, etc.

Freud constantly admonishes those who think that they can understand psychoanalysis, let alone practice it, without having undergone the experiences of psychoanalysis. For educators, this means that the gap between theory and practice cannot be closed without a training program that includes careful supervision of *practical* work. In this experience the teacher would be sensitized to such matters as his repertory and potential for serving as model to the child, his strength and weakness in handling anxieties expressed by children, his grasp of the forms that instinctual expressions take in various children at different age levels.

ADMINISTRATION

A brief word on the administration of the school. The administrator would be the central figure in introducing into the school the theory and practice of education we have just described. He would select the teachers on the basis of their qualifications for the roles we have enumerated (e.g. attractiveness to the children, sensitivity to the needs of children).

---

[30]See *Group Psychology*, S.E., XVIII, 95-96.

[31]See Freud's description of the reward of the scientific life as quoted on p. 162, n. 21.

SOCIETY

In Freud's theory society is clearly important for it is in a society (family) that the inhibitional system is developed. We avoid discussion of a best possible society and will only point to some of the contributions that the school can make as a second society or as a new "milieu."

Although the administrator should be the central figure to the child and the teacher, he is in reality a remote figure. The instrumental central figure in the school society is the teacher. Through his efforts the school, as a new society, can affect the child (inofar as the super-ego can be affected). The teacher would have to be familiar with the various societies in which the child holds membership (family, peer groups, classroom, club, etc.). With the aid of peer leaders the teacher can create an environment that is less restrictive.[32] As we mentioned previously an important asset in the development of this environment is the feeling on the part of the students that they have joined with an unusual adult, the teacher, in a clever and meaningful revolt against the rest of society.

The creation of such an environment is not easily accomplished. Against it are the individual problems that children bring to their groups. There are also the natural enmities which must develop between groups (as they do between families). As to enmities, one counteracting influence might be the creation of a "special" group consisting of the outstanding (elite) members or leaders of each smaller group.[33] This over-arching group committed to a common purpose and supported by the school adminstration would help "stablize" the environment of the school.[34]

We cannot treat here the perennial problem of the relation of the school to society, except to indicate that we see the Freudian structure as requiring that the school's relationship to the society be

---

[32]Because of undue restrictions on man's biological nature all societies prepare the child poorly for living and education. See Chapter Six.

[33]It is true that Freud discussed very special groups, the army and the church, and might have modified his view of group participation had he written more concerning smaller and less formal groups. However, it is our interpretation that there would have been no radical reformulation due to the importance Freud granted to the prototypal group, the family. See Chapter Six, pp. 125-128.

[34]This, of course, presupposes and emphasizes the importance of the school developing criteria and means for early selection of such students.

analogous to the relationship of the teacher to parents. The school would "shrewdly" attempt to minimize the threat of societal control and values. It would avoid at all costs an open confrontation with the society. Indeed its leadership and the values and attitudes which it promotes, would all be taken from, and placed in the service of, the elite of that society. Thus, its minimization of the threat of societal control and values would be a means toward molding the super-ego in two senses: (a) reduction where necessary of its strictness; and (b) modification of its specific content. In this way the school contributes to the benevolent dictatorship of the elite and begins the task of selecting and shaping successor elites.

Thus as far as its relationship with society is concerned the school policy would further the ultimate aims of the highest strata of that society rather than the local class-bound aims.

SUBJECT MATTER

Since Freud was not concerned with specific problems of curriculum and instruction, it is not surprising that there are few implications of his theory for the various subject-matters.

Instinctual gratification via *action* is so central in Freud that the terms with which the subject matter would be viewed are necessarily positivistic or empirical. In terms of Aristotle's analysis *(Posterior Analytics,* 219A) of the steps leading to induction: sense perception, memory, experience and induction, the student for Freud can proceed only as far as experience permits. He is restricted to empirical generalization, which he cannot combine with inductive or imaginative leaps. It is for this reason that we speak of Freud's educational stance as being empirical or positivistic.[35] That is so,

---

[35]The complications for educators who adopt the Freudian frame of reference are most obvious here. First, there is the limitation of the possibility of transfer, i.e. emphasis on empirical generalization would require that each possible and useful generalization would need to be taught in its own right (no over-riding theoretical structures which impose ordered relations among such generalizations). Second, inference (thinking) can become eroticized. Third, regression is possible in thinking patterns. Fourth, memory itself is complicated by non-rational components, i.e. the instinctual needs. In terms of the "structure" of the disciplines as such, the educator will have a very difficult time with such fields as physics which contain such a vast amount of imaginative construction as against empirical generalization. Similarly in art, the school will have a difficult time teaching about the artist's personal world or his symbols.

because the prime function of the ego is to serve the id in its striving for pleasure.[36] Only to the extent that the ego is familiar with and able to cope with reality will it successfully carry out its function, whether in a private or social context. If, however, imagination is considered a part of "the rational," we must remember that rationality would include those "imaginative" and "creative" operations that serve sublimational purposes.

Since the purpose of all learning is to serve the id in relation to coping with reality, the school cannot stop with merely imparting knowledge. It must also provide the training by which knowledge is rendered serviceable. This means that in the first place, the knowledge will be directed toward vocational and professional training; it means second, that the school will involve the child at an early age in experiences requiring mastery of physical, biological and social barriers to satisfaction of instinctual needs. Third, much of what is taught must be chosen to provide channels of sublimation suitable to each child. Fourth, the school must progressively teach the child to control the impulsive expression of instinctual need. We, therefore, conjecture that the school should early involve the child in experiences granting maximum expression of the instincts via suitable sublimations. Simultaneously, the school would introduce experiences designed to teach the child step-by-step to control instinct.[37] These concerns, control and sublimation, would guide the entire school experience and in addition the school would provide the vocational or professional training for adult participation in the society.

The Masses

For the masses, the curriculum follows much of the above outline. Thus, mathematics (arithmetic) would be taught for its practical use. The natural and biological sciences would be presented as guides to effective living, e.g. biology would essentially be a course in hygiene leading to information concerning personal health, thus

---

[36] We remember that the reality principle does not change the aim of the organism; it only postpones the immediate expression of pleasure, in order to attain the maximum amount of pleasure in the light of reality.

[37] In a sense we are suggesting something analogous to the role of music and gymnastics in Plato's curriculum but with a major distinction. In Plato "appetites" can be subdued; in Freud instinct cannot.

avoiding many conflicts and anxieties. Study of the humanities would invite students to identify with certain persons and issues. These identifications in turn would not only reinforce the subordinate role of the masses but would offer scope for constructive sublimation. The arts taught would be arts and crafts, with the hope that hobbies would both occupy leisure time and offer successful means for instinctual expression. The social sciences would be taught so as to facilitate the student's contact with the social reality. Information derived from political science, economics, and sociology would take the form of precepts and aphorisms serving as guides for "proper" action in the society, in accordance with the value system of the elite.

No education would be complete unless it prepared the young for participation in the adult world, i.e. work or vocational training. Freud emphasized the importance of work as a source of happiness and as sublimation of instinct.[38]

The Elite

The gifted student would undergo a similar experience of training in expression, sublimation and control.[39] However, his subject matter instruction would differ from that of the masses. Science would be taught to enable him to master reality so as to construct a physical situation in which he could attain the greatest comfort. In science and in mathematics his elegant theoretical constructions would serve as suitable sublimations. The humanities would serve as an arena for vicarious erotic expression and for free flight of the imagination.

Anthropology would be studied as the history of the development of the cultural and societal psyche, whose stages would be presented as paralleling the stages of individual development.

In the study of history the "facts" would be interpreted in terms of such psychoanalytic concepts as the unconscious, sublimation and aggression. Furthermore, we would search for facts that otherwise might not be introduced into historical investigation, e.g. dreams of

[38]See *Civilization and Its Discontents,* S.E., XXI, 80, n. 1.

[39]Whether the elite should be separated from the masses at an early age or at a later age, or whether they should remain in the group so as to offer leadership, is a question that cannot be dealt with here.

heroes or leaders, psychoanalytic interpretation of folk-myths and culture. Races and nations would be endowed with a *character* as a result of their inheritance over the generations. Special study would be made of the role of the leader and his psychological make-up. The historian himself would be investigated for his own psychological bias.

Economic explanation of present or past problems would be subsumed under psychological explanation.

Political theory would concern itself with the libidinal ties between leaders and groups. Attempts would be made to identify and classify leadership roles on the basis of the erotic needs they fulfill.

Obviously, literature could not be taught without making a psychological analysis of the characters in the drama or novel, the symbols in poetry and the upbringing of the author.

Theoretical and philosophical systems, and political and economic arguments might be distrusted as masking deeper and more basic intentions.

The more narrowly behavioral sciences would be so taught as to prepare the elite groups for leadership. Thus, the arts of rhetoric and "practical" psychology (industrial psychology, group therapy and practice, etc.) would be introduced as necessary skills.

Over and above these somewhat obvious distinctions between education of mass and elite, Freud introduces another and unexpected one.

> There is no golden rule which applies to everyone: every man must find out for himself in what particular fashion he can be saved. All kinds of different factors will operate to direct his choice. It is a question of how much real satisfaction he can expect to get from the external world, how far he is led to make himself independent of it, and finally, how much strength he feels he has for altering the world to suit his wishes. In this, his psychical constitution will play a decisive part, irrespectively of the external circumstances. The man who is predominantly erotic will give first preference to his emotional relationships to other people; the narcissistic man, who inclines to be self-sufficient, will seek his main satisfaction in his internal mental processes; the man of action will never give up the external world on which he can try out his strength. As regards the second of these types, the nature of his talents and the amount of instinctual sublimation open to him will decide where he shall locate his interests.

Any choice that is pushed to an extreme will be penalized by expos-
ing the individual to the dangers which arise if a technique of living that has been chosen as an exclusive one should prove inadequate. Just as a cautious business-man avoids tying up all his capital in one concern, so, perhaps, worldly wisdom will advise us not
to look for the whole of our satisfaction from a single aspiration. Its
success is never certain, for that depends on the convergence of many
factors, perhaps on none more than on the capacity of the psychical
constitution to adapt its function to the environment and then to exploit that environment for a yield of pleasure.[40]

Therefore, the curriculum will contain required courses to protect the student from "tying up all his capital in one concern" and
an area of specialization to permit the development of his "unique"
constitutional potential. We present some of the alternatives that
Freud considered.

One gains the most if one can sufficiently heighten the yield of pleasure from the sources of psychical and intellectual work. When that
is so, fate can do little against one. A satisfaction of this kind, such
as an artist's joy in creating, in giving his phantasies body, or a scientist's in solving problems or discovering truths, has a special quality which we shall certainly one day be able to characterize in metapsychological terms. At present we can only say figuratively that such
satisfactions seem 'finer and higher'. But their intensity is mild as
compared with that derived from sating of crude and primary instinctual impulses; it does not convulse our physical being. And the weak
point of this method is that it is not applicable generally: it is accessible to only a few people. It presupposes the possession of special
dispositions and gifts which are far from being common to any practical degree. And even to the few who do possess them, this method
cannot give complete protection from suffering. It creates no impene-
trable armour against the arrows of fortune, and it habitually fails
when the source of suffering is a person's own body.

While this procedure already clearly shows an intention of making oneself independent of the external world by seeking satisfaction in internal, psychical processes, the next procedure brings out
those features yet more strongly. In it, the connection with reality
is still further loosened; satisfaction is obtained from illusions, which
are recognized as such without the discrepancy between them and
reality being allowed to interfere with enjoyment. The region from
which these illusions arise is the life of the imagination; at the time

---

[40]*Civilization and Its Discontents*, S.E., XXI, 83-84. See also *Libidinal Types*, S.E.,
XXI, 217-220.

when the development of the sense of reality took place, this region was expressly exempted from the demands of reality-testing and was set apart for the purpose of fulfilling wishes which were difficult to carry out. At the head of these satisfactions through phantasy stands the enjoyment of works of art—an enjoyment which, by the agency of the artist, is made accessible even to those who are not themselves creative. People who are receptive to the influence of art cannot set too high a value on it as a source of pleasure and consolation in life. Nevertheless the mild narcosis induced in us by art can do no more than bring about a transient withdrawal from the pressure of vital needs, and it is not strong enough to make us forget real misery.[41]

Freud further discusses work:

No other technique for the conduct of life attaches the individual so firmly to reality as laying emphasis on work; for his work at least gives him a secure place and a portion of reality, in the human community. The possibility it offers of displacing a large amount of libidinal components, whether narcissistic, aggressive, or even erotic on to professional work and on to the human relations connected with it lends it a value by no means second to what it enjoys as something indispensable to the preservation and justification of existence in society. Professional activity is a source of special satisfaction if it is a freely chosen one—if, that is to say, by means of sublimation, it makes possible the use of existing inclinations, of persisting or constitutionally reinforced instinctual impulses. And yet, as a path to happiness, work is not highly prized by men. They do not strive after it as they do after other possibilities of satisfaction. The great majority of people only work under the stress of necessity, and this natural human aversion to work raises most difficult social problems.[42]

The curriculum would then prepare these children for professions able to grant them the greatest instinctual expression (happiness), would prepare them to enjoy the fruits of other professions (e.g. works of arts and literature) and train them to assume positions of power and status in the society.

A Note on the Curriculum

It appears that the curriculum would be guided by the following objectives and that the subject matter-to-be taught would be

---

[41]*Civilization and Its Discontents*, S.E., XXI, 79-81.
[42]*Ibid.*, p. 80, n.

selected and organized to attain these objectives. The first three items are common to both the masses and the elite.

1. Instinctual expression and control.
2. Information and skill.
3. Vocation.
4. Sophisticated channeling of sublimation (appreciation of and amateur participation in art, literature, and the sciences).
5. Professional participation in the arts and sciences.
6. "Professional" utilization of the behavioral sciences.

Some hint of what might have been Freud's *curriculum theory* could also be obtained by looking at the rank order which the commonplace-terms of curriculum theory would take.[43] The child (the student) would be at the top of the educational hierarchy. He is the basic raw material of education and is not very malleable. Any educational theory or practice that makes excessive or improper demands upon the student will be self-defeating.

The teacher occupies the second rank. He is the central person in the group, a potential contributor to super-ego development and in control of the environment of the classroom. He can reduce conflicts and support the ego. Through his role as significant adult he can evoke student interest in the subject matter.

The society occupies third rank (family, school, peers, community and world), since it will continue to affect the child's developing super-ego and the child's ego will have to discover ways of attaining pleasure in his various societies.

The subject matter of education will occupy the lowest rank in the hierarchy. It is (except for the elite) a means for attaining some measure of relief in a perplexing world.

CONCERNING ANOTHER INTERPRETATION

There is another interpretation of the place of rationality in Freud's theory, but we contend that this interpretation cannot be substantiated by analysis of Freud's works, but would have to be based chiefly on post-Freudian developments in psychoanalytic

[43]Joseph J. Schwab. Problems, topics and issues. In Elam, Stanley (Ed): *Education and the Structure of Knowledge*. Chicago, Rand, 1964; Tyler, Ralph. *Basic Principles of Curriculum and Instruction*. Chicago, Univ. of Chicago Press, 1950.

theory. In such an interpretation, Freud's theory would be treated as the initial stages of an evolving inquiry. The point of departure for this interpretation would be the state of psychoanalytic theory at the time and in the mind of the interpreter. For example, Heinz Hartmann's conception of an ego that does not develop from the id but differentiates from a common matrix would result in one variety of this interpretation; Erik Erikson's conception of the epigenesis of the ego would result in another.

With these conceptions, it could be argued that Freud's view of the ego and its relation to the id *developed* during the course of his investigations. The argument would claim that at first Freud conceived of no more than ego instincts in tension with sexual instincts.[44] Then he developed a concept of the ego as a coherent organization that developed out of the id but remained closely related to it.[45] Later he granted the ego the power to suppress the excitations that emanate from the id.[46] Finally, the argument would run, Freud allowed for the possibility of an ego that conquers the id. "Where id was, there ego shall be."[47]

In the light of such a view, the public correspondence between Einstein and Freud could be interpreted as follows: If Freud's "pessimistic" statements limited the possibilities of education for "the vast majority" are intended to counterbalance the "naive" optimism of Einstein, then the reader's attention is improperly focused on the first portion of the passage:

> One instance of the innate and ineradicable inequality of men is their tendency to fall into the two classes of leaders and followers. The latter constitute the vast majority; they stand in need of an authority which will make decisions for them and to which they for the most part offer an unqualified submission.[48]

and *should instead* be focused on its continuation:

> This suggests that more care should be taken than hitherto to educate an upper stratum of men with independent minds, not open to intimi-

---

[44]See *Beyond the Pleasure Principle*, S.E., XVIII, 61.

[45]See our pp. 84-85.

[46]But see pp. 88-89.

[47]*New Introductory Lectures*, S.E., XXII, 80. See our discussion, pp. 91-94.

[48]*Why War*, S.E., XXII, 212.

dation and eager in the pursuit of truth, whose business it would be
to give direction to the dependent masses.[49]

Now the latter portion of this passage would be used as evidence of Freud's hope that education would develop men who
could rise above their instinctual demands.

From these arguments a conception of the enlarged power of
the ego would emerge as well as a different rank order of the commonplaces. The ego would be located at the top of the hierarchy or
it would share this position with the id.

There is a multiplicity of implications for education in this
interpretation of Freud. For ranking the ego highest in the hierarchy of commonplaces opens the door to every conception of education that emphasizes the importance of the rational and the
aesthetic.[50]

The kind of education suggested earlier for the elite would
constitute one curricular program appropriate to this interpretation. So also would most conceptions of "disciplinary education,"
that is, those which emphasized the mastery of intellectual competencies, whether those of the classical liberal arts or the more
modern emphases on the competencies required for enquiry in the
various disciplines.

A source of support for this view of the powers of the ego
might be found in interpretations based on examining Freud's
theory as a product of his personality. For example, we have
argued on pages 91-94 that although there are passages in Freud
that would lead the reader to believe that the ego obtains sub-
stantial power over the id, the overwhelming evidence points to
a conception of an ego that is subservient to the id. Further, in
Moses and Monotheism and in *An Outline of Psycho-Analysis,*
two of his last major published works, Freud maintains his conception of an ego that, for most men, must remain subservient to
the id throughout life. Against this, those who interpret Freud's
theory in terms of his personality might respond that Freud wrote

---

[49]*Ibid.*

[50]Still excluded, however, would be any view of education that did not seriously
consider the power and complexity of the id.

his last works when he was old, sick and despondent.[51]

The introduction of biographical data and the application to it of psychological insight could certainly result in diverse interpretations of this nature. But we know of no way to discriminate among them.

[51]For example, see Eric Fromm: *Sigmund Freud's Mission*. (New York, Harper, 1959); and H. W. Puner: *Freud—His Life and His Mind*. (New York, Dell, 1959), represent interpretations of Freud's work based on his personal life but their conclusions disagree with ours.

APPENDICES

□ □ □ □ □

APPENDIX I

□

THE PROTOCOL:
BEYOND THE PLEASURE PRINCIPLE

CHAPTER ONE

1—Assumes the dominance of the pleasure principle. With the pleasure principle introduces the notion of mental or emotional economics. The above plus the notion of topography and dynamics set the context for his metapsychology.

2—Defines pleasure in terms of stability and quiescence (non-living). Otherwise taken *as* a principle—unaccounted for.

3—Indicates similarity of his concept of pleasure and Fechner's concept.

4—Repeat paragraph two with *striving* to minimize excitation and action. (Presenting a paradox which leads to death as purpose of life. This could have been avoided by conceiving pleasure as consciousess of activity. The price is the Platonic diversity of pleasure.)

5—Qualifies the notion of dominance of the pleasure principle to tendency to dominance.

6-9—Explains those cases that appear to contradict the pleasure principle as actually being in the service of the pleasure principle (a) reality principle—postponement, abandonment, sublimation, (b) expression of repressed and neurosis, (c) perceptual unpleasure (of present danger or forecast of danger). Proposes to examine (c).

CHAPTER TWO

1—Introduces traumatic neurosis caused by fright. Distinguishes fright from fear and anxiety. (Fright—unprepared for

181

danger. Fear—requires definite object. Anxiety—state of preparing for and expecting the danger.) Traumatic neurosis minimized by wound (to be explained later) .

2 and 3—Dreams of the traumatic neurotic are repetitive of fright, therefore (in the light of Freud's theory of dreams) either this is a special kind of dream (not wish fulfillment), or a masochistic wish.

4-6—Examines children's play (re the economic factor) .
Description of the game—"gone," "there."

7—Meaning of game—renunciation and abreaction. Relation to pleasure principle unclear since "gone" solely represents the bad event.

8—Explanation of the bad event in the game (a) abreaction—a separate instinct of mastery—"getting on top of" the bad experience, (b) revenge but still leaves the question of whether there may not be a third explanation unrelated to the pleasure principle.

9 and 10—No resolution yet of the above choice, and no light on whether there is something beyond the pleasure principle.

Resolution of the above will be difficult in view of the ambiguous character of wish fulfillment. But, he does not assume special imitative instinct as necessary to explain the painful in play. (What happened to the possible "mastery" instinct—paragraph eight?)

CHAPTER THREE

1 and 2—Recapitulation of the therapeutic aims of psychoanalysis: (a) interpretation, (b) active recovery of memory, (c) transference, (d) repetition as contemporary experience. (The above in order to use the transference neurosis as another instance of repetition contradicting the pleasure principle.)

3—Details on the transference neurosis. Distinguishes the repressed (instinct) and the repressor (ego) in order to separate the "pleasurable" character of repressing from the painful character (the compulsion to repeat) of the repressed. (Compulsion to repeat likened to play and dreams that repeat the traumatic experience.)

4—Resistance under the pleasure principle. Therapy under the reality principle. That which is unpleasurable to one system may be pleasurable to another, but some repetition (compulsion to repeat) entirely devoid of pleasure.

5—Infantile sexual life as an example of painful acting out.

6—Transference (in therapy) and the repetition of painful acting out of childhood experiences are under the pressure of a compulsion (and hence compulsion to repeat seems to override the pleasure principle).

7—Correlates the above with "normal" experience, i.e. re-occurence of tragic errors such as choice of mate, protégé, friends, etc. (another instance of Freud's view of determinism in emotional life). Distinguishes between passive and active role in terms of repetition.

8-10—The above (transference, "normal" behavior, play and traumatic dreams) indicative of a compulsion to repeat, independent of the pleasure principle. (In each case though he offers the possibility of a combination of the compulsion to repeat plus another motive.) Asks: (1) What function it corresponds to? (2) Under what conditions it can emerge? (3) What is its relation to the pleasure principle?

CHAPTER FOUR

1—Admits the speculative nature of the inquiry.

2—Reviews the basic distinction in psychoanalysis—conscious-unconscious. On the basis of function he assigns consciousness a position on the topography—the perceptual-conscious system, borderline between inside and outside. (He uses function as a principle for the topography. He correlates cerebral anatomy with mental anatomy.)

3—Also distinguishes the perceptual—conscious system on the basis of the presence or absence of memory traces. Absence of memory traces in consciousness is assumed since: (1) memory traces would limit new excitations (thus tape is theoretically limited—see *The Protocol: The Ego and the Id,* page 216 par. 6), (2) no possibility for unconscious memory, therefore, he locates memory in the next system (preconscious). (See *Ibid.,* page 217, par. 7.)

4—Further explanation for absence of memory traces in consciousness is the exposed situation of the system consciousness to the external world.

5—Analogizes to biology to explain the function and nature of consciousness. Extreme specialization leads to perception (Lamarckian). Memory as a trace left when excitation overcomes resistance in passing from one element to another. Perceptual system offers no resistance. Analogizes above to bound and unbound energy.

6—Continues the analogy and explains origin and function of the skin, iris, etc. as protective shield.

7—Digresses to disagree with the Kantian theory on time and space as necessary forms of thought (a) unconscious processes are timeless, (b) the idea of time itself is derived from perceptual-conscious system (it is related to the way the system works), (c) this idea (time) may be a method of protecting the organism from too much stimuli.

8—But to stimuli from within, consciousness has no protection. Hence, the inside predominates over outside. (Handles the problem of being overwhelmed from within by postulating that excitations from within are more commensurate with the system's method of working.) Introduces projection as method of handling overwhelming internal excitation.

A Reconsideration of the Above Problematic Cases

9—Relates traumatic to above as being case of stimuli breaking through protective shield. Energy would therefore be summoned to handle break. Thus *(pcpt.-cs* is too busy with the outside to attend to the inside—pleasure principle) trauma as negation at least of dominance of the pleasure principle.

10—Explains physical pain as breach in the protective shield. This causes excitation to pass from periphery (outside) to mind. He claims that the mind (1) summons cathectic energy to handle breach, (2) as a result other systems are impoverished. (This is necessary to explain paralyzing nature of pain: a limited amount of energy, hence if taken from one system, the other systems are impoverished.) The above necessitates his further assumption that the more highly cathectic, the more potential for binding. Explains discharge and pain as reflex action. Admits the tentativeness of the entire discussion due to little knowledge of excitatory processes, but he assumes that excitatory processes vary quantitatively and possibly even qualitatively (only in terms of amplitude) and that there are two kinds of energy and hence two types of cathexis: free and quiescent. (In any case, a situation to which the pleasure principle is irrelevant.)

11—Explains traumatic neurosis as break in the protective shield. Distinguishes above from shock and psychological explanation —fright. Break due to overwhelming external stimulus plus lack of preparedness, not to physical damage, i.e. the injury is to an organ of *mind* not of body. Distinguishes potential for traumas on the basis of hyper-cathexis of the systems. Now explains traumatic dreams as carrying out task more primitive (hence, instinctive) than dominance of the pleasure principle, i.e. must master the stimulus retrospectively, by producing the anxiety which should have been present at the very beginning.

12—Reformulates the above to make traumatic dreams an explicit example of an exception to dreams as wish fulfillment. He explains them as a response to compulsion to repeat a function more primitive than wish fulfillment. Restates the above and claims that if there is a beyond the pleasure principle then dreams must also illustrate this state.

13—Explains physical wound diminishing traumatic neurosis as hypercathexis of injured organ binding the excess of excitation (chapter ii, par. 1).

CHAPTER FIVE

1—The assumption that the cortical layer has no protective shield from inside makes the inside (instinct) economically dominant and presents the potential for disturbance equal to trauma. (But trauma will be reserved for breach from without.)

2—Uses dreams as basis of investigating instincts. Assumes that instincts are mobile and that cathexes are easily transferable. Distinguishes the unconscious from the preconscious in terms of the above. Describes unconscious processes as primary, and waking processes as secondary, the primary is mobile and the secondary is a bound cathexis. Thus instincts, which are mobile *(ucs.)* require binding by higher strata before the pleasure principle begins to operate. Therefore, there is a task prior to the pleasure principle and that is the binding by the highest strata of the mental apparatus of the instinctual excitations reaching the primary process. Thus he explains the problematic cases for the pleasure principle as being prior but not contradictory.

3—Indicates similarity of characteristics of compulsion to repeat, as manifest in children's games (adults bored at repetition), thus further indicating similarity to primary period of instinctual life. These cases, though, do not contradict the pleasure principle. Compulsion to repeat in analysis is explained as infantile behavior where primary process is dominant, i.e. where no binding has occurred. Dreams explained as primary process plus the residue of the previous day. Explains fear of analysis as fear of compulsion to repeat.

4—The compulsion to repeat is a basic trait of the instincts to restore an earlier state of things that has been disturbed by external forces. (Thus Freud explains apparent contradiction of pleasure principle and is able to explain mental life dualistically.)

5 and 6—Justifies his attributing conservatism to instincts citing animal life (historically determined nature of animal life) heredity and embryology. (Admits the possibility of conservative and progressive instincts.)

An Elaboration of the Conservative Instincts

7—Given the assumption of the conservative nature of instincts he attributes organic development to external disturbances (another instance of a Lamarckian influence). Therefore, the development over generations is explained as the stored up reactions to the earth we live on.

What appear as forces towards change are really the striving towards an "ancient" goal by new and old means. If we assume that instincts are conservative then the goal of life cannot be new but rather an "old" state of things. Therefore, the goal of life must be death (the old state of things). (This also requires the additional assumptions that everything living dies for internal reasons, and that inanimate must have existed before the animate. Therefore, life = circuitous pathway to death. The argument presented here can be outlined as follows:

> If A, then B
> B is [or is not]
> Therefore, A [is or is not].)

8—Postulates the origin of life as due to an unknown force acting on inanimate matter (analogizes this to the development of consciousness) and the first instinct as an instinct to die. Additional external disturbances were necessary to prolong life and postpone death, hence current life is the result of many postponements of death.

9—Explains self-preservative instincts (assertion, mastery) as component instincts that assure that the organism follows its own path to death. (It appears then that the self-preservative instinct becomes an instinct to die in a certain way.)

The Life Instincts

10 and 11—Presents the sexual instinct as contradiction of the above for external forces not sufficient to explain their development. Hence, the germ cells retain the original structure of living matter and they do not move toward death.

12-14—Corresponding to the germ are the sexual instincts. These instincts are conservative and oppose death. They are life instincts. (Note the effort to make the psychological parallel to the physiological.) Brings the data of neurosis to bear, i.e. life moves with vacillating rhythm. Explains sexual instincts in the light of biogenesis as being there, in potential form, from the very beginning. (Calls instincts that result in death ego-instincts.) Negates the possibility of any other category of instinct and denies the possibility of instinct toward higher development. The progressive and the static cases are all due to external forces. The impulsion toward perfection in some men expresses only the energy deriving from repression of sexual instincts.

15—Reaffirms the impossibility of admitting an impulse to perfection but offers an additional explanation of these phenomena. The efforts of Eros to combine into larger entities is added to the notion of the energy resulting from sexual repression.

CHAPTER SIX

1 and 2—Indicates dissatisfaction with the foregoing sharp distinction between ego and sex instincts. It rests on accepting the notion of an inevitable internally determined mortality. This premise is doubtful. (Brings data from primitive societies to support above, i.e. no universal belief in the necessity to die for internal reasons. There seems to be a proportion: infancy is to adulthood as primitive is to present.)

3—No unanimity on this point among biologists.

4 and 5—Cities distinction among biologists of soma (mortal) and germ (immortal) as exact parallel to the distinction made in Chapter V.

6 and 7—But Weismann locates mortality of the soma as product of multicellularity and thus death not basic to life as such —as predicted for the death instincts. (Note that Freud's instincts are ultimate "firsts" not subject to late development in evolution.)

8—Reviews theories of Goette and Hartmann.

9—Reports research which offers to demonstrate immortality of living substance (Woodruff and ciliate infusorian) .

10—Others (e.g. Calkins) report deterioration of protozoa unless special recuperative measures are taken—hence contradictory to Weismann.

11-14—Two points emerge from the above. (1) Conjugation rejuvenates (indicates conjugation is forerunner of sexual). (2) Unicellular organisms do die unless external artificial changes are made.

Freud handles the contradiction (from biology, i.e. immortality of protista) of his notion of death instincts by claiming that the data from which the apparent contradiction is derived conceals the "true" interpretation, i.e. the death instincts in operation. Four arguments are presented in support of the above: (1) the death instincts may be concealed in the primitive organism, (2) the "dynamic" view requires that we assume that the death instincts are there from the beginning, (3) some biologists claim that internal processes leading to death are operative in protista and (4) even those biologists (e.g. Weismann) who claim that death is a later development need not deny the assumption of a process that "tends" towards death.

15—Summary—biology does not negate a distinction of life and death instincts.

16—Compares his dualistic notion of instincts to Hering's theory of two processes that are at work in living substances and Schopenhauer's philosophy.

17—Assuming that conjugation and multicellularity promote life, cellular behavior can be analogized to that of the organism: cells have a "sexual instinct" and "libido" and thus "bind together" all living things.

18 and 19—Reviews the development of the libido theory. (1) Transference neurosis was interpreted as a conflict of sexual instincts (directed toward an object) and ego instincts (reminds us that less was known of this class of instincts). The ego instincts included self preservation. (2) As greater knowledge of the ego was developed (i.e. being more than repressive) and it was realized that the ego was the true and original reservoir of libido (narcissistic libido), neurosis could no longer be defined as ego vs. sex instincts. (Freud indicates that the above division requires no major alteration but a reformulation. "It is merely that the distinction between the two kinds of instinct, which was originally regarded as in some sort of way *qualitative,* must now be characterized differently—namely as being *topographical.")*

20 and 21—Having recognized the libidinal character of the self preservative instincts, Freud is left with the possibility of a monistic theory of instincts. He rejects this and reformulates ego vs. sex instincts to life vs. death instincts. Attacks Jung's monistic instinct theory. Hypothesizes the possibility of other instincts in the ego besides self-preservative.

(Freud must find conflict in the instincts, if life is to be characterized by conflict.)

22—Attempts to relate love and hate to life and death. Brings the data of sadism to bear, i.e. in the oral stage possession equals destruction, then the sadistic separates off and is later represented by overpowering the sexual object. Explains the ambivalence of love and hate as due to the sadistic not having been separated off.

Thus he assumes that sadism is a part of the death instinct.

23—Admits tenuous nature of example of death instinct but suggests masochism as an expression of death, i.e. masochism is a derivative of a "primary" masochism, i.e. death.

24—By analogizing instincts and protozoan conjugation Freud is able to strengthen his treatment of tension (life) as unpleasure, or sexual expression and reduced tension similar to death—pleasure.

25—Indicates that compulsion to repeat can be seen in life instinct in embryological development. (If sex is related to the death instinct then the compulsion must be demonstrated as characteristic of the sexual instinct.)

26—Admits tenuousness of above but claims this due to lack of knowledge of the origin of sexual reproduction and sexual instincts. (Namely, since the compulsion to repeat is basic to instinctual life then it should be manifested in Eros.)

27-29—Reviews theories of origin of sexual reproduction (biological evolution is viewed by Freud here as part of an unfolding of existing potentials set off by chance) and claims them to be tenuous but finds support for his hypothesis in a Platonic myth.

30 and 31—Presents the myth in *The Symposium* and its interpretation: (1) living substance at first was torn to small particles—attempt to reunite to sexual instinct (hence compulsion to repeat), (2) these instincts formed protective layer to handle external world, (3) transferred the instinct to germ cells.

32 and 33—Admits highly speculative nature of theory (life and death instinct) and difficulty in arriving at proper terminology.

34—Admits heavy dependence on biology.

In the footnote, Freud reviews the development of his terminology. (1) Begins with sexual instinct (sex plus reproduction) and then enlarges the notion of the sexual. (2) Enlarges the notion of the sexual to Eros, i.e. combining of cells. (3) Sexual now that part of Eros directed toward objects. (4) Duality now between Eros-life vs. death. (5) The ego instincts that were first viewed as opposed to the sexual are now seen as part of Eros.

CHAPTER SEVEN

1—Summarizes and indicates that the cases that seem to be opposed to the pleasure principle are really prior to it and are obeying the compulsion to repeat.

2—Elaborates on the above by indicating that prior stage is one of binding, moving from the primary process to secondary process, from mobile to quiescent energy. All of the above are in the service of the pleasure principle and insure the dominance of the pleasure principle.

3—Reformulates the pleasure principle to tendency operating in service of a function to reduce excitation and return to inorganic world. (Hence, binding necessary to have discharge which means less excitation, i.e. sexual act. Thus the purpose of life and action is really death. Again we see the extent to which life and even pleasure [next paragraph] are limited at the very outset.)

4—Indicates that binding dulls both pleasure and pleasure principle.

5—Poses new questions:

(1) Claims that consciousness communicates feelings of tension. What are they?

(2) Why are death instincts so unobtrusive?

(3) Why is the pleasure principle in the service of the death instinct?

□

THE PROTOCOL: GROUP PSYCHOLOGY AND THE ANALYSIS OF THE EGO

INTRODUCTION

1—Collapses the sharp distinction between individual and group psychology since the individual relates to other people. (1. It appears from the very outset that the problem will be viewed with an emphasis on the individual. 2. The group will probably be analyzed in terms of an instinct theory since he describes the problem of individual psychology as one in which the individual "explores the paths by which he seeks to find satisfaction for his instinctual impulses." 3. In the light of the above there probably will not be a special group instinct or group behavior.)

2—Elaborates the above by indicating that psychoanalysis (looked upon as individual psychology) has been dealing with social or group phenomena all along (relations of persons to one another), as well as with narcissistic phenomena.

3—Group psychology, as concerned with large groups organized for special purposes, leads to the questionable premise of a special instinct. Rather, suggests that we look for interpretation of the above phenomenon in the analysis of smaller groups, i.e. the family. (Instinct is here defined as that which cannot be reduced.)

4—The limited nature of the present inquiry. Will deal only with those questions that impinge on psychoanalysis not with all group phenomena.

CHAPTER TWO

1—Decides to analyze one of the current interpretations of group psychology—Le Bon's, so as to inquire into the "subject matter" of group psychology.

2—Distinguishes human behavior in the group as requiring an additional inquiry beyond that normally carried on in individual psychology. Therefore, he sets a context for his inquiry with three questions: (1) What is a group? (2) How does it acquire the capacity for exercising such a decisive influence over the mental life of the individual? (3) What is the nature of the mental change which it forces upon the individual? (He will investigate Le Bon within his own framework, i.e. the individual.)

3—Begins the inquiry with the third question, since it is the basis for the inquiry, i.e. it is the change in the individual behavior that is being investigated. (Thus group psychology ends up as a development or extension of individual psychology.)

4—Presents Le Bon. (1) Collective mind—individual thinks and acts differently in the group. (2) Analogizes to isolated cells that form a new entity, a living body.

5—Freud sees lacuna, i.e. what is it that unites the members of the group? (Bond, if similar to individual bonds, might be some kind of libidinal cathexis.)

6 and 7—Continues to quote Le Bon on the alteration that the individual undergoes in the group.

8—Freud interprets Le Bon's statement to mean that in the group the mental superstructure is removed and the common unconscious is exposed. (Le Bon, by reducing to a racial unconscious, is true to his principle and Freud, in the light of his principle, must reduce the group unconscious to an individual unconscious. Le Bon sees the formation of a group in terms of earlier formation of a group. Stated differently the "primitive" for Le Bon is the group.)

9—Therefore explains average character in the group, but as to *new* characteristic, due to the group, he continues to quote Le Bon.

10—Invincible power (numerical condition) makes possible yielding to instincts, i.e. feeling of no responsibility.

11—Freud explains the above not as a new characteristic, but simply as the individuals now being freed from repression. (If no dread of society, no conscience. Freud viewing the group as an aggregate of individuals sees this new characteristic [Le Bon's group instinct] as a variation in the character of the individual involving the disappearance of "restraint.")

(In this paragraph we have another example of what one finds again and again in Freud where such concepts as 'higher' and 'lower,' 'good' and 'evil' are mentioned. These are terms for which there is no ground in Freud. Therefore, we must be alerted to two possibilities: (1) the anticipation of a future theoretical structure in which the higher is not collapsed into the lower, i.e. the fourth Freud; (2) the terms are used ironically.)

12—Continues to quote Le Bon. Second characteristic of a group—contagion (of hypnotic order) in which the individual sacrifices the personal for the collective (rarely possible except in the group).

13—Freud postpones his comment on the above and continues to quote Le Bon on the third characteristic.

14-16—Suggestibility which causes contagion is similar to that of a person in an hypnotic trance.

17—Summary by Le Bon of the characteristics of the individual forming part of the group, (1) predominance of the unconscious, (2) suggestion, (3) contagion (the impact of many people under suggestion) and acting out. Human is now automaton.

18—Freud indicates that Le Bon has actually identified group behavior with that of a person in hypnotic state. This distinction between contagion and suggestibility is not clear (contagion seems to be an effect of suggestibility). Freud feels that the deficiency in the above explanation is that the analogous position of group leader to the hypnotist is not dealt with.

19—Continues to quote Le Bon indicating how the individual lowers his intellect and his status as a civilized being via group membership.

20—Freud now devotes attention to Le Bon's concept of the group mind which he believes can be explained within the present psychoanalytic framework. Freud sees similarity between the group mind and the mental life of children and primitive people. (Group life then would be a type of regression and this would explain the behavior manifested in the group, i.e. the mental superstructure set aside.)

21-23—Continues to summarize Le Bon. Group is impulsive, changeable, irritable, led by the unconscious. Actions not premeditated, feels omnipotent, open to influence, thought is not logical or realistic, but simple and exaggerated—hence the group knows neither doubt nor uncertainty. Freud indicates the similarity of Le Bon's description to that of the affective life of children and of dream life, i.e. no doubts, etc.

24. Continuation of Le Bon. In the light of the above description, group can be excited only by excessive stimulus.

25—The group is intolerant, obedient to authority and hence reacts only to force, wants powerful heroes and is conservative.

26 and 27—Group can be both very moral as well as very immoral, although the intellectual life of the group is always lower than that of the individual. (Compares this to mentality of the primitive epoch.) Freud claims that the above phenomenon again indicates a similarity between the group mind and the mind of primitive people, as well as a similarity to the unconscious in normal man, in the neurotic, and in children. Hence, this is a further indication of the weakening or disappearance of the mental superstructure.

28—Freud sees a similarity between the power of the word (magical power of words) in groups and the taboos in the primitive group.

29—No need in group life to measure concepts by reality.

30—Freud analogizes the mentality of group life to that of the neurotic, i.e. fantasy or psychological reality rules objective reality. Indicates the importance of wishes as compared to the demands of reality in group life as in dreams and hypnosis.

31—Indicates the sketchiness of Le Bon's concept of the leader, i.e. the group is an obedient herd and accepts instinctively anyone who appoints himself its master.

32—Qualifies the above by indicating that Le Bon feels the leader must have certain leadership qualities (in the light of the nature of group needs), i.e. he must be held in fascination by a strong faith and possess a strong and imposing will.

33—Continues summary of Le Bon. Attributes to idea and the leader a mysterious power called prestige. Distinguishes artificial and personal prestige. Only personal prestige will make a man a leader. Prestige is dependent upon success. (This is, in a sense, the objection in paragraph eighteen, and is dealt with but not sufficiently as indicated in paragraph thirty-four.)

34—Freud repeats his feeling that the role of the leader and his prestige is not correlated with the rest of the theory, i.e. why does the group follow him? What is the bond between the leader and the members of the group?

CHAPTER THREE

1—Le Bon's ideas have been previously expounded and even the concept of the unconscious and the comparison to the mental life of the primitive and of children were previously alluded to.

2-5—Le Bon has pointed to certain characteristics of groups. These alleged qualities are correct. However, there are additional properties and when we look at the whole set of qualities we see an inconsistency which is undisclosed by Le Bon's limited description. (Other descriptions of group life see the group as setting high ethical standards. They also point to the intellectual achievements of the group, i.e. language and folk-lore.) This inconsistency points to the possibility of different kinds of groups. The very idea that there might be different kinds of groups would be hard to handle in Le Bon's holistic terms.

6—Introduces McDougall's theory which handles the above apparent inconsistency by introducing the idea of the degree of organization and common purpose as a distinguishing factor within groups.

7-10—Summarizes McDougall: all groups involve exaltation or intensification of emotion and hence lose inhibitions characterizing individuals. This is done by contagion and thus the individual loses the faculty of criticism.

The above is favored by (1) the group impressing the individual with a sense of ultimate power; (2) the group replacing the fear of society; (3) the individual putting his former conscience out of action. The concept of suggestion is to be understood in the light of the above phenomena. Intelligence is lowered since the intensification of emotion inhibits the intellect and the individual is intimidated by the group. The absence of individual responsibility is also deterrent to intellectual quality. McDougall, like Le Bon, is disturbed by these group manifestations and also compares these manifestations to the mental life of children and primitive people.

11—Freud now summarizes McDougall on highly organized groups.

12-17—(1) Continuity of existence in a group. (2) The individual members of a group should have an understanding of the function, nature, composition and capacity of the group and thus they develop the emotional relationships to the group as a whole. (3) Interaction with other groups. (4) Group should possess a tradition. (5) Group should have structure, i.e. members should have definite roles.

If the above conditions exist in a group then the negative features of group life are eliminated and the intellectual ability is not lowered as tasks are delegated to the individual.

18—Freud indicates that McDougall's conditions for the organized group are the characteristics of an individual. (At this point Freud is close to viewing society as an enlarged individual.)

CHAPTER FOUR

1—Summarizes Le Bon and McDougall and again asks for the psychological explanation of the mental change that the individual experiences in the group.

(In this paragraph, we have another statement by Freud that man starts only with his instincts and that what is peculiar to the individual is the unique way he develops an inhibitional system for those instincts and inclinations. ". . . and this result can only be reached by the removal of those inhibitions upon his instinct which are peculiar to each individual, and by his resigning those expressions of his inclinations which are especially his own.")

2—Claims the current explanation of the above problem inadequate, i.e. why do we succumb to suggestion or contagion?

3—Refuses to accept the possibility of suggestion as a primitive irreducible phenomenon, i.e. instinct.

4—Current research has not advanced the understanding of suggestion except as to precise formulation of the concept.

5—Introduces the concept of libido as part of a context with which to approach group psychology.

6-8—Defines libido—the energy of Eros.

9—Offers the hypothesis that the love relationship constitutes the essence of the group mind. He finds basis for the hypothesis in the first instance in (1) the equation of the binding nature of Eros to the power that holds the group together, (2) explaining the submission in the group as the need of being in harmony.

CHAPTER FIVE

1—Reviews various distinctions in terms of the structure of groups (fleeting vs. lasting, homogenous vs. heterogenous, natural vs. artificial, primitive vs. highly organized) and introduces the distinction of the led vs. the leaderless group. Will inquire into highly organized, lasting and artificial groups, the army and the church.

2—Indicates that the army and church are artificial groups (due to external pressure employed to maintain them) and that he chose them since "certain facts" are observable in these groups which are "concealed" in others.

3—Analyzes both groups and compares them to the family, i.e. both have a leader who loves all members equally (father surrogates). The "tie" which unites members to the leader unites fathers and brothers to each other. (Group "tie" then is likely to be similar to the family "ties.")

Distinguishes the army and the church on the basis of structure and super-natural vs. natural leader. Claims that without the above illusion the group would disintegrate.

4—Subsumes idea such as "national glory" as an instance of group ties. Will consider this problem later.

5—Reformulates the above to: members of groups are bound

to one another and to the leader by libidinal "ties." Sets aside, for a moment, the analysis of these "ties." Indicates that this approach, i.e. being bound in two directions, offers a possibility of a better explanation of the loss of freedom in groups.

6—Brings his interpretation of panic in military groups to bear on the theory of psychology of groups, i.e. panic arises when libidinal "ties" disintegrate. Refutes the interpretation that would see panic as set off by real danger i.e. that it causes ties to disintegrate by indicating that where "ties" are in order, panic does not ensue under similar objective conditions.

7—Incorporates McDougall's concept of dread being spread by contagion, for the case of great objective danger and weak "ties." Reformulates the concept of dread and panic as due to either great objective danger or disappearance of the "ties." (Latter is neurotic dread.)

8—Criticizes McDougall on logical grounds and restates his interpretation of panic in a group.

9—Brings the case of the loss of a leader as instance of breaking of "ties" and hence panic. (Is there another way of breaking of "ties" than by loss or weakening of the leader since mutual "ties" depend on the ties to the leader?)

10—The above not observable in the church but claims that similar possibility exists, i.e. the destruction of the illusion of Christ.

11—Analogizes the breaking of "ties" in the church to dread in the army. Indicates that the nature of group mentality requires that the group love its members and consequently be hard to non-members. (Here is another limitation on human nature based on group life.)

CHAPTER SIX

1—In the groups dealt with, the "ties" to the leader appear to be of greater significance than the "ties" between the members of the group.

2 and 3—Enumerates a series of problems that would have to be dealt with in a more complete theoretical framework. Difference between collection of people vs. a group, the nature of the origin

and dissolution of groups, types of groups, led vs. leaderless groups. (Is there a development from a primitive to a mature group, i.e. from tie to leader to tie to idea? The possibility of a negative leader or idea?) Here one sees the typically Freudian analysis in terms of cathexis—Eros and object. If group psychology can be dealt with in Freudian terms then it must involve libidinal "ties." In turn, the demonstration of libidinal "ties" in the group will be an extension of his theory to another area.)

4—A reiteration of the above as introductory to the following paragraphs.

5—Brings data from psychoanalysis and from normal life to indicate that all human relationships (admits the possible exception of mother to her son and this due to narcissism) exhibit a hostile element. (Hence, hostility will have to be handled in groups as well. This would be another demonstration of the notion of conflict as expressed by ambivalence in Freud.)

6—Hostility cannot be wholly explained rationally (in terms of the reality) or due to narcissism. Therefore, he assigns to it an elementary or basic character. (Love and hate are instances of expression of the life and death instinct. See *Beyond the Pleasure Principle,* Chapter VI, par. 2. Hostility as an expression of man's instinctual life will, of necessity, mean a limitation on the potential of education.)

7—Explains the absence of hostility in groups as due to libidinal "ties" created in the group (since narcissism is only countered by love for objects). Denies the possible explanation of the absence of hostility as due to mutual need by arguing that (1) narcissism would return with the end of the need, (2) libido chooses just such situations to form "ties." (From the very beginning Freud assumed this, i.e. object cathexis on the anaclite model. In Freud's attitude toward love in this paragraph, "love alone acts as the civilizing factor in the sense that it brings a change from egoism to altruism," we may be dealing with another instance of the fourth Freud.)

8—Hence, on the basis of the previous assumption (narcissism gives way to object love), the hostility characteristic of all human relations and its absence in the group must be due to a special type of libidinal tie.

9—Offers the possibility that identification (as a type of emotional tie which is not directly sexual in aim)—may lead to an understanding of the "tie" in the group. (What then happens to the ambivalence of love and hate in identification?)

CHAPTER SEVEN

1—Defines identification. (See note on identification in *The Ego and the Id,* Chapter III, pars. 5 to 7 where distinction is made between the first identification and the identification which resolves the Oedipal situation.)

2—Describes the concept of the Oedipus complex. (1) Simultaneous identification with one parent and object cathexis of an anaclitic type to the other. (Here he articulates the leaning of the sexual or preservative instincts on objective need—see Chapter VI, par. 7.), (2) Instinctual development makes the coexistence of these two (simultaneous identification and object cathexis) impossible, thus the Oedipal conflict. (Explains the ability of identification to vacillate as the very nature of identification, i.e. ambivalence. This is consistent with identification's being an early libidinal tie and employing mechanisms of the oral stage. Compares this to the primitive's cannibalism. Hence, the Oedipal complex is another example of the individual living through the history of mankind, i.e. through the primitive stage. Will the later identification indicate this ambivalence as well? See the note in Chapter VI par. 9.)

3—Elaborates on the Oedipus complex, i.e. inverted Oedipus.

4—Distinguishes identification from object choice. Identification equals desire to be, i.e. model. Object choice equals desire to have.

5—Interprets neurotic symptoms in terms of two types of identification: one with the loved one and another with the rival. (1) Hysterical—Melancholic—guilt due to identification with mother as rival; (2) Identification with the loved one and hence object choice has regressed to identification. Indicates that the above identifications are only partial.

6—A third identification: with a person who is not a love object, but possible alter-ego, i.e. infectious hysteria. Denies the possibility of sympathy as a cause of the infection by indicating that the phenomenon takes place where no pre-existing sympathy existed but claims that the sympathy is based on the identification. (This may be a clue that the contagion in groups is due to a common identification. He is now offering an analogy to identification between members in a group.)

7—Summarizes the concept of identification and enumerates three types: (1) original emotional tie, (2) regression, (object cathexis to identification), (3) perception of a common quality shared and no object cathexis. The intensity of identification of the third type depends on the importance of the identification. (Thus the tie in the group will be intense in direct proportion to the need that it meets. Here again Freud has combined libidinal need with physical need as in the identification of the "anaclitic" type.)

8—Indicates that the "tie" in the group is an identification of the third type and the common quality is the tie to the leader. (Did he lay ground for this notion with the concept of the general as a father-surrogate?)

9—He will now use the concept of identification in dealing with two instances of psychoses.

10—Interprets homosexuality as the resolution of Oedipus by identification with the mother. (Ego remodeled on the model of its object.) This is an instance of object cathexis being replaced by identification. Brings similar interpretation to case of a child identifying with a lost kitten. (Thus the concept of identification as a subsitute for the object explains: (1) resolution of the sexual phase, (2) homosexuality, (3) behavior in young children, and (4) melancholia, as indicated in the next paragraph.)

11—Interprets melancholia as identification (introjection) with the lost loved object. Thus the criticism in melancholia explained as the ego taking revenge on the introjected object.

12—Melancholia is seen as evidence of a division in the ego, between the ego and the ego ideal. Thus he explains the critical nature of the ego ideal or conscience. The ego ideal is developed by environmental influences. Brings the data of delusion to show that the ego ideal has its origin in parent and superior powers. Indicates that the range of the development of the ego ideal differs among individuals.

13—Defers application of the above interpretation until he examines other relationships of the object to the ego.

CHAPTER EIGHT

1—The folk use of an inclusive term "love" is validated empirically or in reality, i.e. there are many kinds of love.

2 and 3—Begins to enumerate the cases to be included under the concept of love: (1) object cathexis (direct expression of sexual instincts—the goal being direct sexual satisfaction) equals sensual love. (2) Love as tender preservation of the object between periods of sexual expression. (3) Tenderness as originating in the inhibition of the early object cathexis, i.e. resolution of the Oedipus complex. (As in other cases, if tenderness is to be found in adults then it must be traced back to its origin.)

4—Explains the phenomenon of the male who loves one type of woman and who is excited sexually by another type, as failure to merge the renewed pure sexual (at puberty) with the inhibited sexual (tender) of early childhood.

5—Brings to our attention the phenomenon of "over estimation" (which consists of loving the object for its spiritual merits), which takes place when sensual tendencies are repressed, and says this is due to the repression.

6—Labels the above phenomenon "idealization"and explains the tendency as similar to what occurs in object cathexis, i.e. narcissistic libido flows over into the object. Claims that some object choices actually correspond to the unattained ego ideal. (Thus, he will show how, in the group, idealization of the leader occurs and that the tie between the members and the leader is of a libidinal nature.)

7—Claims that "idealization" can get out of bounds to the point that the directly sexual is completely inhibited, the ego becoming increasingly more modest and the object more sublime. (Explains self sacrifice, humility, limitation of narcissism, and self injury as the partial or complete consumption of the ego by the object.)

8—Sexual satisfaction tends to prevent idealization. Therefore, the absence of sexual satisfaction helps idealization. Thus, the object relationship (in the light of no sexual satisfaction) is now similar to that of sublimated devotion to an abstract idea. (Again proof of one type of energy in Freud that is diverted from its main course.) Idealization curtails the operation of criticism in the ego ideal by replacing ideal with the object. (Thus, in the group, the leader will replace the ego ideal.)

9—Offers a possible distinction between identification and infatuation and decides to reformulate the distinction in terms of whether the object replaces the ego or the ego ideal.

10—Compares love to hypnosis. The hypnotist replaces the ego ideal as the object does in love. Claims that reality is clouded since the ego ideal no longer tests reality. (This concept is reformulated in *The Ego and the Id,* Chapter III, par 2, note 2.) Thus no limit on idealization. Distinguishes hypnosis from love on the basis of complete or partial repression of the directly sexual.

11—Identifies hypnosis as a condition between being in love and group mind. Hypnosis is a group of two individuals, thus leader—member relationship is pervasive. It is distinguished from other groups by limits on number of members.

12—Claims that lasting ties between individuals are only possible with the inhibited sexual (since sexual satisfaction reduces attraction). Sexual love itself is temporary unless it is mixed with the tender.

13—Hypnosis is limited as a model with which to understand the libidinal constitution of groups due to several unknowns: paralysis in hypnosis, its relationship to sleep, individual differences in susceptibility—retetion of moral judgments, etc.

14—In the light of the previous analysis Freud offers a formulation for the libidinal constitution of groups. *"A primary group of this kind is a number of individuals who have put one and the same object in place of their ego ideal and have consequently identified themselves with one another in their ego."* In essence Freud has almost returned to his model of the father-surrogate as the ego ideal and the children identifying with each other through the father.

(There is a further indication here of Freud viewing the group as regressive for he says, ". . . those [groups] that have a leader and have not been able by means of too much organization to acquire secondarily the characteristics of an individual . . .")

CHAPTER NINE

1—Asserts that the above formula relies on an interpretation of hypnosis which is itself incomplete.

2—A further limitation, since the emotional tie in the group explains reduction to the level of "group individuals" but is not sufficient to explain such phenomena as the weakened intellect and the lack of emotional restraint, i.e. the characteristics described by Le Bon. These characteristics are indicative of a further regression which is checked in the organized or artificial groups.

3—Further doubts are based on data—lack of courage, pressure of public opinion, etc.—derived from other areas, which indicate especially that suggestion operates among the members as well as from the leader. (Freud thus addresses himself to what Le Bon considered irreducible in terms of his notion of regression.)

4—Addresses himself to Trotter's concept of the herd intsinct to fill in the above lacuna in his theory.

5—Summarizes Trotter: mental phenomena of group life are an expression of the herd instinct. Trotter analogizes to multicellularity in biology and Freud compares this to the tendency of Eros to combine. (Freud refers to this analogy in *Beyond the Pleasure Principle*.) Trotter explains the fear of isolation as a result of the herd instinct.

6 and 7—Continues the summary of Trotter. There are four instincts: (1) self preservation, (2) nutrition, (3) sex and (4) the herd. The herd instinct often competes with the other instincts. He claims that guilt and duty are unique to the gregarious animal. Repression and speech are also the results of the herd instinct.

In distinction to Le Bon (transient groups) and McDougall (stable groups), Trotter studies the most general form of human assemblage.

8—Objects to Trotter for not dealing with the role of the leader (and as a corollary not being able to explain God—the herdsman) and to the concept of a herd instinct that is not reducible.

9—Freud explains his disagreement with Trotter's concept of a herd instinct, interpreting the data Trotter brought to bear differently. He says: (1) Dread in children—related to unfulfilled desires toward mother or other members of the family. (2) No herd behavior seen in children in early life, hence, claims that herd feeling not primary, but comes into play later as a resolution of sibling rivalry, i.e. since you cannot destroy the sibling without endangering yourself—hence you join with him. (3) Explains the desire for justice on the part of man as a means of self protection in the group situation. The transformation of jealousy to group feeling in the nursery and the classroom and the formation of the "fan" club are explained as a substitute for rivalry by a means of common identification. (The concept of justice as elaborated here and in the next paragraph—a reaction formation—is another one of the examples that the fourth Freud would have to reinterpret.)

10—Reformulates the above: group spirit arises from envy. Thus he explains social justice as assurance of the rights of each individual. He explains duty (what Trotter claimed as characteristic of the gregarious animal) and equality as derivative of envy or need for self protection. The development as in other cases is one of starting with pure id (pure narcissism) which is modified by reality. Thus, values are means by which narcissism is handled. Brings the syphilitic's dread of spreading infection and the Biblical story of the judgment of Solomon as cases supporting correctness of his interpretation. (Freud has now interpreted what Trotter believed to be a herd instinct as a reaction formation necessitated by reality, i.e. common need and no possibility for any one individual to be completed satisfied.)

11—Offers the explanation that the transformation from the hostile to the positive is due to common identification with a person outside of the group. (Thus he will have to find this person in the primitive group as well. This will be the burden of the next chapter.)

The identification insures the process of equalization as the leader would love all the members equally. (Thus the purpose for which herd feeling developed is insured by the leader. The herd feeling came into being to protect member from member through the leader, i.e. there is sibling rivalry and the leader must insure the status quo.) Thus, he now claims that Trotter's concept of a group expressing a herd instinct should be corrected to man as a horde animal directed by a leader.

CHAPTER TEN

1—Discusses his development of Darwin's conjecture that the primitive form of human society was a horde ruled over despotically by a powerful male. (The above related to the development of morality, religion, and social organization—see *The Ego and the Id,* Chapter III, par. 22-23.) This he claims had great effect on man's history.

2—Compares the group and the leader to the primal horde and its leader. Explains the regression in the group as due to the regression to primitive mental activity of the sort to be ascribed to the primal horde.

3—Compares the group to the primal horde. This explains how the characteristics of the primal horde can appear in any random crowd. In the light of the above, group psychology must be older than individual psychology and he realizes the need to indicate the point of departure of individual psychology from group psychology, as well as its development. (In the sentence, "Just as primitive man survives potentially in every individual, so the group primal horde may arise once more out of every random collection," we see Freud working with the principle of ontogeny as recapitulation of phylogeny.)

4—Corrects the above statement. Since the leader of the primal horde was not subject to group psychology, then both psychologies were there from the very beginning. The leader possesses freedom of will and judgment due to the absence of libidinal ties —narcissism.

5—Compares the leader of the horde to Nietzsche's superman. The leader is narcissistic and not in love with anyone else for love checks narcissism. (Here Freud indicates that love is a factor in civilizing in the sense that it checks narcissism and permits man's sharing and building with others. Relates this to Chapter VI, par. 7. However, one must note, in the light of the overwhelming strength of narcissism, how limited the concept of love must be. This is elaborated in *Civilization and Its Discontents*).

6 and 7—Explains succession to the leader of the horde and hence the evolution of group psychology to individual psychology. The father (leader of horde) forced the children into sexual abstinence, and thus into emotional ties with him. Successor was permitted sexual expression and thus narcissism (completed sexual act permits narcissism to return—see Chapter VIII, par. 8) could develop and he was not bound by group ties. Postpones the discussion of the relationship of love to character formation to the Postscript. (Thus he analogizes the libidinal or emotional development of men to biological or hereditary development. Changes occur, as we shall see later—Postscript, pars. 7 to 10, on historic occasion at a moment of weakness. The similarity to Lamarckian biology should be noted.)

8—Outlines the development from the primal horde to the present group as: (1) Common persecution and fear in the primal horde evolving to common illusion of love in artificial groups. (2) The totemistic clan, and (3) the family—presupposes father's equal love.

9-12—Further explains hypnosis and suggestion by tracing it back to the primal horde. (1) The uncanny in hypnosis he believes indicates its archaic origin. (2) Compares the power of hypnotism to the source of ancient taboo, i.e. manna. (3) Hypnotist demands complete attention directed only to him. (4) Introduces Ferenczi's distinction of two types of hypnosis, one modeled on the mother and another modeled on the father. (Both, though, demand withdrawing interest from the world.) (5) Compares the above withdrawal to that of sleep. (6) Sleep is where the archaic is to be found and hence the hypnotist awakens a portion of the subject's archaic heritage. This very characteristic is the source of power parents have over children. This is especially so in the case of the father and the only way to react to the father is as a member reacting to the leader of the primal horde, i.e. passive masochism. (Thus he explains submission in the Oedipal situation—note *The Ego and the Id,* Chapter III, par. 17.) Indicates that individuals differ in propensity to revive the archiac, hence, have differing degrees of resistance in hypnotism.

13—Summarizes. Suggestion and group characteristics traced back to the primal horde and the fear of the leader. Recasts above to fit his formula, i.e. primal father is the group ideal that is substituted by the individual to govern his ego. Hypnotism now a group of two with suggestion the result of the erotic tie.

CHAPTER ELEVEN

1 and 2—Summarizes and indicates how his interpretation of group psychology addresses itself to the data of individual psychology as well as the data dealt with in other theories of the group. If the individual is a member of various groups he shares in various group minds, yet possesses degree of independence. Distinguishes organized groups (McDougall) and ephemeral groups (Le Bon). The loss of individuality is most noticed in the ephemeral group. This loss of individuality is due to the substitution of the group's ego ideal for the individual's ego ideal, the leader. (This is another example of a process in operation, i.e. separation of the ego and ego ideal that is aided from without, i.e. strong leader joins up with the weak ego ideal. Similarly, in *The Ego and the Id,* he borrows from the father to repress the Oedipal feelings.)

3—Explicitly states that his theory of group psychology depends on a previous assumption—the distinction of the ego and the ego ideal, hence identification and the possibility of the substitution of something outside of the individual for the ego ideal. (Here again the outside can be introduced into the individual. Entire character formation is then taking the outside into the inside.) Claims that support for separation of the ego and the ego ideal can be brought from the data of pathology. Will now proceed to indicate that just as the ego related to objects outside of it in a certain manner, so the ego ideal will relate to the ego as an object outside of itself.

4—Mental differentiation causes fresh problems in mental functioning, i.e. instability and the possibility of pathology. (The principle of conflict expressed in this instance indicates that every development offers the possibility of a regression and of the system's going out of gear.) He uses the example of birth—from self sufficient narcissism to changing outer world and objects—as a new condition that cannot be endured for long, hence sleep and no stimulation. (So from the very beginning, every movement forward involves a movement backward, i.e. conflict, instability, and the possibility of regression. Hence, you must have a life and death instinct and you can have but limited progress. Is it possible that you thus have the compulsion to repeat on a much larger scale, i.e. a movement forward requires a movement backward?) Claims that this pattern may have been adopted from the outer world, i.e. night and day. (Is he saying that this polarity exists in the cosmos as well, i.e. no day so no stimulation?)

Brings another example: differentiation of ego from the repressed, which must express itself in dreams neurosis, wit and humor.

5—Offers the possibility that similarly the ego and the ego ideals cannot stand a separation for long. He introduces the example of the festival whose purpose he interprets as release sanctioned by law. The festival par excellence would permit the abrogation of the ego ideal which would mean that the ego would now be comfortable with itself.

6—Reformulates his previous statement by interpreting triumph as the ego coinciding with the ego ideal and guilt and inferiority as tension between the ego and the ego ideal, i.e. in terms of how much distance there is between them.

7-9—Analyzes the pathology of the manic depressive cycle in the light of the above. Admits that there is more basis upon which to assume the explanation of the manic part of the cycle and that he interprets the cycle as the instability of the new institution of the ego ideal and hence weak control.

10-12—Admits the tentative nature of his formulation of the manic depressive cycle especially since he has only dealt with limited cases.

13—Summarizes: rebellion of ego against ego ideal found in both temporary and chronic melancholia.

POSTSCRIPT

1-4—Returns to discuss several of the issues alluded to in the investigation. The first of these issues is the distinction between identification of the ego with an object and replacement of the ego ideal by an object as applied to the two groups investigated, the church and the army. In the army the individual identifies with equals, and hence comradeship, and takes the leader as his ego ideal. In the church, on the other hand, a typical distribution of libido in the group situation is supplemented, i.e. identification added to object choice (relationship to leader) and object choice to identification (members of the group).

5—The second issue to be dealt with is the point in history at which the members of the group advance to the level of individual psychology. (He uses the term advanced, hence another instance of where the group is looked upon as regressive, i.e. more primitive.)

6—Traces the development from (1) primal horde with father as leader (source of notion of creator of the universe, God and justice), (2) totemistic community of brothers in gynaecocracy, (3) new male-headed families, a shadow of the old family, many fathers instead of one.

7-10—Offers the possibility that the transition of group to individual psychology took place at this point with the help of the myth. (Does change take place only when the system is weak, as in this case, for otherwise the historic occasion would have little chance?)

11-13—The next issue is the distinction between directly sexual instincts and inhibited sexual instincts. Summarizes childhood sexual experience as prototype of the repression of sexual instincts, i.e. fusion of tender and sexual to separation between them. Therefore, the sexual and the tender can be fused or defused in adulthood.

14—Admits that the above concept of the relationship of the sexual to the tender requires the acceptance of the notion of a repressed unconscious.

15—Brings the data in adult feelings of tenderness, indicating their relatedness to the sexual. This tender feeling is the beginning of sublimation. Repeats a previous distinction between satisfaction of pure sexual and inhibited sexual (tender) instincts and relates them to the permanence of the "ties." Indicates that fusion of above has unlimited possibilities and brings data of movement in adult life from one type of relationship (friendship) to another type of relationship (love) as another indication of the tender arising from the sexual.

16—Explains the development from purely sexual to inhibited sexual as due to inner or outer obstacles to sexual satisfaction, i.e. repression of latency. Attributes the origin of the obstacle to the father of the primal horde.

17—Continues to explain the relationship of the directly sexual instincts to group ties. The directly sexual instincts are unfavorable for group formation—explains group marriages as prior to sexual love.

18—Brings desire for privacy in sexual acts as indication of a correctness of above assertion. Shame and jealousy explained as protection from group demands. The exception of the orgy is explained as complete absence of the fusion of the sexual and the tender and a regression to an earlier state.

19—Correlates the relationship of the directly sexual to group ties (an inverse one and a late development for man) with his notion of libidinal development, explaining that the sexual expression was inhibited between sons, mothers and sisters in the primal family by the institution of totemistic exogamy and thus explains the phylogenetic origin of the separation of the tender and the sexual.

20—In the light of the above assertions he explains the absence of the love relationship between men and women in the group and the groups he has been discussing.

21—Further indicates that when the love relationship becomes predominant (equates the directly sexual with the individuality of man) then the group ties disintegrate. Alludes to compatability of homosexual ties to the group ties. (Note: *The Ego and the Id,* Chapter III, par. 23.)

22—Reformulates the statement of neuroses to include the inhibited sexual as well as the purely sexual, i.e. neurotic would become asocial when he regresses from inhibited sexual to directly sexual and hence he would lose his group ties. Explain ties in mystic sects as offering distorted cures for neuroses.

23—Claims that when the nurotic loosens ties to his own religion, etc., he ". . . thus recapitulates the institutions of humanity in a distorted way," (Freud claims that this proves dominance of the directly sexual, but might this also not be proof for the existence of the ego and the ego ideal in man from the very beginning?)

24-29—Redefines love, hypnosis, group formation and neuroses in the light of the libido theory. Love = fusion of sexual and tender — only room for the ego and the object. Hypnosis is similar to love. Limited to two people. Not directly sexual. Substitution of object for ego ideal. Group = conditions of hypnosis multiplied plus identification of group members one to another. (Relates hypnosis in group formation to phylogenetic development of man.) Hypnosis predisposition. Group: predisposition plus direct survival. Neurosis is based on the double start of libidinal development. Resembles hypnosis in group—a regression. Takes place when (1) advances from sexual to inhibited sexual not complete, (2) conflict between the two instincts, and (3) manifold possibilities.

APPENDIX III

☐

THE PROTOCOL:
THE EGO AND THE ID

CHAPTER ONE

1—Indicates the summary nature of this chapter.

Introduction to Conscious—Unconscious

2—He begins by distinguishing mental life into conscious and unconscious—the basic premise of psychoanalysis. The data requiring this distinction is derived primarily from pathologies.

3—Further justification of this distinction—sufficient to overcome the traditional prejudice against it—may be found also in the phenomena of hypnosis and dreams.

4—The distinction is also operative in ordinary events of forgetting and remembering (the latency of ideas).

Projection of the Unconscious—Conscious

5—He now elaborates the notion of unconscious by appealing to details of pathological phenomena, namely that activities ("effects") are discernible, identical to those produced by ideas but, with no "idea" present to the consciousness of the subject (one property of the unconscious). This is accounted for by positing a counter-force: a *repressing* activity (second property of the unconscious). Evidence for such a force is derived from its presence-absence, i.e. the removal of *resistance* during analysis and the idea comes to consciousness.

6—Thus, a dynamic unconscious (unconscious proper) and a merely latent or descriptively unconscious (preconscious). (Refers to the "repressed" as a prototype of the dynamic un-

214

conscious thus suggesting that there is further content of this unconscious. Uses metaphor "closer" in reference to the latent, thus implying a topography.) Insists on the generic quality of the content of the conscious and unconscious.

7—Summary of the above but with emphasis on only one unconscious; distinguishes a dynamic unconscious (repressed) from a descriptive unconscious (pre-conscious). In a footnote Freud addresses himself to a criticism (of the distinction conscious-unconscious) which interprets the data as various gradations of consciousness. He attacks this interpretation on three grounds: (1) practical (analogizes to light), (2) dilutes the term conscious, (3) does not explain the dynamic character of the unconscious.

The Ego

8—Now a new set of distinctions, based not on state of content (conscious, unconscious), but upon (a) degree of organization and (b) function. Ego: organized controller of approaches to motility. Function, stated in terms of movement from inside to out, but not vice-versa. Emphasis on overt action of the organism—none on the "inner life" of the ego (point re Plato-thought, ideas, etc.). Mediating function of the ego implies an independent source of originating motives. What is it? Ego further subdivided into conscious and unconscious parts: latter the source of repression (see Par. 6 above). Repeated description of "resistance." This distinction (ego vs. repressed) rather than conscious—unconscious to be the central consideration re neurosis, etc.

9—Summary: Three kinds of unconscious: (1) latent, (2) repressed, (3) repressor in the ego.

CHAPTER TWO
Introduction

1—Now, on the basis of his new set of distinctions, he is to develop further the concept of the ego.

2—He will develop the concept of the ego by investigating the relationship of the unconscious to the conscious, i.e. how the repressed becomes conscious. (In doing this he will describe the history of the ego which is both conscious and unconscious and has control over the relationships between the two.)

The Conscious Perceptual System

3—Assigns consciousness as a function to a system nearest the external world. *(See Beyond the Pleasure Principle, Chapter IV, pars. 1 to 8)*. Thus, he now introduces a notion of a topography so as to explain the mental apparatus (see Chapter I, par. 6.). The principle for this topography is function. Asserts that the position assigned to consciousness in this topography actually corresponds to the anatomical facts. (Freud refers here to *Beyond the Pleasure Principle*.)

4—Enumerates the content of consciousness: (1) sense perception—source outside of man, (2) feeling—source inside man, (3) thought processes—sources inside man. Will now investigate the relationship of thought processes to consciousness, for they were not conscious from the start. (Thus he begins the investigation mentioned above in paragraph two.) Defines thought processes as displacements of mental energy in the interior of the mental apparatus on their way to action. He asks whether thought processes advance to consciousness or vice-versa and decides that neither occurs. (1) Energy—is it of one kind or of different kinds? What does he mean by displacement? (2) Whatever occurs to energy takes place in the interior. (3) Energy actually strives toward action; the problem will occur in blockage. (4) What is thought itself?

5—Distinguishes preconscious and unconscious idea (thought) on the basis of material it is worked out on, and thus reformulates the question of how something becomes conscious to how something becomes preconscious, i.e. comes into contact with verbal images. (This is a clue to therapeutic method—the unconscious must be connected to verbal images.)

6—Verbal images are defined as memory residues. (Memory seems to be defined as traces of perception left on a kind of tape.) This is consistent with Freud's notion that all human actions, thoughts, and feelings have meaning (slips of tongue, etc.) but we must discover the meaning. Hence, anything preconscious that is to become conscious must be linked to external perceptions through memory traces. (Reaffirms the notion alluded to in Chapter I, par. 8—de-emphasis of the inner life of the ego.)

7—Assigns a location on the topography to memory residues—adjacent to perception-consciousness. (Example of topography in relation to function, i.e. memory must be close to consciousness.) Distinguishes hallucination and perception from memory on the basis of the cathexis (in memory, cathexis tied only to mnemic system, while in hallucination, cathexis spreads to entire *Pcpt.* system.)

8—Claims that verbal residues are derived from auditory perceptions and that visual and sensory motor images of words are of secondary importance.

9—Qualifies the above by indicating the importance of optical memory residues and the fact that thought can become conscious through visual residues as well, but claims that this is more characteristic of dreams and the unconscious and cannot express relationships which are the essence of thought. Freud distinguishes here between people in relation to things (visual) and people in relation to words (thoughts—relationships between things). (We have here a recognition of the importance of an intellectual component and an anticipation of Sullivan which is not developed. Visual thinking is close to the processes of the unconscious and is older than thinking via symbols. We see here that in thought as well as in every other area, sexual life, family life, etc., the older or more primitive method to be found in the unconscious. The "unconscious" embodies Freud's notion of determinism: that all of man's experience as individual and as member of the race is effective in the present.) (See *Civilization and Its Discontents,* Chapter I, pars. 4 and 5.)

10—By indicating that thought processes that are unconscious become conscious by first becoming preconscious (by coming into contact with verbal images), he has answered his original question —how the repressed becomes conscious—by analysis forging preconscious connecting links (see note par. 5).

The Ego and Internal Perception

11—Now he is going to investigate the relationships of the ego to internal perception.

12—Describes internal perceptions (pleasure, pain) as (1) arising in the deepest strata of the mental apparatus, (2) more fundamental than external perceptions (again Freud's weighting on the inside), (3) not dependent on consciousness (can come into being when consciousness is clouded), (4) of great economic significance, (5) possibly contradictory.

13—Distinguishes pleasure and pain by impelling quality toward change (pain impelling) or discharge. (Pain, heightening of energy cathexis; pleasure, a lowering.) Describing pleasure-pain as an undetermined quantitative and qualitative element in the mind. Then asks whether pleasure and pain, i.e. feeling, must be transmitted to the perceptual system to become conscious.

14—Claims that clinical experience indicates that pleasure-pain, as such, must be transmitted to the perceptual system. Physical need and physical "pain" (which is intermediate between external and internal perception) can also remain unconscious and act as a compulsion. Hence, he speaks of unconscious feelings as well as unconscious ideas. Distinguishes feelings from ideas on the basis of no preconscious in feelings. (What is perception?)

15—Repeat of paragraph six. Verbal images make thought processes into perceptions.

The Ego and the Id

16—Now that he has clarified perception (external and internal) and its relationship to the superficial system perception -consciousness, he is ready to destcribe and define the ego. He assigns to the ego a position on the topography. Its nucleus is the system perception and it embraces the preconscious. Now he is left with that part of the ego that is unconscious.

17—Handles the unconscious in the ego by correlating his idea with Groddeck's and by dividing the mind into an ego and an id. Ego is that part of the entity which starts off with the system perception, and begins by being preconscious. Id equals the entity into which the ego extends and behaves as though it were unconscious.

18—Further elaborates this division of the mind. The id equals the unknown unconscious and upon its surface rests the ego. Draws an analogy to the germinal layer in the ovum. Ego not separated from the id, lower part merges into it. (Thus he handles the unconscious part of the ego.)

19—Now explains the repressed as part of the id cut off from the ego by the resistance of repression. The ego is thus related to the repressed through the id. Handles ego's great relationship to the verbal by inserting auditory lobe in the diagram of the topography.

20—The ego then is the part of the id that has been modified by the external world. (Man is an acting animal and the ego sets the condition for his action or the discharge of impulse.) Hence, it will be the repressor (Chapter I, par. 8.) He indicates the functions of the ego: (1) brings the influence of the external world to bear, (2) endeavors to substitute the reality principle for the pleasure principle (but the primacy of the pleasure principle, of the inside, is never to be superseded for it is first and basic.) Compares and contrasts the ego and the id: (1) perception is the starting point for the ego—instinct for the id, (2) ego represents reason —id the passions.

21—The ego controls approaches to motility. Uses analogy of horse to rider indicating that the only source of strength is the id, hence the ego often is dependent on the id, even for direction. (Here we have another indication of the supremacy of the biological in man and how man's rationality must always be limited; the ego arises only because the acting animal has difficulty.)

22—Claims that the ego developed not only by the influence of the perceptual system (reality as it modifies the pleasure principle) , but that the body (body image) has great influence on the development of the ego.

23—Ego as body ego, i.e. mental projection of the surface of the body.

24. Denies the identity of "higher" faculties and the intellect with consciousness, e.g. intellectual operations in the preconscious and in sleep.

25—Further proof of the above—(1) self criticism and conscience are found to be unconscious in analytic work, (2) previous example of resistance. Hence, ego itself only a body ego between outside and inside.

CHAPTER THREE

1 and 2—The division of mental life into an ego and an id is not sufficient. There is a third part, the super-ego. (The super-ego was previously introduced in *Group Psychology and the Analysis of the Ego.*) The super-ego is less involved in the testing of reality.

3—Brings interpretation of clinical material (melancholia) to bear—a fundamental process exists consisting of replacement of an object cathexis by an identification. Now claims this is common to the formation of character (character—the result of many identifications), hence super-ego development.

The Development of the Super-Ego

4—Will now trace character development. (Freud, accepting the principle of biogenesis, will have to demonstrate the relationship of adult man to his own history and to his pre-history. He decides to organize the relationship of present to past in terms of stages and epochs.) Stage one—object cathexis and identification very similar in early years because little difference between the ego and the id. Later object cathexis—need and limited to id; while developing ego becomes *aware* of it. The ego (weak, as it is young and developing) either acquiesces to the demands of the id or may sometimes repress them.

5—Freud interprets the phenomena which accompany the giving up of a sexual object (modification of the ego) as similar to the process in melancholia, i.e. reinstatement of the object into the ego (identification). Offers the possible explanation of the above—namely, difficulty of giving up object requires regression to the mechanism of the oral phase (because each step forward is difficult, regressions are quite common and necessary). (See *Group Psychology and the Analysis of the Ego* and *Civilization and Its Discontents.*) In the footnote on page twenty-nine, Freud relates this to the belief of certain primitive people that attributes of animals which are assimilated as nourishment survive as part of the character of persons who eat them. Maintains that identification (introjection of the object into the ego) *may be* the only way the id can give up objects. (Note the extent to which Freud assumes dominance of the id.) Freud explains the early emotional phenomena and distinguishes two types of emotional relationship: object cathexis and identification. He now must explain the phenomena of restraint. This he does by developing another notion of identification, i.e. introjection. This is inherent in man in an early stage in the mechanism of the oral stage.

6—Indicates that by identification ego can in a very limited sense gain control of a part of the id, (1) life is a constant struggle for control; almost no equilibrium, (2) id still the ruler, for in a sense in gaining control over the id, the ego is being modified, i.e. assumes the role of the object.

7—Reformulates the concept of identification in terms of libido, i.e. object libido is transformed to narcissistic libido. This requires a desexualization—a type of sublimation. (Thus Freud indicates that there is only one type of energy, see note, Chapter II, par. 4—libidinal energy which is of a directly sexual nature. This energy must be transformed to be available for other activities: intellectual and artistic endeavors, group ties, etc. Offers the hypothesis that all sublimitation takes place by the ego changing id libido into narcissistic libido. (The id libido is the cause of narcissism, while the ego libido is the cause of secondary narcissism. Will later relate this to his instinct theory.)

8—Digression by Freud to indicate potential for pathology in ego identification when resistances exist between identifications. Explains an aspect of "normal" conflict as due to numerous and contradictory identifications. (Again we see relationship of normal to abnormal as a continuum.)

9—Reminds us of the importance of the first identification and its relationship to the ego ideal. (The effect of man's early life on the present is seen in Freud's emphasis on the primitive period in the history of mankind, and in the case of the individual, in the importance attributed to childhood, as in this case when the first identification stands out as more important than all others.) First identification is to the father. (This I take to mean that every human has this predisposition to identify with his father. The notion of prehistory shows a Lamarckian influence.) This first identification is unique since it is immediate *de novo*, not a result of prior object cathexis.

10—Will now describe the development of the ego ideal, of the Oedipus complex, and the constitutional bisexuality of man. (What precisely caused Freud to introduce the notion of bisexuality?)

11 and 12—Freud sees four stages in the development of the Oedipus complex. (1) An object cathexis to the mother (on the anaclitic model). (2) An identification with the father. (3) Conflict —as the sexual becomes more intense. The father is seen as an obstacle and thus we have the simple Oedipus complex. The relationship to the father is ambivalent (ambivalence inherited), therefore you have the Oedipus complex. (4) Dissolution of the Oedipus complex requires giving up the object cathexis to the mother, and is replaced either by (a) identification with the mother, (b) identification with the father (permits affectionate realtionship to be continued with the mother and consolidates masculinity in boys.) The same is true for girls, though indentification may be taking place to the mother for the first time. (How does Freud explain the identification in girls taking place for the first time at this late stage?)

13 and 14—Whether (a) or (b) above takes place, (a) is more in line with the common notion of identification, i.e. incorporation of the lost object depends on the strength of the feminine or masculine disposition. This is the first way in which bisexuality plays a role. The second way is observed in the more complete Oedipus complex in the boy: both identification with the father and object cathexis to the mother, while behaving like a girl as well, with an object cathexis to the father and hostility to the mother. (As indicated previously, no identification for the girl at first.)

15—Experience with neurotics justifies the assumption of the existence of a complete Oedipus complex, i.e. normal positive and inverted negative. The dissolution of a complete Oedipus complex involves the four trends combining into a father and mother identification. (Father identification permits object relation to mother and identification to father as a result of the negative complex and vice-versa for mother identification.) The strength of the identification depends on the sexual predisposition. Entertains the hypothesis of bisexuality being the cause of ambivalence.

16—Summarizes: the outcome of Oedipus is (1) end of the sexual phase, i.e. beginning of latency, (2) the forming of a precipitate in the ego which involves a combination of the first identification plus the second identification (introjection). This precipitate is different from other previous and future precipitates (in the sense that it is not incorporated into the ego as the other constituents are incorporated.)

17—But super-ego contains reaction formations as well as identifications. This is due to repression of the Oedipus complex, i.e. reaction formation necessary as reenforcement of repression. This is the origin of rebellion. Explains the intensity of repressions as the cause for the dominance of the super-ego over the ego. (Later he will explain where the ego ideal gets the power to dominate the ego.)

18—Summarizes the development of the super-ego. (1) biological (lengthy period of dependence), (2) historical (Oedipus complex). Offers the possibility that the twofold onset of sexual life was necessitated by the glacial epoch. The super-ego perpetuates the existence of the factors to which it owes its origin, i.e. the influence of parents, the race, etc. (Lamarckism).

19—Freud here attacks the notion of a higher and moral-spiritual side of human nature. He indicates that what has been commonly considered higher in man is nothing more than the fear of external authority (parents) that the child incorporates into himself. "Very true we can say, and here we have that higher nature, in this ego ideal or super-ego, the representative of our relation to our parents. When we were little children we knew these higher natures, we admired them and feared them; and later we took them into ourselves." (Values are then means for the id.)

20—Indicates the closeness of the ego ideal to the id. As heir to Oedipus it is the expression of the libido; by setting up the ego ideal the ego further subjugates itself to the id (as is indicated in paragraph 6 whereby identification, the ego both gains control and subjugates itself to the id). The conflict between the ego ideal and the id reflects the contrast of external and internal, the real and the mental.

21—Explains the phylogenetic endowment of individuals as coming through the id to the ego via the ego ideal. He closely connects the "lower" and the "higher" in man. (Here again he negates any separate area of the "higher".) Discourages attempt to introduce super-ego on the topography. (Does introduce it later in the *New Introductory Lectures.*)

22—Indicates how the ego ideal will handle the common notion of that which is "higher" in man: (1) religion = longing for father, (2) censorship and morality = sense of worthlessness, (3) submission to authority, (4) guilt = conscience versus behavior, (5) social feeling = identification with those with similar ego ideal. (Origin of xenophobia, see Bettelheim and Janowitz on anti-semitism.)

23—Traces its development to an undifferentiated beginning; the primeval murder and the band of brothers. The phylogenetic acquisition developed by men and transmitted by inheritance to women (see *Totem and Taboo*). Compares social feeling experienced by man today with that experienced in his early history and brings data of homosexuality to bear. (See *Group Psychology*).

24—Asks whether "the higher" is acquired by the ego or the id. (Theory needs to explain origins even in terms of the human race as a whole.)

25—Postulates the ego and the id (internal vs. external) as characteristic of more than just human conflict (even more simple forms of life.) Super-ego—from experience that leads to totemism. Answers the above problem by claiming that the ego and the id are very close and that predisposition for religion transmitted by the id which has vestige of previous egos. Hence when the super-ego develops it may be reviving images of previous egos. (Freud shows Lamarckian influence here as well, "The experiences of the ego seem at first to be lost for inheritance; but, when they have been repeated often enough and with sufficient strength in many individuals in successive generations, they transform themselves, so to say, into experiences of the id, the impressions of which are preserved by heredity.")

26—Summarizes and reviews closeness of super-ego to id and hence super-ego as a repressor—that part of the ego that is unconscious. (Thus, the distinction between "higher" and "lower" in man is in a sense collapsed for the very highest situation is in intimate contact with the very lowest in man.) Thus the super-ego can control (via reaction formation of the unresolved Oedipus complex) the earlier conflicts of the ego and id.

CHAPTER FOUR

1—Summarizes and indicates that though the starting point for the ego is perception and the starting point for the id is instinct, the ego is also affected by the instincts, since it is only a specially modified part of the id.

2—Reviews life and death instincts (death conservative): (1) Eros —sexual, the sublimated, and self preservative (which he assigns to the ego), (2) death—purpose to lead organic back to inorganic (only sees a representative of this instinct—sadism). Admits that they differ in their accessibility to study. Life at its very outset then is a conflict and compromise between two trends. He claims that the origin of life would remain a cosmological problem, the purpose and goal of life would be answered dualistically.

3—Describes instincts as being active in every particle of living substance, (in unequal portions) thus Eros may be thought of as a substance. As with physiological particles each of the instincts will be associated with the processes of anabolism and catabolism. (Note the biological tendency in Freud here.)

4—Assumes that instincts fuse and mingle with each other— fusion would make it possible for the death instinct to be neutralized and to be diverted through musculature. (If you postulate a death instinct at the very beginning, it, like the id, must be neutralized but it can never be fully neutralized and therefore destruction must always occur.) In addition, death must be diverted outward, too, as destructiveness.

5—Notion of a fusion, then the counter notion of defusion. (See *Civilization and Its Discontents.*) Gives example of fusion (sadistic component of the sexual), and of defusion. Death habitually in the service of Eros. Reinterprets clinical data in the light of these concepts. The epileptic fit, the obsessional neurosis, and regression are examples of defusion and the movement from stage to stage would be an example of fusion and the accession of the erotic. (By fusion there always is neutralization of the death instinct.) Offers the possibility that ambivalence may also be a case of defusion, though it is more likely that it is a case of the incomplete fusion. With the notion of fusion and defusion, Freud explains the power behind development and regression.

6—Now he is going to relate the parts of the psyche, the instincts and the pleasure principle. Admits difference in reliability of the concepts to be inter-related, the distinction between the instincts being relatively unsubstantiated.

7-11—Freud introduces a thought experiment to test the instinct differentiation. The problem he poses is that of ambivalence (shifting of hate to love and vice-versa) and he considers two possibilities: hate and love are two manifestations of one instinct or they are the representative of two instincts. He does not consider cases where (1) succession of love to hate due to external reasons, (2) love has not as yet become manifest; rather he considers the data from paranoia, homosexuality and desexualized social feeling (all of which manifest a change from love to hate). Freud decides to solve his problem by introducing a new assumption—movable energy. With this assumption he claims that the ambivalent attitude present from the beginning shifts from love to hate by means of a shifting of the cathexis (energy) withdrawn from the erotic energy and used to supplement the hostile energy. Thus Freud claims it is not different manifestations of one instinct, but two instincts that gain mastery, depending on a neutral energy that shifts the cathexis from one instinct to the other.

12—The only evidence Freud brings to justify this assumption (movable energy) is the data that point to the fact that component instincts communicate with each other via energy exchange, i.e. reinforcement, substitution, etc.

13—Now assumes that this movable energy is desexualized—Eros employed in the service of the pleasure principle. (How can desexualized libido exist in the id?) It is to be discharged (pleasure-avoidance of pain). The path of discharge is unimportant. This neutral energy would help explain (1) transference in analysis, (2) neurotic revenge and (3) the indifference in erotic cathexis. The indifference of path of discharge is supported by what is observed in dream work (there it was a looseness in displacements of the primary process). The ego though, he claims, is more careful in its choice and is choosing a path of discharge (more careful but still not really careful, for it is a product of the id). (Discharge or the pleasure principle must rule. This may explain how Freud could develop the notion of identification and of an Oedipal complex—since pleasure must win, i.e. you must have gratification. Therefore, if the object cathected is not possessed, then identification; if there is an attraction to the mother, then it must be gratified and hence the Oedipus complex and identification.)

14—Equates desexualized energy with sublimated energy. The intellectual processes are an example of sublimated energy. Note intellectual activity here is a death activity.

15—Desexualization is a function of the ego similar to giving up object cathexis by identification. Thus the ego is working in opposition to Eros and placing itself at the service of the opposing instinctual trend. (Here we have another example of how easy it is to tip the balance and develop pathology.)

16 and 17—Summarizes libido development. Originally libido resides in the id and it is sent out into an erotic object cathexis. As the ego develops, it attempts to get hold of object libido and transfers itself into a love object of the id. Thus, he distinguishes primary narcissism of the id and secondary narcissism of the ego. (Admits again that he has little evidence for the death instinct, but since he must be dualistic [conflict] then he must postulate death.)

18—Summarizes; relates the parts of the psyche to the two classes of instincts. The pleasure principle guides the id in its struggle with libido. (Representatives of Eros [libido] which constantly introduce tensions. Without these tensions life would soon terminate in death.) (a) By gratification of sexual need, especially through intercourse. He describes the discharge in intercourse as "sexual substances which are saturated vehicles, so to speak, of the erotic tensions." Compares sexual act to the operation of soma and germ plasm (thus he compares higher and lower forms of life.) Explains the death of some lower forms of life after reproduction and the condition following complete sexual satisfaction as Eros being spent and therefore the death instinct now has a free hand. (b) The ego, through sublimation, assists the id in mastering the libido.

CHAPTER FIVE

1-3—Reviews the development of the super-ego and its special position in relationship to the ego; (a) first identification, (b) heir to the Oedipus complex. The super-ego is not very amenable to change and throughout life it rules the ego (as father ruled the child). (Values are not chosen for rational reasons, but as means to deal with the id.) Being a derivative of the id it contains the phylogenetic endowment of the individual and is in close touch with the id.

4—Will now reinterpret clinical data in the light of the framework he has developed.

5—Describes patient who exhibits negative therapeutic reaction.

6—Discounts several possible explanations for the above: need for illness, defiant attitude to the physician, fixation, various kinds of advantages derived from the illness.

7—Interprets the sickness as due to an unconscious sense of guilt.

8—Claims that the unconscious sense of guilt plays a role in all severe neurosis and therefore he now examines guilt per se.

9—Explains "normal" conscience—guilt as tension between the ego and the ego ideal. Relates feelings of inferiority to guilt. Melancholia and obsessional neuroses are enumerated as instances of conscious guilt.

10—Explains certain types of obsessional neuroses as conscious guilt that the ego does not accept—the super-ego being influenced by the repressed (and here we have another example of the super-ego in closer contact with the id).

11—Distinguishes melancholia from obsessional neuroses in terms of whether the ego acquiesces or rebels against the guilt feelings. Explains the distinction in terms of whether the criticized impulse has become part of the ego.

12—Admits that he must explain why guilt is so intense in these cases, but turns at this point to examine cases of an unconscious sense of guilt.

13—Hysteria is commonest form of expression of unconscious guilt. The ego has repressed the guilt, (though the ego usually represses at the behest of the super-ego, here it represses the sense of guilt.) Are there two repressors in the ego? The super-ego and something else? This and the material in paragraph 24 may be the basis for what psychologists call ego-psychology. It is important to note that this only indicates a role for the ego in curbing the id; it does not at all imply controlling the id (see paragraph 23). Distinguishes hysteria from obsessional neuroses.

14—Offers the hypothesis that a great part of guilt must normally remain unconscious (since the origin of the conscience is closely connected to the Oedipus).

15—Claims that unconscious guilt can be the cause of crimes. (The guilt is able to fasten itself to something.)

16—The above cases he uses as data for the independence of the super-ego, and its closeness to the id. The super-ego is derived from the auditory perceptions as is the case for the rest of the ego. Distinguishes the super-ego from the ego as to cathected energy —ego from the external, super-ego from the id.

17—Turns to the question: "How is it that the super-ego manifests itself essentially as a sense of guilt (or rather, as criticism—for the sense of guilt is the perception in the ego answering to this criticism) and moreover develops such extraordinary harshness and severity towards the ego?" Explains melancholia as super-ego plus sadism, i.e. the death instinct. This would drive the person to death were it not for the reversion to manias.

18—Accounts for differences between obsession and melancholia in terms of the tendency to suicide. This, he explains, is due in the case of obsession to the object being retained and regression to the pre-genital where love impulses can be transformed into impulses of aggression.

19—Death instinct can be rendered partially harmless either by (a) being fused with the erotic, (b) directed to the external world (musculature) (but part of the death instincts continue to operate). Why then (in the light of the above possibilities) is its gathering place in melancholia the super-ego?

20—Digresses to relate the parts of the psyche to morality (defines morality as the control and restriction of instincts). Claims that the more the id is checked, the more tyrannical the super-ego. (The id can be limited but not ruled. If it is checked to too great an extent it will express itself by other more devious means.) Claims that morality has a harsh restraining quality and that this is the origin of the concept of the inexorable higher being who metes out punishment.

21—Assumes that sublimation unbinds the death instinct from fusion with Eros. (Hence, again limitation in terms of controlling and id—too much sublimation and you have pathology.) Thus harshness of the ego ideal and its dictorial "Thou Shalt."

22—Answers the question in paragraph nineteen (ego having gained possession of libido is punished by super-ego through aggressiveness) and explains that in all of the cases he has been discussing, the harshness of the super-ego is due to instinctual defusion.

23-25—Now redefines the role of the ego. (1) Organizes process in the mind and tests reality. (2) Controls (by thinking) discharge (greatly limited here). Freud again explicitly states here the ultimate limitation of the ego. This last power is, to be sure, a question more of form than of fact; in the matter of action the ego's position is like that of a constitutional monarch, without whose sanction no law can be passed but who hesitates long before imposing his veto on any measure put forward by Parliament." (3) Enriched from without and within (by gaining libido from the id). (4) Through the super-ego draws upon past experience (heritage). (5) Two ways that the id penetrates into the ego (a) direct, (b) through the ego ideal. (6) The ego first perceives and then controls instincts. (Much of the control of the id is taken over by the ego ideal.) The purpose of psychoanalysis is to enable the ego to further conquer the id. (This is difficult to understand and seems to be an instance of the fourth Freud). (7) The ego owes service to three masters and hence is open to three dangers: (a) The external world, (b) the libido of the id, and

(c) the super-ego. Therefore, it is menaced by three types of anxiety. (8) The ego is a mediator. It attempts to get the id to comply with the world and accommodate the world to the id (by muscular activity). It is not only an ally but a submissive slave to the id. (9) The ego's attitude to the two classes of instinct is: (a) When it identifies and sublimates, it releases the death instinct. (b) To save itself, it floods itself with Eros.

26—Always open to dangers unleashed by defusion of sublimation. (Constant possibility of upsetting the relationship between the parts and the instincts.)

27—Examines the relationship of the ego to the super-ego. (The very title of this chapter indicates that this cannot be an ego psychology.)

28—The ego is the abode of anxiety. Handles danger first by withdrawing from anxiety and then by protective cathexis—phobias. Introduces the question of what the ego fears. All analysis is able to say is that it obeys the pleasure-principle and offers the hypothesis that the fear of the super-ego is a derivative of castration fears.

29—Denies that all fear is ultimately fear of death. Distinguishes fears: (1) fear of death, (2) objective anxiety, (3) neurotic or libidinal anxiety. Admits the difficulty of explaining death psychoanalytically for it "is an abstract concept with a negative content for which no unconscious correlative can be found." Offers a possibility of relinquishing narcissistic libidinal cathexis (difficult to lose as in any object). Involves an interplay between the ego and the super-ego.

30—Examines fear of death and distinguishes such fear as due to objective reality from that of melancholia.

31—Explain melancholia (neurotic fears as ego giving in to persecuting super-ego). He postulates living as requiring love and thus the living ego requires love from the super-ego (narcissism); if no love, than death. The super-ego is again similar to the father (protection) and therefore the notion of providence or destiny. Hence, he explains objective fear of reality, namely, a fear of being deserted by forces that normally protect. Explains birth and infantile anxiety similarly.

32—Relates the fear of death to castration fears and offers the possibility that ordinary neurotic anxiety may be reenforced by fears of castration and death.

33—The id is then seen as the abode for the instincts and their struggle under the rule of the pleasure principle. It has no means of showing the ego love or hate. It has no unity (organization) or will. (Man is seen as a step forward from previous biological forms. The id is the starting point and therefore the most basic point. The ego and its subdivision, the super-ego, are what distinguishes men, but super-ego is a newly won, shaky, and limited structure.)

APPENDIX IV

☐

THE PROTOCOL: CIVILIZATION AND ITS DISCONTENTS

CHAPTER ONE

1 and 2—Freud introduces the view that religion has its origin in the "oceanic" feeling which all men experience.

3—Denies its universality and turns to its ideational content on "methodological" grounds. Doubts that it is properly interpreted by those who experience it and whether it is the origin of the need for religion. (Again we see how Freud will move back to the sources or instincts, as he says in the next paragraph—to approach the problem genetically. This volume, then, will be an application of his theory of the psyche to another area.)

4—Does not admit the possibility of a direct feeling which immediately expresses man's connection to the outside world. (Of necessity, the only original and direct feelings can be in the pleasure-pain series.) Compares oceanic feeling with states of shifting ego boundaries: ego in its relationship to the id, the ego of people in love, and the ego's relationships to the outer world in certain types of pathology, to support his assumption that the notion of an immediate, intelligible primary feeling or entity may be misleading.

5—Reviews the development of the ego from inability to distinguish itself from the external world, to rule by the pure pleasure principle to pleasure plus the reality principle and indicates that earlier feelings and notions may coexist with present feelings (see *The Ego and the Id* and *Group Psychology and the Analysis of the Ego*), and thus the oceanic feeling, believes to be primary, would be a vestige of a primitive or infantile state.

6-9—Bolsters the above (original feelings coexist with later feeling) by appealing to his conclusion that all memories survive. In a limited sense the above is demonstrated in biological evolution. Also in history—archaelogical remains of Rome through the ages.

10—Qualifies the above by the condition that the brain remain intact.

11—Points out that this marvelous conservation is purely mental; is not the case for the developing body. (Here we have an instance where Freud cuts loose from the biological.)

12—Reformulates his assertion that in most cases in the mind the past survives along side the present. (See *The Ego and the Id,* where Freud describes the mind as though it were a tape.)

13—Hence, oceanic feeling may exist in many people but is to be related to early stages in ego feeling. (Thus it would be infantile and illusory as claimed in the next paragraph.) The next problem is what claim this feeling has to be regarded as the source for the need of religion.

14—The oceanic feeling, though related to the religious feeling, is not its primary source. Feeling possesses energy when it expresses a strong need. Freud sees the source of need for religion as the child's feeling of helplessness and the longing for a father (later the fear of a superior power or fate). Thus the oceanic would be a later stage derived from the child's feeling of helplessness.

15—Relates oceanic feeling to later stage in individual development, i.e. a way in which the ego handles the threatening external world. (See *The Future of an Illusion.)*

CHAPTER TWO

1 and 2—Summarizes the manner in which religion was dealt with in *The Future of an Illusion* (the religion of the ordinary man—infantile and unrealistic) where it is indicated that man imagines Providence as a greatly exalted father.

3—Enumerates the categories of escape used by man to make life more palatable (diversions, substitute gratifications, intoxications). (Another indication of Freud's notion that all activities can ultimately be traced to the id. All reactions, including work, science and art then become means for satisfying id needs.) Will now relate religion to the above.

4—Identifies the central religious question as: What is the purpose of human life?

5—Freud reformulates the above question (which he claims to be both unanswerable and presumptuous) to "What men themselves show by their behaviour to be the purpose and intention of their lives." The answer, he feels is "happiness" (pleasure or avoidance of pain).

6—Reviews his assumption of the supremacy of the pleasure principle. Defines happiness (in terms of pleasure) as the satisfaction (most often instantaneous) of pent up needs. Thus pleasure itself is of a transitory nature. Indeed sustainment of "pleasure" means diminution of pleasure (see *Beyond the Pleasure Principle,* Chapter VII). Thus Freud sees man's potential for happiness as limited *constitutionally.* In addition, life abounds in suffering (he lists three sources: (a) our own body, (b) anxiety and pain from the outer world, (c) human relations—probably the most painful of all).

7-9—Since reality forces postponement and, in some cases, abandonment of pleasure, man throughout history has recommended different ways (philosophies, religions) to gain pleasure and avoid suffering. Reviews various approaches: (a) unbridled gratification, (b) isolation, (c) power of cooperation, (d) science, (e) intoxication, (f) curbing or influencing the needs of man, i.e. his psyche, by the higher mental apparatus. (This produces a feeble experience of pleasure.)

10—Another method of handling reality is through libido displacement (sublimation is the outstanding example). Thus, expression is made possible despite circumstance. Compares the satisfaction of the artist and the scientist to the direct instinctual satisfaction as being "higher and finer" but also as tempered and diffused. ("It does not overwhelm us physically"—pleasure and happiness are biological-physical.) Indicates limitation of this way of life as well, i.e. limited to only a few and does not protect one from fate.

11—Similar to the above is fantasy of which art is the chief example—similar to a mild narcotic.

12—Another method of substituting something for reality is delusion. Religion is explained as a mass delusion. (What is reality for Freud?)

13—Admits incompleteness of his list of ways of handling reality. Introduces another method—love—which he claims comes closer to positive pleasure than any other method. Its great risk, however, is that the love object may be lost.

14—Elaborates on the pursuit of beauty as a source of happiness. Admits several problems that psychonalysis cannot answer, e.g. the nature and origin of beauty, but it seems that beauty is derived from the sexual realm via inhibited aim.

15—Summarizes. Pleasure is not easily attainable (either in its positive or negative form). In the final analysis, happiness is a problem of economics of the libido, unique to each individual. There are many variables that affect the individual: (a) the way the external world relates to him, (b) the individual's mental constitution, (c) the individual's instinctual constitution. Introduces another way of dealing with the tasks of living—neuroses and psychoses.

16—Religion promulgates the doctrine that happiness is to be achieved in the same way for all by inducing a mass delusion (an enforced infantilism).

CHAPTER THREE

1—Reiterates the three sources of human suffering and indicates that though they can never be eradicated they can be diminished. Offers the possibility that the third source (social) of suffering is inconquerable due to our mental constitution. (Is he thus indicating that instinctual life itself makes happiness in this area impossible?)

2—Presents the paradox resulting from the point of view which is hostile to civilization—regarding it (civilization) as the source of suffering when it has been through civilization that the first two sources of suffering have been diminished.

3—Traces the above point of view historically to two sources: (a) contact with primitive societies (they seemed to live simple, happy lives); (b) analysis or understanding of the neuroses (cultural ideals cause great privation).

4 and 5—Presents the argument that technological advance has not been accompanied by an increase in happiness and indicates that it is difficult to ascertain whether man is happier today than in an earlier period. (Thus Freud opens the possibility for evaluating various cultures in terms of happiness.)

6—Will now analyze culture in relationship to "happiness." Defines culture ". . . the whole sum of the achievements and the regulations which distinguish our lives from those of our animal ancestors and which serve two purposes—namely to protect men against nature and to adjust their mutual relations." Will proceed by listing the features of culture as mainfest in human communities.

7 and 8—1. Protection and dominion over nature (by producing tools, man improves on his own organs). Through science man has achieved the very role he previously attributed to the gods. (Freud alludes here to the fairy tale where man attributes ideals to a god. In *Group Psychology,* he speaks of the myth as giving man the strength to move forward.) Despite the scientific advance man remains in a state of unhappiness.

9—2. Cultivation of beauty (which is not utilitarian). 3. Cleanliness and order. (Explains order as imitated from nature—as a repetition compulsion it removes doubts and hesitation in future, similar occasions.) Asks why in man there seems to be a natural aversion to order.

10—Reminds us that he has not explained why beauty, order and cleanliness are requirements of civilization—certainly not for their obvious utility.

11—4. The value it sets on the higher mental activities. (This feature seems to characterize culture more than any other.) Intellectual, scientific, and esthetic achievement. The various systems of thought: a—religious, b—philosophical, c—ethical. Claims that these activities must indicate the fulfillment of a great need. (Since the force behind all human activity is striving for pleasure, then above will also be explained in these terms.)

12—5. The regulation of social relations. (Restrictions of the rights of individuals for the sake of the group.) Defines justice as ". . . the assurance that a law once made will not be broken in favour af an individual."

13—Hence, individual liberty has been restricted with the advent of culture. The desire for freedom may either be in revolt against injustices or the primitive personality's protest against culture. (Sees the conflict of individual vs. society as one of the basic conflicts of any culture.)

14—Claims that common to all the characteristics of culture is a modification of man's instinctual disposition. Compares or analogizes the development in culture and libidinal development (brings his notion of anal traits as the example), i.e. both involve sublimation. Offers the possibility that sublimation of an instinct is the result of culture. Cultural privation is seen as problematic, for instincts being repressed may cause disorder. (There are just so many sublimations possible. See *The Ego and the Id*.)

15—Having presented the analogy of the evolution of culture to the normal growth of the individual, he asks: (a) What are the influences to which the evolution of culture owes its origin? (b) How did it arise and what determines its course? (As man grows there are many possibilities for regression, neuroses, etc., so in society there must be similar possibilities. ("The city is a man writ large.")

CHAPTER FOUR

1-3—Attempts to answer the above questions (Chapter III, par. 15) by tracing the development or origin of culture. (Freud more fully develops this in *Totem and Taboo*.) Attributes the development to a two-fold foundation: (a) compulsion to work (external necessity) and (b) power to live, i.e. disappearance of seasonal sexual cycle.

4—Digresses to indicate that man, having discovered genital love most satisfying, left himself open to another source of unhappiness: the loss of the loved one. (Freud, due to his system of checks and balances, claims that every step forward, be it a human development or a cultural development, opens up new dangers and new potentials for unhappiness as well as for regressions.)

5—One way of handling the above problem is to attach love to mankind. (This, of course, is a type of sublimation.) Claims that this is an area in which the pleasure principle has been linked with religion. Objects to this approach on two grounds, (a) indiscriminate love does injustice to the object, (b) not all men are worthy of love.

6—The many uses of the term *love* are justifiable genetically. Distinguishes genital love from aim inhibited love (though all love originally genital in nature). Genital love produces new families and aim-inhibited love, friendships. As culture develops it conflicts with love and love with culture.

7—This conflict is inevitable. (Implication for education but especially group work. See *Group Psychology.*) In the first stage it exists between the family and the larger community. (In *Group Psychology* this problem is seen as between members of the group and outsiders.) This is due to this form (family) being phylogenetically older (and that which is older is more basic and hence more deeply rooted). Brings data of difficulty in culture, of breaking away from family, thus need for initiatory rights. (Again example of development requring outside help as in the case of individual psychology and character development. See *Group Psychology and Analysis of the Ego* and *The Ego and the Id.*) Claims that the above difficulty is in the very nature of mental and organic development, i.e. conservative nature of the organism. (See *Beyond the Pleasure Principle.*)

8—Another problem in cultural development is caused by the conservative nature of women. (Men more capable of sublimation.)

9—Culture introduced sexual limitation from the very beginning and has continued to do so, with the greatest restriction to be found in Western European civilization. (Brings inhibition of sexual life in children as data to support his thesis.) Culture ignores the highly individualized nature of emotional economics.

10—Though much of the cultural regulation of the sexual is not heeded, the damage is very great—by diminution of the satisfaction to be achieved in the sexual. Offers the possibility that something in the sexual itself limits full satisfaction. (In the footnote on pages 105-106, Freud elaborates by indicating that bisexuality in man, expressed psychologically in passivity and activity [and thus conflict] exists in the sexual from the very beginning. Thus Freud would claim that conflict exists even within Eros. Also, suggests that repression may be caused by man's adoption of the erect posture.)

CHAPTER FIVE

1—The neurotic suffers especially from sexual frustrations (the substitute gratifications are painful in themselves or cause reactions from others which are painful). Claims that creating a substitute satisfaction that is painful in itself poses a problem (due to demands of the pleasure principle).

2—Reviews his assumption that cultural development manifests the difficulties of all evolution—inertia of libido. This is manifested (inertia of libido) in the conflict between civilization and sexuality where Eros, though tending to combine, is satisfied with the combination of two people—the lover and the beloved.

3—Culture could proceed as a company of couples combining for work but culture is not satisfied with this. It requires investment of aim-inhibited libido (thus greater privation for the individual). And this is yet to be explained. It involves a factor as yet unidentified.

4-7—Offers the possibility that a factor in the cultural antipathy to the sexual in man is due to the "values" of civilized society (which do not sufficiently address themselves to man's nature). Brings an outstanding example: "Love thy neighbor as thyself." Attacks this notion on several grounds: (1) not found in primitive man (not natural or primary), (2) not to be justified rationally, (3) the love will not be repaid. Finds it even more difficult to accept the notion of "Love thine enemies." Sees ethics as neglecting a basic factor, the variations in human behavior which are predetermined. (We have here an example of "crosstalk." Freud viewing man as striving for pleasure cannot possibly see values as anything but "sublimation" or "illusion." The theories which emphasize an "ethic" maintain quite a different notion of man's nature.)

8—Claims that the above value and other values reflect a naive view of human nature. Aggression is basic to man's nature, is instinctual in man. (Any education theory based on Freud will have to take this into consideration).

9—The aggressive nature in man is the reason for cultural restrictions and demands. Civilization uses the sexually inhibited relationships, sexual restrictions, and ethical ideals as means of checking the aggressive in man.

10—Disagrees with Communist explanation of man and society as misunderstanding the basic nature of man (since it does not accept an aggressive instinct) and claims that elimination of private property would open new avenues of expression of human aggression and hostility. (A Freudian theory of politics would, of necessity, have to coincide with his views of man's nature and the Freudian explanation for the use of social institutions.)

11—Furthermore men feel ill at ease with no outlet for their hostility and aggression. Brings historical data to bear that all "in" groups expressed hostility to "out" groups, as well as made use of scapegoats (see *Group Psychology*).

12—Summarizes. Happiness limited since civilization inhibits both the sexual and the aggressive (expression of both instincts). Civilized man has traded part of his happiness for security. Compares the state of primitive man to man's present state and indicates that man may not find himself at a greater disadvantage in the present era.

13—Though culture can improve—impose fewer restrictions—there is a limit to such improvement (due to instinctual inhibition and the problem of group living). (Thus presence of strong leaders important for quality of group life.) Attacks American culture as an instance of group members identifying only with one another, without a significant leader.

CHAPTER SIX

1-3—The hypothesis of an instinct of aggression does not require a modification of his theory (see *Beyond the Pleasure Principle*). Summarizes development of instinct theory (Ego vs. Libido to Eros vs. Death). (Freud himself, in a footnote on page 118, indicates that the notion of Eros as spreading is problematical in the light of the notion of instincts being conservative in nature.

Freud claims here that the death instinct is difficult to observe and is assumed to be working silently within the organism towards its disintegration. Thus, it appears that the investigation in *Beyond the Pleasure Principles,* as to whether death occurs for internal reasons, is the only proof at that point for the existence of the death instinct. Aggression would be an example of the death instinct directed to the outer world. This is an extension of the notion of the death instinct being handled by musculature, and further indicates that this notion is in harmony with the feeling that the instincts are intermingled, i.e. aggression in the service of Eros (by destroying outside instead of inside). (See *The Ego and the Id,* Chapter IV and V.) Sadism (strong death plus weak sex) and masochism (sex plus death working internally) are mentioned as instances of the instincts being intermingled.

4—Claims that the data of non-erotic aggression and destruction have given greater support to his notion of a death instinct. Man finds it difficult to accept the notion of a death instinct. (This is due to his cultural background and education. See *Civilization and Its Discontents,* Chapter VIII, page 90, footnote 1.)

5—Libido is now the energy of Eros and there is another energy for the death instinct. (He does not name this energy.) Admits the tentative nature of his notion of a death instinct due to the difficulty of observing it in life (brings as additional data for the death instinct the intense pleasure experienced when the destructive, unaccompanied by the sexual, is expressed).

6—Thus Freud claims that the death instinct (aggression) is a great obstacle to culture. Culture is a manifestation of Eros (binding together of families, etc.) thus it must conflict with death, for he feels that necessity could not hold them together. (You cannot beat the id death by necessity, which is not instinctual or primary, but only by libido, hence culture must be expression of Eros.) The evolution of culture equals Eros vs. Death (life vs. destruction or aggression). Civilization then, is the struggle of man for existence (the social again approaching an oversized individual). (Freud indicates in a footnote on p. 122 that culture began at some moment, or due to some event. This is in harmony with his notion of the development of consciousness and of the super-ego, etc. Namely, some historical event caused the movement forward—the new solution.) The illusion of religion, Freud claims, attempts to handle this very real struggle.

CHAPTER SEVEN

1—Admits his inability to answer why the cultural struggle exists in man and not in the animal world. Offers the possibility that in the case of the animal world a deadlock exists between environment and instincts (while in man a new spurt of libido may have kindled a new spirit of destruction via the check and balance system—inside vs. outside) and therefore they are in a static state.

2—Turns his attention to the question of how civilization holds aggression in check. The solution is to be found in the manner in which the individual handles his aggression—by introjection. The super-ego takes it over and rules aggressively over the ego. (See *The Ego and the Id,* where Freud explains how restraint is developed.) Civilization is well protected from aggression by this institution in the mind (thus the super-ego is called the Dread of Society).

3—Analyzes the source of the sense of guilt. Rejects a natural sense of guilt (since evil need not necessarily endanger the ego or deny pleasure and these are the only terms in which something can be natural or original in Freud). Thus guilt must originally be outside of man (all you have inside, originally, is instinct, thus everything else must come from without) and there must be a reason (force or power) for obeying it (or else all men would not accept it). Freud claims the reason is to be found in the fear of the loss of love, which implies the loss of protection and possible punishment (he has no other choice, for aggression could only be checked by a need of Eros), and thus the feeling of guilt, does not require evil action, intention is sufficient. The objection though, begins when the authority has discovered the action.

4—The above state of mind described is called "bad conscience" but Freud points to the fact that the feeling is only one of social anxiety. This is the state in children and may not be surpassed by many adults (society replaces the parents), fear is only one of detection.

5—The above situation is changed when the authority becomes internalized in the form of a super-ego. (It is at this point that we may speak of conscience.) Fear of discovery no longer important (for super-ego sees all) and reality no longer to be feared (i.e. loss of love, see par. 3) but super-ego as a derivative continues to torment the ego.

6—Addresses himself to a manifestation that appears at the second stage of development—the more virtuous one is the more strict and punitive the conscience (hence check and balance required for the "normal" life, if not, then one part gets the upper hand and destroys the other parts). External deprivation also intensifies the strength of the conscience. This phenomenon is observable in nations as well as in individuals. Explains this as due to the infantile stage of conscience being coexistent with the second stage, namely, fate replaces parents, adversity means loss of love and the individual humbles himself before the super-ego (representative of the parents). The above intensified as destiny is viewed as the will of God. Points to the phenomenon in peoples as manifested by the Jews (who considered themselves a favorite child) who explained adversity as due to their sinfulness and out of a sense of guilt constructed the stringent commandments of their priestly religion.

7—Distinguishes between the effects of two sources of guilt:
A) Arising from the dread of authority—requires instinctual renunciation so as not to lose love and then no further pain.
B) Dread of the super-ego—punishes even after instinctual renunciation, for the wish persists and cannot be concealed from the super-ego.

Thus man's happiness is now further limited (from the inside) for in the second stage a sense of guilt has been established that is not satisfied with renunciation.

8—Summarizes and reformulates chronological development of conscience:
A) Instinct renuciation—due to dread of external authority (loss of love)

B) Internal authority—dread of conscience (wishes, acts, intentions—sense of guilt).

Poses question of misfortune increasing the stringency of the conscience. Introduces data disclosed by psychoanalysis, that, though conscience is the result of instinctual renunciation, renunciation increases the severity of conscience.

9—Defends the plausibility of the above notion and minimizes the contrast between this view and the previous view (conscience more rigorous after renunciation) by applying it to the aggressive instinct. The super-ego received its initial aggressiveness by an identification introduced to compensate for the renunciation of the aggressiveness. ("The relationship between the super-ego and the ego is a return, distorted by a wish, of the real relationships between the ego, as yet undivided, and external object.") The aggressiveness of the super-ego represents the child's aggressiveness to an external object. Thus, in the light of the above explanation, Freud claims that the conscience is formed and intensified by the renunciation of aggressive impulses. (This explanation makes it possible for Freud to demonstrate aggressiveness in the primary state.)

10—Claims that apparent discrepancy between the two theories: (a) Conscience the result of fear of loss of love; (b) Super-ego the result of an identification with the threatening external object can be explained. (They coincide at the point where aggression is provoked by the amount of punishment anticipated by the father.) And both theories can be derived from the data. Namely, stringent super-ego can be the result of lenient or severe upbringing. (On page 130, in a footnote, Freud refers to the work of Franz Alexander who discussed how aggression may be turned inward or outward depending on whether the child was neglected. Thus Freud says that a strict conscience can arise from instinctual deprivation plus love, which turns aggression inward.)

11-13—Deprivation followed by aggressiveness and a severe super-ego is in harmony with a phylogenetic prototype, i.e. primitive father both terrifying and aggressive. Introduces problem of origin of guilt from Oedipus, where aggression was not renounced while in present guilt, the aggression is renounced. Explains the above by distinguishing remorse from guilt (remorse the feeling after gratification has restored the balance of conscience vs. instinct and the person feels badly about having committed the act). Explains the guilt felt at the very first, i.e. after the father-murder, as due to remorse resulting from the original, primal ambivalence between love and hate of the father. After act (caused by hate) the love came forward in remorse and established the super-ego by identification and thus set up the restriction preventing a repetition of the deed. Future feeling of aggression was thus suppressed and additional guilt felt increased stringency of the super-ego and so on. Love then played a role in the origin of conscience and guilt. Guilt then is the expression of the eternal conflict of Eros vs. Death. It first expresses itself (since the child cannot avoid living in a family) in the Oedipus complex which causes a super-ego. As life becomes more complicated, the conflict intensifies, and thus more guilt. Eros binds man and intensified guilt help to keep them bound. "If civilization is a necessary course of development from the family to humanity as a whole, then—as a result of the inborn conflict arising from ambivalence, of the eternal struggle between the trends of love and death—there is inextricably bound up with it an increase of the sense of guilt, which will perhaps reach heights that the individual finds hard to tolerate." Thus one sees to what extent Freud charges civilization with causing great guilt and greatly limiting man's life and opportunity for pleasure.

CHAPTER EIGHT

1 and 2—Restates his position that guilt is the most important problem in the evolution of culture. In a footnote, Freud claims that besides diminishing pleasure, the effect of the sense of guilt is to prepare the young for the world poorly, i.e. guilt gives them a distorted picture of the reality. (This must be considered in an education theory based on Freud.) Will now relate guilt to consciousness. Remorse is clearly conscious. Takes another look at neurosis in the light of its relationship to guilt. In the obsessional, guilt is unconscious. Claims that guilt is essentially a variety of anxiety and that later it coincides with the dread of the super-ego.

As anxiety may be experienced consciously or unconsciously so guilt may be expressed both ways and thus much of the uneasiness that is really a manifestation of the unconscious guilt is assigned other motivations. Religion has understood the great importance of guilt and has offered to save mankind from the sense of guilt (i.e. sin). Refers to his explanation of the Christ figure in *Totem and Taboo*.

3—Defines more precisely some of the terms he has been working with:

    A) Super-ego—agency in the mind which has been inferred.
    B) Conscience—one of the functions of the super-ego (censors and ego).

Sense of guilt, severity of super-ego and rigor of the conscience are all the same, the result of the tension between the desires of the ego and the standards of the super-ego. The anxiety felt as a result of this tension is an instinctual manifestation on the part of the ego which has become masochistic as a result of an erotic attachment to the sadistic super-ego. He reserves the use of the word conscience for the super-ego, but claims that conscious guilt is earlier, i.e. a fear of the external authority. Thus, at a very early stage, there exists a conflict between instinctual gratification and parental love. The thwarting of the instinctual gratification provokes the aggression. There are two sources for guilt: one from the fear of the external authority and the other from the fear of the internal authority. The term remorse he reserves for a reaction of the ego under a special form of the sense of guilt which also may occur before the conscience has developed.

4 and 5—Reviews several apparent contradictions and their resolution: the sense of guilt seems to be both the result of an act as well as an intention. Resolution—the development of the super-ego altered the situation (omniscient super-ego made intention guilt bearing). As to the sense of guilt and consciousness, he reviews his previous explanations of the relationships and the apparent contradictions. Discusses the problem of whether any privation results in a sense of guilt (namely, does this apply to erotic as well as aggressive wishes) and suggests the following: instinctual repression results in the libidinal elements being

transformed into symptoms, only the aggressive components result in a sense of guilt.

6—Reviews the struggle of Eros and Death as related to a) humanity, b) the individual, c) organic life. Distinguishes between the struggle in the individual and humanity. a) In the individual, development is ordered by the pleasure principle, with an interplay between two forces, an egotistic and an altruistic, with the main emphasis on the egotistic. b) In culture, the main, and almost only emphasis is on combining individuals and happiness seems almost unnecessary.

7—Clarifies: society vs. the individual is not a result of Eros vs. Death, but rather a struggle within Eros, comparable to the struggle of the Ego and its objects for the libido. (Conflict exists in the inside of each of the instincts.) Hopes that both problems may be solved eventually (i.e. Society and the Individual, and Ego vs. Objects).

8—Claims that society has a super-ego as does the individual. It originates in a manner similar to its development in the individual, i.e. the impression left behind by great leading personalities in whom some one tendency has developed beyond proportion (again his heavy reliance on biology). (Is it possible that the tri-partite division in the psyche exists in society as well? This might explain certain group phenomena.) In many cases, the great person may have been ridiculed or even killed, as the case with the primal father. The cultural super-ego also sets up high ideals and punishes by anxiety. The cultural super-ego is more easily discernible than the individual super-ego.

9—Freud defines ethics as the demands of the super-ego which deal with the relations of human beings to one another and attempts to achieve, by imposed standards, what has been unattainable in other ways. Criticizes the values that are the expression of the cultural super-ego (especially the command to "Love thy neighbor as thyself" as being unpsychological, i.e. doubts whether man can live by the standard. It assumes that man's ego has unlimited power over the id.) Sees the values of the Socialists as equally unpsychological.

10—Admits the possibility of the analogy of the individual in the society being carried further, i.e. neurotic societies. (See Chapter III, par. 15.) Cautions against improper transfer of concepts developed in individual psychology to the area of social psychology. Brings to our attention that one basic element is missing in the case of "sick" societies—an environment to supply a norm. (Here we have another indication of the importance of the notion of the conflict in Freud.) Points to the fact that there would be no power to force society to accept the therapy.

11—Does not evaluate the merits of civilization, or culture, but accepts them as necessary realities. Claims that both the revolutionary and the pious believer are basically searching for consolation in world that is full of unhappiness.

12—Feels that the fateful question is: "Whether and to what extent their cultural development will succeed in mastering the disturbance of their communal life caused by the human instinct of aggression and self-destruction." Ends with the hope that Eros may at this point thrust itself forward.

BIBLIOGRAHY

WORKS BY AND ABOUT FREUD

Freud, Sigmund: *The Standard Edition of the Complete Psychological Works of Sigmund Freud.* James Strachey (Trans. and Ed.), in collab. with Anna Freud. 24 vols. London, Hogarth Pr. and the Inst. of Psycho-Analysis, 1953-1974.

Freud, Sigmund and Pfister, Oskar: *Psycho-Analysis and Faith: the letters of Sigmund Freud and Oskar Pfister.* Meng, Henrich and Freud, Ernest L. (Eds.). Mosbacher, Erich (Trans.). London, Hogarth Pr., 1963.

Fromm, Erich: *Sigmund Freud's Mission.* New York, Harper, 1959.

Jones, Ernest: *The Life and Work of Sigmund Freud,* 3 vols. New York, Basic, 1953-1957.

Puner, H.W.: *Freud—His Life and His Mind.* New York, Dell, 1959.

OTHER

Aristotle: *Posterior Analytics.* In McKeon, Richard (Ed.): *The Basic Works of Aristotle.* New York, Random, 1941.

Arnold, Magda: An excitatory theory of emotion. In Reymart, Martin L. (Ed.): *Feeling and Emotions.* Chicago, McGraw, 1950.

Belth, Marc: *Education as a Discipline.* Boston, Allyn and Bacon, 1965.

Bernard, Claude: *An Introduction to the Study of Experimental Medicine.* Henry C. Greene (Trans.). New York, Dover, 1957.

Bettleheim, Bruno: *Love is Not Enough.* Glencoe, Free Pr, 1950.

......: *The Informed Heart: Autonomy in a Mass Age.* Glencoe, Free Pr., 1960.

......: Truants from Life: *The Rehabilitation of Emotionally Disturbed Children.* Glencoe, Free Pr, 1955.

Coleman, James S.: *Equality of Educational Opportunity.* Washington, D.C.: Government Printing Office, 1966.

......: *The Evaluation of Equality of Educational Opportunity.* Santa Monica, Rand, 1968.

......: Policy research in the social sciences. New York, General Learning Pr., 1972.

Cremin, Lawrence Arthur: Curriculum making in the United States. *Teachers College Record, 73:* 2, 207-220, 1971.

......: *The Transformation of the School,* New York, Knopf, 1961.

Cronbach, Lee and Suppes, Patrick (Eds.): *Research for Tomorrow's Schools.* New York, Macmillan, 1969.

Dunkel, Harold Baker: *Herbart and Herbartianism; An Educational Ghost Story.* Chicago, U. Chicago Pr., 1970.

......: *Whitehead on Education.* Columbus, Ohio State University, 1965.

Erikson, Erik H.: *Childhood and Society,* 2nd ed., revised. New York, Norton, 1963.

......: *Young Man Luther.* New York, Norton, 1958.

Fox, Seymour: A practical image of the practical. *Curriculum Theory Network,* no. 10, 45-57, 1972.

Frost, J. L.: The rediscovery of Piaget. In Frost, J. L. (Eds.): *Early Childhood Education Rediscovered.* Readings. U. of Texas at Austin. Holt, Rinehart and Winston, 1968.

Hilgard, Ernest R. (Ed.): *Theories of Learning and Instruction.* The Sixty-Third Yearbook of the Nat. Soc. for the Study of Educ. Part I. Chicago, U. of Chicago Pr., 1964.

Kaplan, Abraham: *The Conduct of Inquiry.* San Francisco, Chandler, 1964.

Locke, John: *Two Treatises on Government.* New York, Hafner, 1961.

Lukinsky, Joseph S.: "Structure" in educational theory. *Educational Philosophy and Theory, 2:* 15-31, 1970; *3:* 29-36, 1971.

Martin, Jane R.: The disciplines and the curriculum. In Martin, Jane R. (Ed.): *Readings in Philosophy of Education: A Study of Curriculum.* Boston, Allyn and Bacon, 1970.

Piaget, Jean: *Six Psychological Studies.* New York, Random, 1967.

Plato: *The Republic.* In Jowett, B. (Trans.): *The Dialogues of Plato.* 2 vols. New York, Random, 1937, vol. I.

Redl, Fritz and Wineman, David: *The Aggressive Child.* Glencoe, Free Pr., 1957.

Rogers, Carl: *Client-Centered Therapy; Its Current Practice, Implications, and Theory.* Boston, Houghton and Mifflin, 1951.

Sarason, Seymour B.: *The Culture of the School and the Problem of Change.* Boston, Allyn and Bacon, 1971.

Scheffler, Israel: Philosophy and the curriculum. In *Reason and Teaching.* London, Routledge and Kegan, 1973.

Schwab, Joseph J. (Supvr.): *Biology Teacher's Handbook.* BSCS, New York, Wiley, 1963.

......: *High School Biology Teacher's Handbook.* BSCS, 1st and 2nd eds. New York, Amer Inst Bio Sci, 1960, 1961.

......: On the corruption of education by psychology. *Ethics, 68(1):* October, 1957; also *School Review, 66(2):* 169-183, 1958.

......: The practical: A language for curriculum. In NEA Center for the Study of Instruction (Pub.): *Schools for the 70's.* Auxiliary Series. Washington, D.C., Nat Educ Assoc, 1970.

......: The practical: Arts of eclectic. *School Review, 79:*493-542, 1971.

......: The practical 3: Translation into curriculum. *School Review*, 8 (4) 501-522.

......: Problems, topics, and issues. In Elam, Stanley (Ed.): *Education and the Structure of Knowledge*. Chicago, Rand, 1964.

......: What do scientists do? *Behavioral Science, 5(1)*:1-27, 1960.

Sullivan, Harry Stack: *The Interpersonal Theory of Psychiatry*. New York, Norton, 1953.

Tyler, Ralph W.: *Basic Principles of Curriculum and Instruction*. Chicago, U. of Chicago Pr., 1950.

Walton, John and Kuethe, James L. (Eds.): *The Discipline of Education*. Madison, U. Wisconsin Pr, 1963.

SELECTIVE INDEX

A

Activity-passivity, *see also* Change, Energy,
  of ego, 105, 219
  in Freud, 42-44
  in personality theory, 25-26
Affect, 27-28, 44-45, 129-130, 145-146, 234
Aggression, 146, 199, 200-201, 241, 243, 249
Ambivalence, 63, 111
Anatomy, mental, 80-81, 100, 147, 183, 215-217
Animal psychology, 104-105, 110-112, 144 n. 4, 147, 243
Anxiety, 89-90, 146 n. 15, 231
Archaic heritage, *see also* Phylogenesis, 63, 107, 111, 114-115, 117
Aristotle, 27, 168
Art, 78, 135, 168-170
Authority, 127-128

B

Beginning orientation,
  in Freud, 31-35, 38-45, 101-102, 115-116, 144-145
  in holistic theory, 23-24
  and rationality, 101-102
Bernard, Claude, 25, 79-80
Bruner, Jerome, 4

C

Cannon, Walter, 44-45
Change, *see also* Lamarckism, 22-23, 31, 42-44, 97, 105, 159-160
Character, *see also* Groups, 65, 110-111, 127, 153-154, 209, 220-225
Chemistry, 52, 57-58 n. 33
Childhood, early, 65-67, 69, 70, 153-154, 221
Commonplaces, *see also* Freud,

defined, 26-28
  in Freud, 147-148
  of personality, 27-28
  ranking of, 61-62
Communism, 241
Compulsion to repeat, 183, 186, 190-191
Comte, A., 51
Conflict, 60-62, 119-120, 124, 143-147, 236, 240
Conscience, 37, 117-118, 228-229
Conscious system, 80-81, 183, 214-218
Consciousness, 72, 80-81, 100, 147, 183, 215-217
Conservatism
  of instincts, 58-59, 186-187
  of mental life, 64, 75-76
  of women, 239

D

Darwin, C., 61, 207
Death, 55-57, 129, 132, 139, 187-190, 229-230, 231-232, 241-243
Determinism 32-34, 75-76, 101-102, 183
Development, 68-69, 71-73
Dreams, 63, 65-66, 89, 185
Dualism, 60-62, 139, 189

E

Education
  administration, 166
  aims of, 159-163
  and the child, 153-155
  and the curriculum, 4-5, 168-174
  and the ego, 157-158, 160-161
  and instincts, 153, 155-159, 163, 169
  and the peer group, 156-157, 167
  and Piaget, 6-7
  and school milieu, 155
  and society, 167-168
  and structure of knowledge, 4